Lydgate's Reson and Sensuallyte: Vol. II

EARLY ENGLISH TEXT SOCIETY

Extra Series, No. 89

1903

PRICE 35s.

Lydgate's
Reson and Sensuallyte

EDITED FROM

BODLEIAN MS. FAIRFAX 16

AND

BRITISH MUSEUM
ADDITIONAL MS. 29729

BY

ERNST SIEPER

VOLUME II
STUDIES AND NOTES

Published for
THE EARLY ENGLISH TEXT SOCIETY
by the
OXFORD UNIVERSITY PRESS
LONDON   NEW YORK   TORONTO

FIRST PUBLISHED 1903
REPRINTED 1965

𝕮𝖝𝖙𝖗𝖆 𝖘𝖊𝖗𝖎𝖊𝖘, No. 89

ORIGINALLY PRINTED BY
RICHARD CLAY & SONS, LTD., BUNGAY, SUFFOLK
AND NOW REPRINTED LITHOGRAPHICALLY IN GREAT BRITAIN
AT THE UNIVERSITY PRESS, OXFORD
BY VIVIAN RIDLER, PRINTER TO THE UNIVERSITY

PREFACE.

At last I am able to put into the hands of the members of the *Early English Text Society* the second part of my edition of Lydgate's *Reson and Sensuallyte*. This volume contains Notes and Studies on the text.

The following remarks may be made as to the Studies. The first chapter enters into the question of the date of the poem. With the fixing of the date at which *Reson and Sensuallyte* was written the chronology of the more important poems of Lydgate is completed; and when this task is accomplished the way is prepared for an inquiry into the development of Lydgate's poetical manner.

The study of the metre brings us to the conclusion that as in his other octosyllabic lines, so here also Lydgate's metrical art offers no occasion for serious fault-finding. May this chapter give the lie for good and all to the reproach that the good monk of Bury could not write three consecutive lines without offending the rules of his metre. If we follow a critically pure text and do not allow ourselves to be deceived by corruptions of transmission we find that even the careless scribbling of his later days kept tolerably to its metre. The comparatively easy flow of his verse and the fire and sonorousness of those recurring poetic expressions which came to him from Chaucer, explain to us the puzzle why Lydgate has been so highly rated by some undoubtedly great authors of modern times. Poets like Chatterton, Gray, and Mrs. Browning have suffered themselves to be led by this element of musical rhythm in his language to assign to the works of the monk a worth out of all proportion to their value as poetry. For it cannot be too clearly asserted that as poetry Lydgate's works are absolutely worthless. I have gone through all the productions of the monk—a service of doubtful value, which probably none other in Germany has accomplished, except Prof. Schick—and from page to page I became more and more convinced that the poetical fame of the once so belauded pupil of Chaucer has no basis to rest upon in fact.

But this, however, does not lessen the importance of a study of Lydgate for the knowledge of English philology.

The chapter on Lydgate's style will, I trust, be found to add something to our understanding of the history of the English language. The effort after parallelism of expression which Lydgate consciously pursues was not without influence upon the English style of later times. The following are a few examples of similar features in the *Book of Common Prayer* of the English Church (composed mostly in 1549 and 1552): "acknowledge and confess our manifold sins and wickednesses" (from the Exhortation in Morning and Evening Prayer): "we have erred and strayed from Thy ways" (General Confession in Morning and Evening Prayer): "to declare and pronounce" (Absolution): "vanquish and overcome all his enemies" (Prayer for the King): "desires and petitions" (Prayer of St. Chrysostom, where the original Greek, from which the translation is made, has only the one word τὰ αἰτήματα).

The study of Lydgate's style has also led me to the conviction that the poem *The Assembly of Gods* which Trigg has edited under the name of Lydgate, cannot possibly be assigned to him.

The chapter on the source of Lydgate's poem is intended to supplement in some respects my own work on the *Échecs Amoureux*. Certain additions and corrections are made in what I there said about the commentaries on this Old French Love-romance. The relation of the *Échecs Amoureux* to the mediæval encyclopædias is settled in its most important points. Guido da Colonna's *De regimine principum* proves to be the principal source for the second and lengthy part of the poem.

I may be allowed here to allude to some of the criticisms which have been raised against my book on the *Échecs Amoureux*. I will confine my attention to those critics who have a right to be heard as authorities on the subject. In the front rank of these is M. Ernest Langlois, the well-known student and scholar of the *Romance of the Rose*. M. Langlois has subjected my book to a thorough examination in Vollmöller's *Krit. Jahresbericht über die Fortschritte der Roman Philologie* (V, 3). The result of his examination is the following criticism: "L'étude de M. Sieper est faite avec soin, et les inexactitudes que nous avons remarquées dans les citations ne diminuent en rien son mérite." It will be seen from these words and the few corrections which follow that the supplement to my book had not yet come into M. Langlois' hands. I should like to call attention therefore a second time to the fact that I have myself in a contribution to the *Englische Studien* (xxviii, pp. 310-312) corrected these "inexactitudes dans les citations."

A second criticism which I should not like to leave unnoticed is that of Herr Joseph Mettlich, who has been occupied for several years in establishing a critical text of the *É. A.*, and also intends to publish a definitive essay on the question of its sources. Meantime he has made a valuable contribution to our knowledge of the *Échecs Amoureux* in a publication called *Wissenschaftliche Beilage zum Programme des Königl. Paulinischen Gymnasiums zu Münster*. His work bears the title: *Ein Kapitel über Erziehung aus einer altfranzösischen Dichtung des* 14. *Jahrhunderts*. In this treatise he sets forth with great skill and considerable artistic taste the interesting information which the mediæval poet gives about the education of boys. By way of introduction Herr Mettlich deals amongst other matters with my book. He also acknowledges that I have gone into the poem thoroughly and in a way deserving of commendation. Thankful as I am, however, for the kindly praise which he bestows, I cannot say that I am convinced by the criticism which he proceeds to pass on the book.

At the outset he thinks that the title of the book, describing the *É. A.* as an imitation of the *Romance of the Rose*, was not happily chosen. " Der Titel der Arbeit erscheint insofern nicht ganz glücklich gewählt, als die *Échecs amoureux* zwar der Form und auch stellenweise dem Inhalte nach zu dem 'Roman de la Rose' Beziehungen haben, der eigentlichen Tendenz nach aber eine Lebensauffassung vertreten, die der im Rosenromane dargelegten feindlich entgegensteht. Schon der altfranzösische Kommentator Fds. franç. 143.[1] schreibt fol. 337 r⁰ col. 2 : ' Car c'est la principal entencion de l'acteur dessus dit et la fin de son livre que de reprendre et blasmer leur folye come chose a raison contraire sicome il peult apparoir clerement par le proces de son livre ryme.' Die Hingabe an die Sinnenlust wird hier verworfen, dafür aber uicht etwa Weltflucht, sondern richtiger Lebensgenuss in der 'vie active' gelehrt und empfohlen."

I really cannot think that Herr Mettlich would have written thus, if he had kept clearly in mind at the time what I said on p. 207-9 of my book about the idea of this poem. In that passage attention was drawn to exactly the same point which Herr Mettlich here makes about the tendency of the *É. A.* When therefore I described the

É. A. as an imitation of the *Romance of the Rose*, I was led to this by the consideration that the poet as far as concerns the artistic form of his work relies entirely on the *Romance of the Rose*, from the contents of which moreover he borrows remorselessly.

Herr Mettlich further objects to my statement on p. 143 relating to the poet's attempt to make Pallas surrounded by flying swans (chienettes) in place of the traditional owl. " Wenn auch," he says, "bei der ersten Schilderung der Pallas ' chienettes' in der Handschrift steht, so liess sich doch in Cod. Dresd. Fol. 72 am Schlusse (wo von der Kurzsichtigkeit des Menschen gegenüber dem Wesen Gottes die Rede ist) in den Versen :

> ' et, briefment ne que la chieuete
> peut, pour sa veue feblette,
> la clarte du soleil comprendre,
> ne puet li homs,—tant sache apprendre,—
> le hault dieu comprendre de plain.'

das Wort, auch bei nur oberflächlichem Lesen, nicht als eine Nebenform von afrz. ' cisne ' auffassen. Die Notwendigkeit der Einsetzung von ' chieuette (= nfrz. chouette) an Stelle von ' chienette ' in dem obigen Falle ergab sich von selbst."

My reply to this would be as follows. Naturally I could not help noticing on Fol. 72 the variant form "chieuete" which manifestly in this place can only mean an owl. When in spite of this in the first description of Pallas I kept to the *chienette* (swan), it was in deference to the authority of my Lydgate who not only knew how to read his French author, but also could follow him in his deeper conceptions. He read *chienette* (swan) and has carefully explained to us the reason why the swan was here chosen to be the companion of Pallas. Nor does the fact that Rudolf Tobler takes a different view (cf. *Herrig's Archiv* civ, p. 399 f.) alter my opinion, much as I have reason to agree with the rest of his remarks on my work. He says that the explanation of the swans as attributes of Pallas is "far-fetched" (gesucht); but it is no more so than thousands of other allegorical explanations of passages in the works of mediæval writers.

I feel compelled to make a few remarks as to the scope and purpose of the notes. In many instances I have tried to show that we have to note in Lydgate's phrases constantly recurring formulas. Very often these formulas could be shown to be common property of the Chaucer-school.

Preface.   ix

The question of the relation between Lydgate's poem and its original, which I have already dealt with in a connected form in my book on the *Échecs Amoureux*, will be found to have further light thrown upon it here and there in the notes. It is hoped that the citations, short and long, from the *Échecs Amoureux* will make the understanding of the Lydgate text an easier matter. In the case of single and fictitious personages in the poem (*e. g.* Dame Nature and Dame Fortune) I have tried to draw out the connection with the other allegorical poems of the Middle Ages, and also to point to the fruit borne by these and fictions in the later poetry. Lydgate takes excessive delight in going off into allegorical interpolations: in two passages we meet with this tendency displayed in the most arbitrary way: once when it serves to describe the attributes of the various gods who were present at the judgment of Paris, and the second time when he has to explain the stones and animals employed on the chessboard. Here our task extended itself on the one side into the study of the mythological writers, and on the other into that of the mediæval books on stones and animals used in Lydgate's sources. In the case of the numerous stories from the classics which Lydgate touches on, it was necessary to point out their source and also their appearance in other specimens of contemporary literature.

In conclusion it is my pleasant duty to thank all those who have come to my help with counsel or work. Dr. F. J. Furnivall, Prof. Schick, the Rev. S. C. Gayford, and Prof. Weyman, to whom I was under heavy obligations for their assistance in the volume on the text, have again been unwearied in their kind services to me in the preparation of this second volume.

I have further to thank Mr. Henry Bergen for the help he has given me. And it is a pleasure for me to be able to announce that his edition of Lydgate's *Troy Book*, at which he has been working for some years, will appear in the course of the next few months.

Last of all, I should like to express my thanks to Dr. Eugene Oswald, the excellent secretary of the *English Goethe Society*, who, as many others besides myself have good reason to know, is always ready to help Germans coming to England with the intention of pursuing serious studies.

E. SIEPER.

Munich, May 1904.

STUDIES.

I. *Authorship, Title, and Date*, p. 1.
II. *Structure of the Verse*, p. 9.
III. *The Inflexions*, p. 20.
IV. *The Rhyme*, p. 40.
V. *Lydgate's Style*, p. 43.
VI. *The Source of Lydgate's Poem*, p. 59.

CHAPTER I.
AUTHORSHIP, TITLE, AND DATE.

In his article on *Reason and Sensuality*,[1] Professor Schick has already established Lydgate's authorship of that poem. As the result of my own observations and investigations I should like to add the following remarks.

Both MSS. assign the poem to Lydgate. But the heading in F, in which the words "compylid by John Lydgat" follow the title, was written, without doubt, at a much later date than the text. After carefully comparing the hand in which this heading is written with that of A, I have arrived at the conclusion that both are of the same person—John Stowe. Thus the two proofs are reduced to one; and it is on Stowe's authority alone that the authorship, according to the MSS., is ascribed to Lydgate.

There is no doubt that Stowe's statements are of great value; still, they are by no means invariably trustworthy. The Add. MS. itself proves this, for on leaves 8 and 9 is an epitaph on Edward IV., designated by Stowe as the work of Lydgate. The error, it is true, was recognized and corrected later, the name of Skelton taking that of the monk; but it is a question whether this blunder would have been seen, had there not been so palpable an anachronism, Lydgate's death having taken place even before the reign of Edward IV.

However, in spite of Stowe's questionable authority, there is not the slightest room for doubt as to the authorship of Lydgate. In addition to the external proof, the internal evidence is convincing.

At first I should like to mention that during the literary decay of the fifteenth century, when the creative art of Chaucer began to crumble down into dead formulas in the hands of his successors, internal evidence is not always to be trusted, and is, in fact, often of doubtful value in deciding points of authorship.

For example let us take the verses by Ashby, printed by M.

[1] *Anglia*, Beiblatt. viii, p. 134, etc.

Förster in *Anglia* (xx, p. 140–152). Here we find—besides the improper use of *champartye*—all the tricks of style usually pointed out as Lydgate's united, thus forming a most Lydgate-like work. Indeed, it would be hard to believe, were we not certain of the authorship, that this is not one of the monk's productions.

On the other hand, in the *Assembly of Gods*, attributed to Lydgate on the very good authority of Wynkyn de Worde, metre, rhyme, final -*e*, vocabulary, even method of expression, are totally different from those we are accustomed to judge the property of the monk. Certainly, as Triggs remarks, Lydgate discloses himself in his writings as scarcely any other poet does, but he does not do so in the *Assembly of Gods*. If this poem is really Lydgate's—which I very much doubt,—it can be said quite as truly that the monk knew how to conceal his peculiarities as scarcely any other poet could.

In short, an editor must be very cautious with regard to so-called internal evidence; it is only of relative importance, and does not count at all unless there is an overwhelming number of extraordinary coincidences. The latter is the case in our poem.

My investigations as to the final -*e* and metre have led to practically the same results as those reached by Schick[1] and Krausser.[2] In the chapter on the style, I have shown how that most characteristic of Lydgate's peculiarities, the doubling of expressions, is especially noticeable in our poem. But I would like to lay even more stress upon the striking resemblance between *Reson and Sensuallyte* and two special Lydgate-works, the *Troy-Book* and the *Pilgrimage*.

The resemblance between portions of the *Pilgrimage* and *Reson and Sensuallyte* is indeed of an extraordinary character. The description of the principal figure of the first-mentioned book, Grace Dieu, frequently calls to mind the very words which are used in *R. and S.* about the appearance and decoration of Dame Nature. I limit myself to the following lines, which read almost as a quotation from *R. and S.* l. 665 ff. (Dame Grace Dieu appears to the author):

"And whil I dyde my besynesse,
A lady of ful gret ffayrnesse
And gret noblesse, (soth to say,)
I dyde mete vp-on the way."
679 ff. : . . . "thys lady gracyous,
Most debonayre, & vertuous,
. . . .
And in the Awmaylle ther was sette
Passyngly a rechë sterre,

Wych that cast hys bemys ferre
Round aboveten al the place,
. . . .
This lady, of whom I ha told,
Hadde on hyr hed a crowne of gold
Wrouht of sterrys shene & bryht,
That cast aboute a ful cler lyht."
758 f.: "I pray yow that ye wyl me lere
Your name & your condycioun."

---

[1] See *Temple of Glas*, p. lxv ff. and lvi ff.
[2] *Complaint of the Black Knight*, p. 13 ff. and 21 ff.

Compare also the descriptions of the two paths, one of which is to be chosen by man.[1] Here the resemblance is so great, certain expressions and formulas being so strikingly alike, that no further comment is necessary.

Finally, I would like to call attention to the peculiar manner in which the appearance of the goddesses and other allegorical figures is announced; this manner of announcing, as well as the introductions to the speeches of the various figures, is very much the same in the *Pilgrimage* as in *Reson and Sensuallyte*. There is, of course, a general resemblance between the French originals, but this correspondence even in words and phrases is only to be found in the Lydgate versions.

The *Troy-Book* too has many points of striking resemblance with our poem. The judgment of Paris is there also related in all its details. Especially in the speech made by Mercury, there is much that reminds us of his oration in *R. and S.* The same rhymes and the same wording often occur at the very same points in the two narratives.

But in other respects also the phraseology of the *Troy-Book* is the same as that of our poem. There are many lines in the *Troy-Book* which by the dropping out of an adjective, or adverb, etc., can be converted into verses of *R. and S.*:

II, 2525 " for to declare [sothly] in sentence."
    2641 " That Iubyter helde at his [owne] borde."
    2648 " She toke an appel rounde of [pure] golde."
    2652 " [To] the fayrest of them euerychone."
I, 1556 " I wante connynge [by ordre] do discryue."
    2063 " And [trewely] yet as I shall deuyse."
    2381 " Truste right well me lyste nat [for to] fayne."
    2385. " Without chaunge or [any] doubylnesse."
    2502 " But ye had leuer [shortly] for to dye."
    2560 " This is the fyne [and sume] of my requeste."
    2588 " And fayrest eke [in sothe] it is no naye."

Finally we have one more, and, in my opinion, the strongest proof of Lydgate's authorship. Our poem is a translation from the French. From the *Pilgrimage* we can form a clear idea of Lydgate's peculiar method of rendering a French text, and we have now to discover whether this same method is followed out in *R. and S.* Deguileville's work has about 14,000 lines, in Lydgate's version 22,000. This relationship in the length of original and translation is also the same with *R. and S.* and its source. But apart from this

---

[1] See *Pilgrimage*, l. 3344 ff., and l. 12205 ff.

coincidence we find in the *Pilgrimage* exactly the same peculiarities of translation which we have previously pointed out as existing in *R. and S.*,[1] viz. the tendency to render one French line by two English ones, the extraordinary lengthening out of the original which takes place at the beginnings of the chapters, and the frequent bringing in of expletive sentences in order to obviate difficulties brought about by rhyme and metre.

Thus our investigation has led to the result that both external and internal evidence bear each other out in establishing Lydgate's authorship. There is not the slightest doubt that *Reson and Sensuallyte* was translated by the monk of Bury, the writer of the *Troy-Book* and of the *Pilgrimage*.

Here I think is the proper place to settle the questions connected with the title and the marginal notes of our poem.

The title, there remains little doubt, is an invention of Stowe, who supplied it in the Fairfax MS. It is well suited to the subject. It was natural for Stowe to take it, since it is the superscription of many similar allegorical works. Perhaps it was suggested by the following writing:

Lvcii Annei Senecae ad Gallioneni de Remedi[i]s Fortuitorum. The remedyes agaynst all casuall chaunces. Dialogvs inter sensum et Rationem.

A dialogue betwene Sensualyte and Reason. Lately translated out of Latyn into Englyshe by Robert Whyttynton poet Laureat, & nowe newely Imprynted. London 1547.

As to the marginal notes,

α. they belong only to the English poem, as is amply proved by the note to l. 763-64, which cannot refer to the quite different French version.

β. The annotator was intimately acquainted with the relationship of Lydgate's work to its original. This appears from the notes to ll. 1245 and 1279, which inform us where Lydgate's additional interpretation begins, and where the translator returns to his original.

γ. The annotator in most cases starts with his remarks, when Lydgate leaves the ground of his original.

δ. The sources which Lydgate followed in his deviations are correctly pointed out.

These facts permit of the conclusion that, if Lydgate did not write the marginal notes himself, they originate from a man who knew perfectly all the conditions of his work.

[1] See *Échecs Amoureux*, p. 213 ff.

But when did he write it? Schick expresses his opinion in his edition of the *Temple of Glas*. See p. cviii : " For *Reason and Sensuality* I know of no external evidence which would warrant a certain date for the year of its composition. The work is of considerable length (about 7400[1] four-beat lines), and there remain only three periods in which Lydgate could possibly have found time to write it, namely, 1422–1426, 1439–1445, and the time immediately before 1409. I believe that 1422–1426, and still more 1439–1445, are quite impossible dates . . . He can only, I believe, have written the best production of his life in his prime, and I consider the *Flour of Curtesie*, the *Black Knight*, the *Temple of Glas*, as works which lead up to the only one of Lydgate's poems which we can read with real interest and enjoyment. Thus we are, perhaps, not far wrong in believing that *Reason and Sensuality* was written between 1406 and 1408."

In fixing the date at a comparatively early period, Schick is influenced by the consideration that the work is much more poetical than the long and wearisome translations of Lydgate's later years. However, the monk is not responsible for the poetical excellence of *R. and S.* Although the French original has not perhaps suffered greatly in his hands, it has certainly gained nothing by the Englishing. In consequence, for the present, we are face to face with absolute uncertainty in all that concerns the date of the work.

It is only by internal evidence that we obtain even approximate results:

The final -*e*, as our investigations have proved, is treated more or less as in the *Temple of Glas* and in the *Black Knight*. The dropping of the final -*e* in the rhyme, however, shows a considerable advance beyond the *Temple of Glas*. This, of course, leads us to date *R. and S.* certainly not before this poem. Now it is true that we do not gain much by this result, as the time after the *Temple of Glas* includes almost the whole literary career of Lydgate. But, as we have seen from the passage quoted above, there remain only three periods in which Lydgate could have found time to write *R. and S.* In which of these three periods, then, is the work to be placed?

The method to solve this question is to examine the style of *R. and S.* in its relation to the manner of writing, exhibited in those poems, which temporarily limit the above-mentioned periods, viz. the *Pilgrimage* and the *Troy-Book*. If we pursue such a course, we

---

[1] This must be a misprint for 7040. The exact number is 7042.

are led by the supposition that there is a certain development of style visible in the monk's writings. Previous Lydgate editors have had but little to say upon this point; Schick alone has touched on it with some excellent remarks. He has already pointed out that the early works of the monk, led Parnassus-ward by enthusiasm for Chaucer and love of nature, are written in a spirit entirely different from that of the productions of his "fordulled" age. Moreover, it is quite natural that an author who wrote and translated—in such a mechanical way—must have gradually fallen into certain peculiar mannerisms and formulas, which, as time went on, became more and more developed and apparent. Thus we shall see in the chapter on the style of *R. and S.* that the doubling of expressions, the most significant of Lydgate's peculiarities, becomes much more frequent in his later works.

Before beginning to compare the peculiarities of style in our poem with those found in the *Pilgrimage*, I would point out how natural and valuable such a comparison must be, as both poems are translations from the French, and resemble each other in metre and species of poetry.

We find, as we have hinted, that in the *Pilgrimage* double expressions occur far oftener, and that individually they are more finished and perfect. Especially numerous are the alliterative synonymous expressions. The number of examples to be found in *R. and S.* is but scanty; a far greater quantity can be collected from a proportionately small part of the *Pilgrimage*.

I adduce some of the instances in the first 2500 lines: 657 nedful *and* necessarye; 778 thus yt stant *and* thus yt ys; 1059 lyff *and* liberte; 1507 Enoyntynge *and* oynementys; 1560 cruel nor contrayre; 1624 pyte and compassyoun; 1687 portreye or peynte; 1757 tavoyden . . and tenchase; 1814 robbe or reue; 1845 fredam *and* fran*n*chyse; 1956 forfet *and* folye; 2016 malys *and* malencolye; 2476 kutte *and* kerue; 2515 peyne *and* penau*n*ce.

That the metre of the latter work shows the more practised versifier, who has a greater store of formulas at his disposal, and in course of longer exercise of his art has learned to avoid metrical irregularities by means of sundry more or less unpoetical manipulations, is to be settled in the chapter on metre, p. 9. Also, judging from the way in which the final -*e* is employed, the *Pilgrimage* must certainly belong to a later period; for the cases in which the -*e* loses its value as a last syllable are much more numerous in this work than in *R. and S.* In addition, there are other grammatical peculiarities appearing in the *Pilgrimage* and in later works, which are not to be found in our poem.[1] In short, it seems to be almost certain that *R. and S.* could not have been written after the completion of the *Pilgrimage*, but must have been composed at a considerably earlier date. Therefore, of the three periods, in any one of which, at first sight, it seemed our poem could have been written, there remain to us now but two—either the one immediately before the commencement of the *Troy-Book* or that immediately following its completion.

In order to decide in favour of one of these we must of course resort to a comparison of both poems. It has already been said that their resemblance, at least in some parts, is striking enough, and that, therefore, it is quite probable that they do not lie very far apart in respect to date. The question is, which is the earlier of the two?

In the *Troy-Book* there are many traces of peculiarities characteristic of Lydgate's later period. It contains numerous examples of the double expressions of which but few, as has already been said, are to be found in the *Temple of Glas*, and which, as can easily be shown, appear in their greatest numbers in the later works. Alliteration is very frequently met with in the *Troy-Book*, which in this respect takes its place nearer to the *Pilgrimage* than to our poem. Moreover, certain grammatical peculiarities of later Lydgate works—for instance, forms like the above-mentioned "of myn," "of her," "of his," instead of "myn," "her," "his,"—are now and then noticeable in the translation of Guido's work, whilst in *R. and S.* they do not occur at all.—Lastly, there are certain standing formulas in his later works and already in the *Troy-Book*, which Lydgate avoided in *R. and S.*, e. g., "al and somme," "in al the hast he can."[2]

It would be difficult to compare the two poems from a metrical standpoint, as the one is written in heroic verse and the other in octosyllabic couplets, but nevertheless I should like to mention that, as Schick and Krausser have already pointed out, in his earlier works Lydgate avoided writing verses in which a syllable is wanting at the beginning and also in the middle of the same line.—I have shown in its proper place that there are some such lines to be found in *R. and S.*, although their occurrence is rare. But in the latter part of

[1] Comp. especially forms like "an hous of hers" (l. 852); "A sergaunt of myn" (l. 941), which are not at all to be found in *R. and S.*
[2] This expression occurs only once in *R. and S.* From the *Troy-Book* we can adduce heaps of examples. Compare Notes.

the *Troy-Book* Lydgate employed this type without hesitation. Comp. the following instances from Book IV:

"Prudently or he wold assent."
"Though that thou outward shewe fayre."
"Fynally as ye haue it shape."
"Sodaynely fylle in a drede."
"Crowned sat in his regalye."
"Gredyer nor more rauynous."
"Satirye nouther Dryades [ffawny]."

That the occurrence of such lines cannot be accounted for by oversight or through errors in the MSS., is proved by their consistent structure (trisyllabic adjectives filling the first half of the line).

For these reasons I am inclined to consider *R. and S.* to have been written before 1412, the year in which the *Troy-Book* was begun.

These considerations had been already noted down some time, before I met with a literary testimony which seems to confirm my results. A. Schmid in his book *Literatur des Schachspiels* (Wien, 1847) gives an account of those manuscripts relating to chess which are described by Th. Hyde.[1] Then follows: "Th. Hyde giebt noch eine Handschrift an, welche wahrscheinlich zu Oxford befindlich ist. Lydgatus, Joh. in Poemate amatorio Anglice MS. Shahiludii et Belli Amatorii comparationem scite et eleganter instituit (S. Hyde, Mandragorias. Oxon. 1694. 8. Prolegom. und dessen Syntagma Dissertat. Ibid. 1767. 4. Tom. II, Prolog. (!)) In diesem, um das Jahr 1408 geschriebenen Gedichte wird das Minnespiel mit dem Schachspiele verglichen." Now we read in Thomas Hyde, *Mandragorias seu Historia Shahiludii*. Oxonii, 1694, under the heading *Prolegomena Curiosa* as follows: "Johannes Lydgatus Anglus, Monachus de Burgo S[cti] Edmundi, hunc Ludum suo tempore usitatum vocat the Game Royall: idemque Lydgatus Librum suum per modum Poëmatis Amatorii conscriptum, hujus Ludi (quam Bello Amatorio assimilat), Aestimatoribus dicat dedicatque, his verbis, uti in Codice MS. legitur:

"To all folkys vertuouse,
    that gentil bene and amerouse,
which love the fair pley notable,
    of the Chesse most delytable,
whith all her hoole full entente,
    to them this boke y will presente:

---

[1] Hyde, Thomas, D.D., 1636–1703, orientalist, chief librarian of the Bodleian.

> where they shall fynde and son [!] anoone,
> how that I nat yere agoone,
> was of a Fers so fortunat
> into a corner drive and Maat."

Here no date is mentioned for the composition of the Lydgate poem. Neither does Hyde in other places give information on this point, at least so far as I can see. Nevertheless, it seems to me absolutely impossible that Schmid made his statement without any solid ground to stand on.

CHAPTER II.
STRUCTURE OF THE VERSE.

THE great admiration which was felt for Lydgate by his contemporaries is only to be understood on the ground that his verses were not quite bare of a certain rhythmical music. Schick in his essay on our poem has brought a direct literary proof of this proposition.

No less an authority than the great Scotch poet Dunbar has left us his opinion of the metrical perfection of Lydgate's verses:

> " O morale Goweir, and Lidgait laureat,
> Your suggarat toungis, and lippis aureat
> Bene till our eris cause of grit delyte:
> Your angelic mowthis most mellifluat
> Our rude langage hes cleir illumynat."

Diametrically opposed to this stands the judgment of recent critics: Ritson does not hesitate to declare that there are scarcely three lines together of pure and accurate metre; and Skeat (*Kingis Quair*, p. xxxii) points out how totally different James I.'s musical verses are to the halting lines of Lydgate. On the other hand, Schipper in his *Englische Metrik*, 1, § 196, and, as we shall have to explain later on, Schick in his Introduction to the *Temple of Glas*, p. lvi ff., have done greater justice to the metrical system of our monk.

But even with this, the question does not appear to be finally settled. A criticism like that of Steele (*Secrees of old Philisoffres*, p. xviii), it is true, does not weigh much, as his conclusion is based upon a totally uncritical text. But there are other scholars, too, who fail to find in the verses of at least some of our monk's works anything but a " barbarous jangle." (Cp. Triggs, *The Assembly of Gods*, chapter iii, p. xiv.)

[1] See Th. Prosiegel, *The Book of the Gouernaunce of Kynges*. München, 1903.

I do not think that matters are advanced by further general statements, and, uninfluenced by the conflict of diverse opinions, and taking the standpoint of an agnostic, I enter into an unprejudiced metrical examination of our poem in order to find out, first of all, how its verses are to be read.

In the first place, it may be desirable to give a few remarks as to the general rules which Lydgate used to follow in building his verses.

The most important matter, that of sounding the final -e, will be thoroughly dealt with in the next chapter. Here we have only to point out some special peculiarities:

1. With regard to elision, on the whole, the same rules are followed as in Chaucer, but hiatus is, especially in the caesura, not at all unfrequent. Again, Lydgate limits elision much less exclusively to the unaccented final -e. That the article *the* and the preposition *to* before a vowel are elided is in Chaucer, also, very often met with, as well as the fact that a final -y is combined with a vowel following to make one syllable. But elision goes further in cases like: 199, "I was so ententyf for to here;" 932, "The ayre so atempere was and clere;" 1847, "Mercurie in al the hast he kan)." Compare further from the *Pilgrimage:* 483, "By vertu off crystys gret suffravnce;" 6386, "The valu and the magnyfycence;" 7878, "That vertu ha domynacïoun;" and 10561, "She abrayde by good avysëment."

2. Synizesis is comparatively rare. Of decided examples we can adduce the following:

    1078   "For to lyve vertuously."
    1180   "Makythe mensyon of her armoure."
    1439   "As ye shal here, cerjously."
    2406   "But best and most specjaly."
    2435   "To reherse compendjously."
    6445   "That al[le] bestys specjaly."

3. Diæresis is met with in *treës*. In some cases, too, a good metre would permit us to read *virtuës:* 503, etc.

4. Under the heading of syncope we could put together two rules, with regard to which Lydgate again, there is no doubt, goes much farther than Chaucer:

a. Sometimes the endings *-el*, *-en*, *-er* do not count as syllables. Not only are such words concerned as: whether, outher, rather, thither, evene, evele; but also a number of nouns, adjectives (especially of Romance origin), and verbs:

Ch. II. General Rules for Lydgate's Verse. 11

1422 " A ful ryche sceptre she helde."
3170 " Or any spot of evel menyng."
5936 " With my brother, the god Cupide."

β, Slurring takes place almost always in words like: naturel, spirit, perseueraunce, soueraynte, subtylyte,[1] perilouse, Cerberus, semelynesse,[1] syngulerte.

5. Finally I have to call attention to a peculiarity which is frequently enough to be met with in Lydgate: the suppression of a final -e between two dentals which is otherwise sounded. Examples:

97 " Alle the erthe, this verray trewe."
844 " To holde the wey[e] of resoun."
966 " For the grete dyuersyte."
4252 " For which take good hede therto."
4969 "To be-holde the purtreytures."
6088 " And y-bounde to his emprise."
6178 " Nor of kynde they be nat lyke."
6202 " Of her trouthe dooth never fade."
6605 " Which hath by kynde the dignite."

The instances, of course, are not limited to *Reson and Sensuallyte*. The *Pilgrimage* has:

448 " Who lyst taken hed ther-to."
3089 " The cause to me yn-knowen ys."
6252 " They sholde the plesë neueradel."
6742 " And to spede thy pylgrymage."
20647 " In erthe, ther sholdë non greyns sprynge."

Compare also *Temple of Glas*, 855, " And eke my sone Cupide, þat is so blind."

The lines of our poem are composed of four iambic feet, a metre which the poet took from his French original. As a rule the caesura falls after the second foot, but now and then we must look for it at the end of the first or the third foot.

If we examine the structure of the verse a little more closely, we perceive at the outset that Lydgate by no means confines himself to the strict exactitude of the French octosyllabic line, but varies the regular march of the original metre very much.

In reading the poem we are first of all struck by the frequent omission of the first thesis. The poet is far from being a stickler in this respect, for the first unaccented syllable is wanting in no less

---

[1] In *subtylyte* and *semelynesse* the vowel in question is not in accordance with the etymology of the respective words; its existence was perhaps merely graphic.

than nearly 300 out of every 1000 verses. Such verses in which the opening syllable is wanting are strictly of trochaic metre. The poet himself seems to have been more or less unconsciously influenced by this fundamental alteration in the metre; for frequently, after falling into the trochaic step, he adheres to it for some time, and then suddenly drops back to his usual measure.

This is shown by the following list, which gives an enumeration of the acephalous or headless lines occurring in the first 500 lines of our poem: 4, 8, 12–14, 18, 24, 27–28, 31, 45, 47, 52, 55–57, 59, 61, 66, 70, 76, 81, 85, 88–90, 97, 103–105, 107–108, 113?, 117–18, 123, 127, 140, 151, 157, 162–64, 167, 169, 175–76, 178, 180, 185, 190, 195, 198, 204, 213, 215, 217, 219, 224, 227, 229, 230–32, 235, 238, 241–42, 245, 250, 260, 262, 266, 268, 270, 273, 275, 278–80, 283–84, 287–88, 293, 296, 297, 299, 302–4, 308–9, 314, 316?, 317, 329, 334–35, 338, 342, 348, 352, 355–56, 364–68, 370, 373–74, 377, 390–94, 396, 400, 403, 408, 415–17, 420, 424, 426, 428–29, 431, 438–40, 442, 448, 455–56, 459, 471–72, 478–80, 482, 484, 486, 494, 498–99.

Occasionally also in the opening foot of the verse we notice another irregularity which consists in the substitution of two, instead of the one, unaccented syllables of the iambic. Examples of this are however extremely rare. In the first 2000 verses we meet only two decided instances: 261, "Non man may contrarie nor with-seye;" 652, "By exaumple of the firmament." With regard to *contrarie* see ten Brink, *Chaucer's Sprache und Verskunst*, § 261. Of the rest the following lines belong to, or might easily be brought under, this type:

> 2099 "For she semys, shortly for to telle."
> 2107 "Al this worlde gooth the same trace."
> 3623 "Of which in ysidre ye may se."
> 4480 "Of the kyng Nabugodonosor."
> 4776 "And I neuer after with hir spake."

The same licence which we have noticed in the opening foot meets us also in the caesura. Thus (α) the thesis is omitted so that two accented syllables clash together. To be sure, this does not occur so frequently as the omission of the thesis in the first foot, but still it is frequent enough to constitute one of the metrical characteristics of the poem. Such lines to a modern ear have a harshness of which the ears of Lydgate and his contemporaries do not seem to have been sensible. (β) There are two light syllables in the caesura.

This ceasura is properly called trochaic. Only three conclusive instances occur: 1235, 1239, 1471.

It is, then, indisputable that Lydgate allows himself this amount of licence at the beginning of the verse or in the caesura. But the further question arises: Does he combine the two in the same line? Cases in which irregularities in the caesura occur in combination with a double thesis in the opening foot can be set aside at once. The few verses which have a double thesis at the beginning, are in other respects regular. Only two cases, then, remain with which we need concern ourselves: (α) when the thesis is wanting in the first foot and in the caesura at the same time. That there are examples of this cannot be denied, for it is impossible to scan the following verses upon any other principle:

741 " Wher as man), in sentence."
968 " Est and West, norṫh and southe."
5980 " I kam) forṫh to presence ;"

(β) when the trochaic caesura is found in the same line with the omission of the thesis in the first foot. There are a good many verses which could be easily brought under this scheme:

1452 " For the membres that y of spake."
1799 " Wonder kene the point to form)."
3924 "Faire witḣ-oute, but corumpable."
5873 " And fortune shoop so for me."
5936 " Witḣ my brother, the god Cupide."
6748 " Whan) a wommaṁ) hath no rewarde."
6678 "Curse hem newe for her dysdeyne."

In these instances, the superfluous thesis in the caesura supplements the missing syllable of the first foot, and offers a possibility of reading the verses as regular ones.

The only question is, whether the accentuation of the words will permit such an explanation. That Lydgate allows himself a somewhat arbitrary licence in regard to the accent, which he sometimes puts on the inflexions, or other light syllables, is, as we shall see later, certain enough. But the question is, whether this licence has its limits. Can we go so far as to say that the writer of a poem, the metre of which offers in other respects no foothold for serious censure, could twice or even three times in the same line have done violence to the natural accentuation?

Again, we might ask, why should exactly this kind of measure be impossible in our poem? Granted, first of all, that variations from

14   Ch. II.   Lydgate's 3 Kinds of Metrical Lines.

the regular form occur in the same line, both in the first foot and in the caesura, which our previous examples have shown to be indeed the case, we have no ground for denying the existence of this kind.

On the other hand, it can be justly said that a line with eight syllables formed on the model of the regular French octosyllabic line, should not be scanned on other principles.

Of course, in some cases the difficulty would vanish, if we were to slur over the final -e after the second arses. But the conclusions of our inquiry are such as to make us hesitate before doing this; for we cannot point to a single other instance in the whole poem where the -e of the adjectival *ja*-stems is not counted as a syllable. Nor is there any certain occurrence of wĭthóutę, fŏrtúnę, etc.

We are really compelled, if we would avoid an arbitrary method of accentuation, to take refuge in the supposition of a special type of verse which, however, like the preceding, is only to be regarded as an exceptional resort in case of difficulty.

We can distinguish, then, in our poem, leaving out of consideration those lines which only exceptionally occur, three large groups of verses, which are enumerated in the order of their frequency:

1. The regular line; 2. the headless or acephalous line; 3. lines without a thesis in the caesura.

There is a comparatively small number of verses, which cannot be placed in any group.

Examples of these are:

        3900 "Ay tendre, fresh, and grene."
        4805 "Ha noon) occasion)."[1]
        6879 "That for to stynte her mone."

It needs no proof to see that this analysis of Lydgate's metre into its *external structure* is far from giving us a truer and deeper insight into its metrical art. Much more important is the question: How does his verse stand as regards its *quality*? Of course the answer to this question is not entirely independent of the structural analysis. The problem is, namely, whether the above-mentioned variations are consistent with the nature of the four-foot iambic line. To see this point clearly we must go a little further afield and lay down a few necessary presuppositions.

By the pause after the second foot, our four-foot iambic is divided into two exactly equal halves, each of which can be properly counted as an independent line, and, as the development of modern metrical

    [1] Here we might perhaps read: Há[vě] nóon) ŏccásĭon).

Ch. II. Omission of a First Syllable justified. 15

art teaches, was actually conceived as such. Now the indulgence of a certain amount of licence in the rhythm—whether in the transference of the accent or in the doubling or the omission of the thesis—is much less repellent, if it occurs at the beginning of the verse. See the admirable remark of ten Brink, *Chaucer's Sprache und Verskunst*, p. 156: "wie die Betrachtung der Verskunst der Gegenwart bei verschiedenen Völkern lehrt, will der Schluss eines Verses unter allen Umständen in seinnem Rhythmus respectiert sein und wird dies sogar in der syllabisch accentuirenden Versart der Romanen (ebenso, kömen wir hinzufügen, in der syllabisch quantitirenden Versart den alten Inder) [anerkannt], währendandrerseits der Versanfang sogar in den rhythmisch-accentuirenden Metren der Germanen Abweichung vom streng rhythmischen Schema bzw. Verschleierung desselben gestattet." Indeed, at the beginning of a verse, a monosyllabic or trisyllabic foot scarcely breaks the rhythm at all. At the same time, after the caesura, which to our sense of rhythm constitutes the beginning of a new and independent line, the omission or addition of a thesis does not offend. In this way it happens, that we are not, so to speak, thrown off the track by these variations from the strict iambic, and do not lose the sense of an even and regular motion.

But further, this licence in the verse structure not only constitutes no violation of the fundamental metrical form of the poem, to which the most refined ear could object, but is even, if used judiciously, a positive advantage to the rhythm. It breaks the wearisome monotony of the French octosyllabic line with a refreshing variation, and imparts a touch of sprightliness to a somewhat ponderous measure.

We must, however, once more expressly point out that this holds good only in the case of the regular four-footed iambic with the caesura in the middle of the line. The case is very different when the caesura comes after the third or first foot. In the former case we are forbidden to indulge in licence for fear of offending the rhythm which belongs of right to the last foot of the verse. In the latter case, it is quite impossible to introduce a second arsis immediately after the first.

We now come to that point which is of the most radical importance for the metrical perfection of a poem, viz. the correspondence between the logical intonation and the metrical accentuation of the words.

How far has Lydgate reconciled the metrical accent with the

proper emphasis demanded by pronunciation and by the sense of the sentence? A closer examination shows us that, as in Chaucer's poems, the accent of the *sentence* seldom conflicts with the rhythm of the verse, but that the *word-accent* often does so. The result of my investigations on this point are shortly put together in the following lines:

Most frequently we find the accent on the *-ing* of the present participle, and indeed this accentuation seems to be almost the rule with present participles. Of the extremely numerous instances I give as examples:

makyng 129, cleymyng 395, goynge 430, syngyng 460, havynge 545, knowyng 573, 1157, takyng 651, biddyng 822, 1481, smyling' 1547, laughyng' 1548, persyng' 1587, brennyng' 1588, fleyng 1597, semyng 1598.

There are also a fair number of instances,—mostly confined to the first foot,—where the *-eth* of the 3 sing. pres. ind. is put in arsi: duelleth 2595, clotheth 96, semeth 113, holdeth 790, singeth 1248, falleth 4152, graunteth 3335, maketh 3338, yiveth 3348, singeth 1248, myneth 6918.

In the following instances the *-eth* forms the third arsis : causeth 102, turneth 654, bereth 2621, sorweth 5034, chaungeth 6214, stauncheth 6491, techeth 6634.

All other cases of the accent occurring on inflected syllables of the verb, appear only as isolated exceptions. We may note these instances:

(*a*) of the inf.: sywe[n] 660, resten) 6870; both infinitives stand in the middle of the verse, *sywen* after, and *resten*) before, the caesura.

(*β*) of the past part.: couered 919, named 1054, cromped 1800, pulshed 6080, prentyd 4622, medled 6070.

In all these instances the past. part. begins the verse. In *getyn*) 1611, the accented ending stands before the caesura.

The fact, that the plural ending *-es* bears the verse-accent, is confirmed by several cases: herbes 536, membres 1300, goddys 2987 [?], folkys 6653. In the adjective, the superlative termination is found in arsi, a fact which in itself can scarcely surprise us, since the *-est* cannot be regarded as a light syllable.

Cp. fairest 2197, trewest 2604, gretest 5115, swyftes[t] 6977.

The *-er* of the comparative also occasionally takes the place of an accented syllable: bryghter 436, fairer 2175, fressher 3434, feller 3622, fairer 4554, swetter 5737, ferther 6016, lever 6369, lyghter

Ch. II. Lydgate's Licence in accenting Proper Names. 17

6709, rather 6908. *fressher* in l. 3434 follows the caesura, *swetter* in l. 5737 antecedes it; in all other cases the comparative begins the verse. Lydgate also often lays the stress on the naturally unaccented final syllable in prepositions, conjunctions, and other similar words of a merely formal character: after 77, 160, 4620, 6168, vnder 1485, 3700, nouther 2553, 4174, 4205, 4535, 4632, outher 5345, 5970, 6330, ellis 1640, ouer 4166.

The licence which Lydgate takes in the metrical accentuation of proper names is, however, much more marked than we have yet met with, so that it seems really impossible to lay down general rules. The dissyllabic proper names appear with the accent, in one place on the first, in another on the second, syllable, according to the demands of the metre: *e. g.* Argus, Phebus, Pallas, Juno, Venus, Atlas, Paris, Deduit, Arthur, Jason. Still greater is the confusion with names of 3 and more syllables. In these, not only does the accent shift about, but syllables also are sometimes dropped. Examples: Sătóurnĕ 1295, 1306, 1346, Sátŭrnús 1462, Sátoŭrnę 3103; Mĕrcúrĭús 1528, 1606, 1646, Mĕrcúrĕ 1623, 1655, 2102, Mĕrcúrĭe 1847; Cŭpýdĕ 2438, 3891, Cúpĭdó 2488; Ŏuídĕ 3261, 3965, Ŏuídĭuś 3847.

Unnatural as these arbitrary alterations in the word-accent may appear, still when we read the verses, their harshness is much less felt than we should at first imagine.

It is not difficult to understand how a language, which in a state of rapid development shows itself capable of a remarkable degree of assimilation, is somewhat arbitrary in the accentuation of rare and foreign proper names.

As to the accentuation of inflected syllables, it must be remembered that such instances are always exceptional, and in comparison with the far more frequent cases where the right accentuation is preserved, are hardly matter of urgent concern. Secondly, it is a noteworthy fact that this licence of accenting the inflected syllables is almost exclusively confined to the first foot of the verse, where a variation from the strict rhythmical form or a slurring over is permissible. The poet allows himself this licence in the first foot after the caesura also, but with much greater reserve. Thus, of the examples given, in which the ending *-eth* is put in arsi, ten occur at the opening of the verse, and only seven after the caesura. The prepositions, etc., mentioned occur almost without exception at the opening of the verse.

Let us sum up now in a general judgment:

Taking it all in all, we may fairly speak of the metrical qualities of *Reson and Sensuallyte* with praise. At any rate, the poem offers no occasion for severe criticism. It satisfies all the demands which we are justified in laying upon it in accordance with the general conditions of its production. As far as this work is concerned, we must emphatically deny a statement to the effect that "there are scarcely three lines together of pure and accurate metre." One can read whole pages of the poem in which even a classically-trained ear would not be conscious of a shock to its sensibility.

It might be supposed that this comparatively great perfection was due to the finer cast of the whole poem, but we are not able to accept this opinion. It would indeed be incorrect to make the higher poetical value of *Reson and Sensuallyte* responsible for the smooth metre.

In order to settle to what extent the metrical peculiarities of our poem are connected with the peculiar poetical character, we have to examine how the four-beat line reads in other productions of Lydgate. I leave the minor occasional poems out of consideration, which in other respects also differ much from one another, and turn at once to the other great poem written in four-footed iambic, the *Pilgrimage*.

This poem was commenced in 1426, later therefore than our poem. The noticeable fact that the monk, in advanced age, grew more and more wearisome and careless in his writing should lead us to expect a worse metre; it is consequently a surprise to find that the metre is certainly not worse, but occasionally better than in *R. and S.*

It is true there are also some doubtful verses. I am however quite sure that simple, easy conjectures will, in general, suffice to put them right. For the others the metre is unquestionably smooth and flowing.

The violence done to the natural accentuation of the words, which in *R. and S.* now and then falls harshly upon the ear, is not met with so frequently here. Also the type C, where in the caesura two accented syllables clash together, is more rare; a fact which proves that Lydgate, too, felt the harshness of such a verse, and therefore tried more and more to avoid it.[1] Of the whole 22,000 lines which

---

[1] The recognition of exactly this fact has induced me, by adding a final -*e* in the caesura, to do away with type C as far as possible. If Lydgate avoided as much as he could the clashing together of his accented syllables in the caesura, he will have also done so in all those cases where the sounding of a final -*e*, historically justified, and in most cases retained, afforded an easy means of doing so.

I have carefully examined, there occur but a remarkably small number which can be read only according to the peculiarly Lydgatian type, in which the thesis is wanting in the caesura. By my calculation they amount to 0·58 per cent. A redundant syllable before the caesura is even still scarcer.

We see therefore that also in this work the four-beat line is treated comparatively skilfully; and it might therefore be maintained that this kind of Lydgate's metre offers little scope for censure, and that all the adverse criticism which has been delivered on the good monk's metrical art does not touch his four-beat line.

Let us now compare our conclusions with the researches hitherto made on the subject of Lydgate's metre. The first successful attempt to put in order the metrical principles of Lydgate was (next to Schipper's) that of Schick in his *Temple of Glas*. Schick submitted the iambic five-beat line of that poem to a vigorous examination, at the conclusion of which he came to the following results:—

"We may say, roughly speaking, that Lydgate has five types of the five-beat line.

A. The regular type, presenting five iambics, to which, as to the other types, at the end an extra-syllable may be added. There is usually a well-defined caesura after the second foot, but not always. Example:

Line 1 :   For thóuȝt, constréint,
            and gréuous héuinés[se].

B. Lines with the trochaic caesura, built like the preceding, but with an extra-syllable before the caesura. Example:

L. 77 :   There wás eke Ísaude—
           & méni anóþir mó.

C. The peculiarly Lydgatian type, in which the thesis is wanting in the caesura, so that two accented syllables clash together. Example:

L. 905 :   For spéchelés
            nóþing máist þou spéde.

D. The acephalous or headless line, in which the first syllable has been cut off, thus leaving a monosyllabic first measure. Example:

L. 1396 :   Únto hír
             & tó hir éxcellénce.

E. Lines with trisyllabic first measure. The occurrence of such lines in our poem is uncertain; but two lines may belong to this class, if we read them in the following way:

L. 781 : Thăt wăs féiþful foúnd, til hem depárted déþe;
L. 1029. Ănd ăs férforþe ás my wíttes cón concéyue."—

If we compare with these conclusions the results of our inquiry, we find a remarkable agreement between the two. In both species of verse the same liberties in the opening foot and in the caesura lead to the same metrical groups or types, the last of which (lines with trisyllabic first measure) on account of its extreme rarity is scarcely worth counting. Only in the frequency with which the various other forms occur do we perceive any remarkable difference. The headless line is much rarer in the five-beat line than in the four-footed iambic, while instances of irregularity in the caesura are comparatively more numerous.

In spite, however, of the external similarity of verse structure, the four-beat line is, as a rule, of a higher metrical quality and reads more smoothly than the five-footed iambic, for which fact I am inclined to advance the following reason : In the four-footed iambic we have two equal and independent halves, each of which admits a certain rhythmic licence at the beginning. But in the five-beat line the halves are unequal and therefore not independent of one another, but essentially going together, so that irregularities now at the beginning and now in the caesura, if frequently repeated, cannot fail to jar upon the ear.

CHAPTER III.

THE INFLEXIONS.

LYDGATE'S treatment of the final -*e* has also been thoroughly dealt with by Schick in his edition of the *Temple of Glas*, and by him the most essential points have been settled once for all. Nevertheless it does not seem to me that the editor of a poem by Lydgate is justified in wholly ignoring the subject (Steele, *Secrees of old Philisoffres*, p. viii). There is but little doubt that the gradual loss of inflectional endings is clearly visible in the works of Lydgate, whose literary activity extends over a period of more than half a century. Difference in metre and versification, too, had a certain influence on the treatment of the unaccented syllable. In short, I believe it is imperative that in each of Lydgate's works the question regarding the final -*e*'s should be specially dealt with. In cases where there is no external evidence for deciding the date of a poem, the settlement of this question (taken together with an investigation of the rhyme) may be the only ground

Ch. III. Inflexions. The final -e. Strong Substantives. 21

upon which to base a trustworthy conclusion touching the date of composition. I believe, therefore, I am fully justified in again raising the question, to what extent the final -e was sounded.

First of all some remarks as to the method to be followed in the treatment of this vexed point.

The issue, of course, hinges upon the structure and nature of the metre; but a decision based upon it would naturally be of absolute accuracy only in the event of absolute regularity in the metre throughout the entire poem. Now not a single one of Lydgate's works presents such a phenomenon. The apparent difficulty of formulating available conclusions need, however, not appal us. The case is not a hopeless one. Even a cursory glance at the text under consideration will reveal the fact that, however bold the licences the author allows himself in the first foot of a line or at the caesura, he never indulges in any in the second or the fourth foot. Hence, in spite of the variety of ways which some lines admit of scansion, there are a great many verses that can be scanned in one, and only one, way. These afford us examples of positive value in the attempt to get at the root of the matter. With their aid we may formulate a law, which, even in dubious cases, will help us in deciding how the final -e should be sounded.

Thus we have always added a final -e in the caesura in order to prevent the clashing of two accented syllables, when such an addition is found to agree with the rules we believe Lydgate to have followed. I have pointed out my reasons for doing so in the chapter on the structure of the verse.

Of course, I have confined myself in my investigations to the poem which is the subject of this work, citing examples from Lydgate's other works only when of a particularly interesting character.

1. SUBSTANTIVES.

Strong Declension. 1. *Singular.* (a) *Masculines and Neuters.*

Nom. and Accus. of the *a*-stems without ending. To heap up examples would be useless.

We find an inorganic *e* in weyë (nom. and accus.) 811, 2722, and 602, 790, 798, 858, 883, 4105. In *morowë* 75, 449, 906, 1074, 1185, *ë* remains after the apocope of a final -*n*; also in *gamë* 6933. dalë 4785 (rhyming with *valë*) and gatë 4990, 6958, belong to those short-stemmed words which in nom. and accus. assume an *e* taken from plural (O.E. *u*). See ten Brink, *Chaucer's Sprache und Verskunst*, § 203, 5. In *kole*, 1578, we have another word of this group, but here elision takes place.

Genitive in *-ës* (*ÿs*): goddÿs 632, 2269, 2273, 2637, 4106, 4321; kyng*ës* 1899; borës 3741; lordÿs 6832.

Dative usually without ending, but instances of *-ë* not unfrequent: kyndë 103, 174, 254, 304, 390, 462, 1085, etc.; hedë (rhyming with *hede, rede,* adj. plur. or *drede*) 1208, 1410, 1782; wayë 4780; goldë 1946; swerdë 4662; brondë 2023; wal[lë] 4961.

Dissyllables either remain unaltered or assume *ë* after having syncopated the vowel of the final syllable: hevenẹ 114, 383, 846, 1224, 1675; siluer 1320, 1325; coper 1328; appul 1923, 1947; wynter 5163; somer 5164; mayden 2357, 6732;—toknë 1045, 1056; bothmë 5753; maydë 1617, 3650, 5817.

ja-stems: *ë* in all cases: Nom. endë 895, 3996; hiwë 1103; lechë 5151; Dat. hewë 98, 138, 150, 234, 363, 536, 1167, etc.; endë 3669; Accus, endë 1091, 3740; witë 6768.

i- and *u*-stems: Also a fair number of examples in *-ë*. Nom. lyë 4011 (dye, inf.); Dat. wood[e] 1970; wodë 3749; stedë 1573; Accus. sperë 1196; lyë 11, 997; but sonẹ 2879 [?] Of abstracts in *-shipë* (O.E. *scipe*) occur the Accus. wórshĭpé 6803 [?]; lórdshĭppẹ 546, 1477.

(β) Strong *Feminines*.

The *ë* in the nom. is either the remnant of O.E. *u* or foisted in from the oblique cases.

Examples: quenë 432 (shenë); talë 960, 1149;[1] nasë (*u*-stem) 1715; dredë 2053, 6710; lovë 2517, 5434; trouthë 2821, 3175, 6857; botë 3441, 4130; help[e] 3454; shamë 3520, 6705; shadwë (*wa*-stem) 4011; ryndë 4955; hyndë 3727; merthë 5559, 6883; youthë 6231; sorwë 6876.

The final *-e* is silent in worldẹ 3092; lovẹ 3167, 4301, 6061, and quenẹ 1343 (sene, inf.), 1569, 4336.

Gen.: in *-ës* (*is, ÿs*) lowës 2428; lovës 4866, 5188, 5466, 5806, 6284; youthës 6236; youthis 6241; quenÿs 6667.

Dat. and Accus. in *-ë*. The examples are too numerous to be cited in full. I confine myself to giving exceptional instances. We find always: sight, myght, and, apart from l. 1875 (where the regular metrical type would demand hondë), also hondẹ: 1196, 1200, 1577, 1590, 1735, 1750, 3573, 3986, 4724, 6934; *worlde* seems

[1] The word rhymes in both cases with smale (adj. plural) following the noun.

Ch. III. Inflexions. The final -e. Strong Substantives. 23

likewise to permit both ways of reading: worlde 1323, 1343, 2033, 2215, 3234, 4212, 5349, 6069, 6983; but ll. 559, 618, 1027, and 4510, read after our first type, exhibit *worldë*. See further: youthe 334, blysse 1093; trouthe 6197; quene 6025, 6251; hede rhymes thrice with *dede* (adj. sing.) 2962, 4124, 4264, once with *renomed* 5138. Such instances as l. 3752 ("who that kan take hede ther-to") are, of course, dubious. In l. 5877 we must, I think, also read *hede*.

Abstracts in -*hede* (O.E. hâd, *hǽdu), of which examples only occur in dat. and accus., seem to be felt as feminines. In l. 6759 I should certainly read *womanhedë*; comp. further: flesshlyhedë 5058, (dedë), woman-hedë 212, (dredë), frendelyhedë 5854 (hatredë).

Words in -*nesse* (-*nysse*) rhyme frequently with Romance nouns in -*esse*: ydelnesse 463; fairnesse 1860, 2052; worthynesse 1510; lyknesse 1733; besynesse 1638. In cases like swetnesse 82, where the accent is thrown back, the final -*e*, of course, is dropped.

2. *Plural.*

A few neuters sometimes retain the original form without any termination: folke 2143, 2385, 3422, 3449, 6675, 6766; thing 259, 298, 2291, 4194; swyn 3428. The *wa*-stem *tree*, now and then, assumes the ending of the weak substantives: treen 2750, 3898, 4372, 4387, 4389 (treën), 4407 (treën). Apart from these instances, the ending of the plural is always -*ës* (-*ÿs*) or -*s* (-*es*). -*s* (-*es*) seems mostly to be confined to dissyllables: fethers 1428; meremaydenes 1773, maydenes 3129 [?], maydens 3248; appuls 2752; lovers 6996, 6999, 7004. Dissyllables which syncopate the vowel of the final syllable have -*ës* (-*ÿs*): fethrës 5358, 5461, 5490; applÿs 3916; watrÿs 3832, 3884. Monosyllables, as a rule, terminate in -*ës*; comp. arwes (earh) 2852, 2860, 5413; instances where -*es* does not count as an extra-syllable are quite exceptional: thinges 732, 744; rynges 1568 [?]

As to the plural of words ending in a vowel, see the following instances: trees 2729, 3915, 4002, 5159; but treës 4009, 6281, 6871; weyës 621, 640, 2300, etc.; dawës 851.

n-stems.

With the exception of *lady*, *pley*, and (*h*)*adder*, which have lost their final -*e*, and *woo* (O.E. wêa, wâ), the ending of nom. sing., to which dat. and accus. correspond, is generally -*ë*.

24   Ch. III. *Inflexions.*   *The final* -e.   *Weak Substantives.*

The following list, I hope, contains all the weak substantives of our text. We scarcely need note down all the lines where they occur.

a. Masculines :
Nom.: namë, willë, tymë, makë, harë, phanë, snakë; dat. and accus.: namë, willë, tymë, tenë, wonë, hopë, ferë, bowë, stedë.

β. Feminines :
Nom.: sonnë, erthë, hertë, wellë, swalwë, dowë, tonnë, nyghtyngalë; dat. and accus.: hertë, tonnë, sonnë, sydë, erthë, wisë, wellë, molberye, tongë, dowvë, trappë.

γ. Neuters :
Nom.: eyë; Accus.: erë.

Instances where the final *-e* is suppressed are only sporadic :
Nom.: eye 6967 ; dat. and accus.: wil 2252 (but comp. O.E. gewill), erthe 97, tyme 1064, pithe 740,[1] eye 996,[2] tene (trene) 5204. In l. 6185 f. we must read *to donë moonë*. Comp., however, *Temple of Glas*, l. 394.

Examining these exceptional cases, we must confess that, save those instances where the weak noun is a rhyme-word, they are more or less dubious, and that there is scarcely one conclusive example of the suppression of the final *-e*.

Genitive in *-ës (-ÿs)* or *-ë* : hertys 5020, 6962 ; sonnë 938 ; hertë blood 6823. Schick (*Temple of Glas*, lxvi) adduces two similar examples: hertë roote (*Falls of Princes*) and sunnë bemes (*Pilgr.*).

Plural : The old ending is retained in : eyën 423, 826, 1258, 1548, 1715, 1782, etc.; fon) 1195, 3134. In all other cases we find *-ës (-ÿs)*. Examples :

a. Masculines : sterrës, sterris 118, 269, 274, 417, 420, 752, 1005, 1133, 1277, l. 1676 we had better read *sterris;* blosmës 139, blosmÿs 535 ; dropës 140, 453 ; assës 3428 ; stedÿs 4210 ; ebbÿs 4617 ; bowës 5412 ; knottÿs 5427 ; namÿs, namës 5441, 5445, 6724, 6728 ; husbondÿs, -ës 6584 6877.

β. Feminines : hertÿs 93, 1508, 5432, 5473, 5855 ; wellÿs 934 (tellys), 4365, 4484 ; wellës 4143 ; ladyës (dissyll.) 1021, 2423, 3128, 3187, 3249 ; dowës 1596 ; asshës 3920, 4115 ; berië (dissyll.) 4001 ; trappüs 4139 ; harpÿs 5579.

γ. Neuters : erës 4128, erÿs 6396.

---

[1] "To know the prevy pithe withinne."
[2] "Myn eye so as I caste a-syde."

Ch. III. Inflexions. Final -e. 1. Accent of Romance Nouns. 25

Other consonant-stems.

We subjoin a complete list of the instances occurring in our text.
1. Items in *-r* :
Nom.: fader 1614, 4167, 4170; brother 2981, 3265, 6236; doughter 1034, 1050, 1618; doghtrë (doughtrë) 1042, 1437, 1793, 2975; moder 5267, 5939; stepmoder 1642.
Gen.: fader 4175; faderës 4180, 4202.
Dat.: fader 1451, 4311, 4324; brother (brothir) 4800, 5264, 5936, 5946.
Accus.: fader 3086, 4288; suster 874, 4948; doghter 3260; moder 4292.
Plural: stepmodres 1648, 1651; brethre 2521.
2. in *-nd:*
Voc.: frende 722, 1850, 2117, 2257, 2298, 3481, 4106.
Plural: frendës 1404, 3157.
3. in *-os, -es:*
Nom.: lambe 6259. Nom.: childe 1275.
Voc.: childe 445, 2937.
Plural: children 1649, 4330.
4. Minor groups of monosyllabic consonant stems:
A. Masculines:
Nom.: man 237, 261, 313, 317, 384, etc.; woman 6224, 6405, etc.; tothe 3578.
Gen.: mannÿs (mannës) 1159, 1367, 1423, etc.
Dat.: man 405, 531, 542, 563; woman 6219, 6365, 6547.
Accus.: man 624, 673, 1085; foot 4096.
Plural: men 84, 104, 295, 389; fete 1429; tethe 1717, 3576; womën 1775, 3190, 6346, 6571; gentilwymmen 3181.
B. Feminines:
Nom.: boke 1030, 1035; night' 100. Gen.: gootÿs 6893.
Dat.: goot 4286; boke, book 19, 4859, 6843.
Accus.: boke 6; nyght' 365, 2866, 3675; mylke 1630, 1639, 1644.
Plural: bookës (bookÿs) 1038, 1306, 1344, 2282, 3263, 3647, 4297.

Romance Nouns.

At first I think some elucidation might be desirable as to what extent the accent is thrown back. The original accentuation is retained in the following cases: cŏmfórt 192, cŏunsaýl 803, guérdón

26 *Ch. III. Inflexions. Final -e. 1. Accent of Romance Nouns.*

506, 593, měríte 590, mětál 1325, pŭrpós 787, sŏláce 887, ărmoúre 1180, 1192.

How far the tendency of throwing the accent back is proceeded, we see from the following instances:

áuctoŭr 933, 1028, 1129, 1179, 1433, ăuctoúr 1391; crístăl 124, crĭstál 436; cóloŭr 1103; beáutĕ 113, 147, 213, 315, 1109, 1120, 1212, 1231, 1370, 1389, beăuté 151, 207, 220, 251, 319, 322, 325, 523, 924, 999; fórtŭne 1358 [?], fŏrtúnĕ 47, 74 [?], 1364; góddĕsse 217, 437, 1031, 1286 [?], 1434, 1487, gŏddéssĕ 256, 316, 408, 481, 491, 1044, 1075, 1161, 1232, 1343, 1355, 1365, 1406, 1456; hŏnoúr 1059, hónoŭr 1070; málўce 30, 371; mátĕr 526, mătér[ĕ] 42, 1151, 1278; mánĕr 57, 59, 173, 657, 736, 838, 841, 984, 1242, 1264, 1430, mănérĕ 144, 630, 1146, 1227, 1236; méschĕf 1073, mўschéfe 1294; nóblĕsse 544, nŏbléssĕ 241, 496, 553, 567, 592, 693, 1515; pléntĕ 64, 68, plĕnté 127, 1313; pórtĕr 378; pówĕr, póvĕr 268, 530, 1379, 1388, 1475, 1530, pŏwér, pŏvér 285, 865; prófўt 542; prócĕsse 1280; résŏn 742, 757, 761, 788, 853, 870, rĕsów 341, 505, 553, 588, 672, 724, 769, 776, 818, 844, 1219; sésŏw 94, 101, 160, 163, 176, 180, 915, sĕsów 95, 122; súrplŭs 989; trávăyle 610 [?]; trésoŭr 1356, 1361, 1406; vértŭ 471, 576, 586, 687, 698, 716, 777, 818, 920, 1087, etc.

With regard to the final *-e* our investigation bears out Schick's statement that it is usually retained (see *Temple of Glas*, p. lxvi). In fact, in the first 1500 verses there is not one dissyllabic word which loses its final *-e*. There are some instances later on, but even these are not conclusive.

Polysyllables too, as a rule, appear with their original final *-e*, except when read as proparoxytona:

aventurë 46, creaturë 173, 550, 1483, constableryë 1470, damagë 171, 1155, engendrurë 1300, 1446, fortunë 47, 74 [?], but fórtŭne 1358, iupartyë 12, materë 42 [?], 1278, but mátĕr 526, manerë 144, 630, but mánĕr 57, 59, 173, 657, etc., marchandysë 946, naturë 164, 167, 1111, 1365, norturë 988, pasturë 956, philosophie 1170, tavernë 55, vysagë 329, 335, 1435; vesturë 1144, viagë 608. The very frequent substantives in *-avnee*, *-ene*, *-esse* also retain the final *-e* when read as paroxytona. As to the words in *-orie* see the following instances:

glórië 682, 1059; mĕmórye 1183, vĭctóryë 1060, 1184.

Plural always in *-es*. The cases where the ending does not count as a syllable are comparatively rare in our text:

mănérs 689, pŏétes 1051 [?], 4209 [?], 4291 [?], formes 710, pártyĕs 1170.

II. ADJECTIVES.

Strong Form:

Singular: The *ja-* and *i-*stems retain their *-e*:
sootë 135, 939, 3638; nywë 1104; trewë 97, 297; grenë 108; wildë 3678; senë (quenë) 332; shenë 413 (sustene, inf.), 1320 (wene), 1828 (quene); derë 1349 (lere, inf.), stillë 5564; dryë 6938; clenë 6704.

In a few cases the rhyme does not agree with the sounding of the final *-e*: in l. 5419 we find *smothe* rhyming with *sothe*.

Other adjectives, as a rule, assume no *e* in the sing.; sometimes *e* appears as the remnant of an earlier more complete ending:

Comp. l. 1742 of so gret[e] force; 2644 in gretë fere; 3784 to gret[e] shame; 5591 of gret[e] melodye; 6842 of gretë prys; 6352 of wit they ha so gretë grace; comp. further: 1241, 4423, 6206, 6435, 6721, 6777, 6953. See also *Pilgr.* 593 with gretë peyne; 603 on echë party; 706 off gretë prys; 890 I have of helpe so gretë nede; 998 in allë wyse; 1362 so goodë cher (acc.); 1811 at allë tyme; 2164 in swychë cas, etc.

Plural. It goes without saying that the above-mentioned *ja-* and *i-*stems keep the final *-e*. *e* is also added to all other adjectives except those with a vocalic ending:

fairë 265, 2746, 5481; bright[e] 420, 962; redë 962, 3644; smalë 1150, 3719; kyndë 1648; oldë 1755; horë (more) 2870; lowë 2871, 3031; sharpë 3631; strongë 3884; vnkouthë 4519; sykë 5158; yongë 5637; wanë 6179.

Again, there are some cases, where the rhyme would seem to demand the suppression of the final *-e*:

fair (repair) 951, brou*n* (condicio*w*) 5484, wood (vnderstood) 5506, lyke (lunatyke) 6178, good (blood, Dat. Sing.) 6894.

Twice the apocope of the *e* is proved by the metre: foule 5485, hool 6774. In all these exceptional instances the adjective is used predicatively.[1] The attributive adjective never seems to drop the *e*, at least, when it precedes the substantive. It is a special question how it is treated when it follows the latter.

Generally here too the *e* is preserved:
whitë 1409, 6887; redë 388, 1409, 3940, 4019; fairë 621, 2147,

---

[1] Compare ten Brink, l. c. § 234: "Im Praedicat kann das Adjectiv auf ein pluralisches Subjekt bezogen, auch unflectiert bleiben."

28 Ch. III. Inflexions. The final -e. 2. Strong Adjectives.

2182, 3916; smalë 959, 1150; gretë 3472; yelwë 4019; blyndë 4091; falwë 5199; blakë 5199; donnë 6200, 6529.

There are comparatively few instances without *e*:
bright' 1133, v̆prýght' 2730; wis 6431 (cp. 6494), 6608.

Weak Form: it is employed

1. After the definite article:
samë 87, 99, 181, 192, 912, 1441, 2107, etc.; brighte 114, 133, 269, gretë 190, 404, 573, 1295, 3490, 3499, 3529, etc.; freshe 185, 432, 2732, 4022, 4926, 5984; firthë 186; lessë 552; ryghte 634, 655, 674, 800, 847, 2724, 4782; thilkë 855, 924, 931, 1064, 1207, 2152, 2537, etc.; wrongë 858; cold[e] 937, 3870; saltë 942, 1453, 4166, 4613; highe 1224, 1524, 5117; silvë (selvë) 1441, 2108, 3992; longë 1761; proudë 2041, 5772; hool[e] 3326; next[e] 4787; feyrë 4867; softë 5184; ravysshingë 5212; sharpë 5469.

2. After a demonstrative pronoun:
ilkë 73, 1709, 2121, 3998, 5524; gladë 906, 5179; oldë 551; derk[e] 1754, freshe 2593, 3538, 4807; vnkouthe 2751; yong[e] 3691, 3704, 5843, 5934.

3. After the possessive pronoun:
hoolë 5, 601, 1638, 1841, 2535, 4991, 5540; brighte 218; best[e] 238; ownë, oonë 302, 874, 1042, 1164, 2117, 2965, 3846, 3988, 4106, 4261, 4288, 4292, etc.; highe 5275, but high 496, 554, 1231, 1449, 1516, 2318, 4315; gretë 1003, 1052, 1289, 5292, 6882; oldë 1291; proudë 1520; fairë 3315, 3481; swartë 3791; quyk[e] 5720; ryghte 6690.

4. Before proper names:
feyrë 1456, fresshe 1859.

5. Where an adjective is used as a substantive:
samë 2096, 5926; fairë 2887, 5984; yong[e] 5823; sothe 4017.

When there are two adjectives following an article or pronoun, the second remains without ending:
fresh 4867, 4887, 5633; high 2124, 3499; fals 4032; best 5041.

In our poem which has been taken from a French source, we find the adjective very frequently placed after the substantive. The question arises, whether in such a case the *e* of the weak ending is preserved or not?

In Chaucer it is usually dropped. See ten Brink, § 235. There is no doubt that this law, on the whole, holds good for the language of our poem. But the rhymes sometimes seem to point to the conclusion that the *e* is preserved.

Ch. III. Inflexions. The final -e. 2. Romance Adjectives. 29

Compare the following examples: siluer fair (ayr) 453; salt (halt, 3 pers. sing.) 1458; vnkouthe (southe) 967; olde (tolde) 3268, 4234; longe (stronge) 1403, 5653; smal (at al) 1566; sad 5692; bright 6196, 6531. But: redë (medë) 105; donnë (sonnë) 4178; fayrë (debonayrë) 4485; blakë (makë) 6929.[1]

Romance Adjectives.

The strong form preserves the original ending. Thus with *-e* appear, also in singular: primë 27, 3950; attemprë 130, 932; sagë 344, 1105, 2009; noblë 1071; treblë 1140, 3648, 6975, 6988; debonayrë 266, 1503, 2063, 4745, 5411, 6259; ragë 1583; senglë 3225; troublë 3887; doublë 3888; sobrë 5297; straungë 5341. Here are to be enumerated also the adjectives ending in *-arië* (*-ayre*) and *-ablë*.

The O.F. participle *du* is always dissyllabic: dewë, dywë, diwë 304, 816, 1837, 2811, 5291; duë 4578.

Exceptions: enterë (entier) seems to be rhyming always with words in *-ë*: 41 (materë), 874 and 1617 (dere), 2528 (y-fere). Ten Brink (§ 242) has raised the question as to whether the feminine form of a French adjective may be adopted in connection with a feminine noun. In our poem there are indeed many instances which would seem to confirm this view: hert enterë 41, mayde enterë 1617; lady souereynë 2264; wounde profoundë 4664.

Plural:

Adjectives ending in a consonant assume no *e*. This goes without saying as far as paroxytona are concerned: dyuers 294, 367, 619; foreyn 703; sotil 1150; futire 1707; present 1892; gentil 2379; mortal 3717.

But even monosyllables and dissyllables with the original accent appear without the plural *-e*: fals 3279; pleyn 6299; dyuers 641, egal 100; present 1897 (absent, adj. sing.); vileyn 1508; mortal 3406; enter 6192.

There are also a fair number of polysyllables which bear out the above given statement: amerous 3400; bestiall 406, 814, 3425; celestiall 668, 831, 1014, 6455; temporal 680, 3279; accidental 703; apparent 738; tempest[u]ouse 958; fortunat 1084; pertynent 2292; diligent 3160; vertuous 3173. In l. 5745 the metre demands orient[e], and in l. 5746 persë.

[1] Here might be added an example of a Romance adjective clerë (materë) 1277, (sperë) 269, (y-ferë) 4484.

Weak declension:

It follows from our text that Romance and German adjectives are treated alike. Comp. ten Brink, l. c. § 241, and Schick, p. lxviii. Instances: clerë 90, 934; fals[e] 972, 1932; dyvynë 4697. It is true, there are some instances which seem to point to another conclusion, but these are not conclusive: chefe 256, 547, 1684, 3470; veyn 972, fers 2761. *chefe* may be regarded as a subst., *veyn* and *fers* are preceded by another adj.

Proparoxytona with a second accent upon the last syllable remain without -*e*: excellent 416, 1778, 3264, 3840, 5135; amerouse 1470[?]; mervelous 3380; preciouse 5721. Comp. however l. 4844.

III. (a) ADVERBS.

Adjectival adverbs have the ending *e*. Our text offers a great many examples: allonë 2796, 3053, 3065, 3984[?], 6874, rhyming with moonë: 899, 3060, 3137, etc.; depë 6121; clenë 2851; fairë 1504, 5244; fastë 1372, 2605; kenë 2852; longë 168, 447, 3974, 3883, 4393; lowë 401, 2674, 4174, 4185; alowë 4186; lyche (y-lyche) 1104, 1117, 1381, 2565, 2740, 2746, 2769 etc.; latë 6401, 6957; newë 298, 308, 364, 1728; sharpë 5440; shenë 1969; sorë 2890, 6368, 6483 (always rhyming with more); swythë 5812, 7030 (rhyming with sythe); vnnethë 1334, 3132. Forms with *of*: of latë 3281; of newë 152, but comp. 6416; rounde 420 and brood 3646 are to be read as monosyllables.

Adverbs formed by composition of the simple adjective-stem with -*ly* are found in considerable number.

The adverbs enough, full, high, representing adjectival accusatives, remain without *e*. Also the compounds in -*ward*: bakward 211; ageynwarde 650, 1266, 1517; westwarde 658, 799; outwarde 738, 4034, 4051; aftir-warde 3443; thiderwarde 6726.

The following adverbs are derived from substantives: aloftë 451, 3222, 4176; asydë 5231, 6556, 6706; a-rowë 6023; besydë 4946, 4952; wronge (perhaps adj.) 616, 855, 2242, awronge 1716, 6754; *somwhile* occurs in l. 3938 as a dissyllable; in l. 957, however, the regular metre would demand *sommwhilë*.

Other adverbs in *e* are: abovë 574; about[e] 258, 412, 560, 2764, 4514, 5068, 5234, 5600: ageyne [O.E. ongegn, etc.) 146, 226, 654, 850, etc.; amonge 797; behyndë 4956 (ryndë); doun (always monosyllabic) 940, 1032, 1291, etc.; fer 3633, 5053; here 618, in compounds: her with al 823; yondë 2656[?]; morë

(O.E. mâra), rhyming with sorë : 2889, 6367, 6484, with lorë 3252 ; ll. 3200 and 4455 we find *mor*, and 3677 *evermorẹ* ; *mo* (O.E. mâ) occurs twice 3934, 4009 ; *nerë*, occurring only in the rhyme, 7026 (dere), but *ner* (penser) 6972 ; oftë (dissyllabic from original *oft*) 862, 3207, 6166, 6712, also in the adverbial phrase *oftë sythe* 768, 2314, 3320 ; outë (doute) 2590 ; *sonë* is a dissyllable also in the middle of the line : 3906, 4470 ; seldë 2574 ; tha*n*në 3190 ; *therẹ*, always monosyllabic, but comp. rhymes like : erë : there 5216,[1] withinnë 230, 740, withoutë : no conclusive instance where the final -*e* is not sounded ; dubious cases : 3924, 5548.

Adverbs in -*es*, -*s* : certës (certys) 579, 603, 1142, 2800, 3220 ; ellës (ellis) 579, 1640, 2503, 2509, 3501, 3520, 5015, 5046 ; ellës-where 2785, 5899 ; hens 6990, but henÿs 2659 ; in myddës 6839 ; for the nonÿs 3113, 3212, 5744, 6032 ; somwhilës 3938 ; thens 3595 ; vnnethis 2148 ; al the whilës 4967.

Regarding expressions like : the most[e] sage (2360) I refer to ten Brink, l. c. § 246, Anm.

III. (β)

Many of the above-enumerated adverbs are used as prepositions : abovẹ 752, 1132, 1277, 5713, but in l. 351 the metre demands abovë[n], comp. also l. 4551 ; among, amongẹ, 1963, amongë 1022, 2423, 4815 ; amongÿs 5179, 5263, 6455 ; ageyn 171, 868, 938, 1203, etc. ; ageyn[e]s 857, 860, 2134 (ther ageyn[e]s) 2897, 3227, 3229, 3413, 3441, 4586, 4764, 4824 ; in l. 771 also, I think, we had better read ăgeɣn[ë]s ; to fornẹ 826 ; syth 2152 ; withoutë 11, 51, 142, 155, etc., withouten (mostly before a vowel) 58, 95, 1445, 1375, 3052, 4779, 5052, 5069, wĭthóut 4547. Only as a preposition occur : ătwénẹ 4445 [?], atwenë 783 ; atwixen 1942, 4205, atwex 5902.

IV. NUMERALS.

In our text we find the following examples : oon (often used as a pronoun) 1023, 2142, 2148, 2174, 2280, 2281 ; compare here forms like : oonẹs (onÿs) 2316, 3211, 3609, 3869, 4088, 6091, 7010, al attonës 3114, for the nonÿs 3113, 3212, 5744, 6032 ; two 692, 2261, etc., ; tweynë 785, 1163, 1815, but compare ll. 73, 826 and 1116 where the rhyme demands *tweynẹ* ; the word (in Chaucer dissyllabic) rhymes also with *peyne* : 2502, 4186, 6396, etc. See Schick, l. c. p. lxii.   thre 1020, 1168, 1186 etc. ; fourë 352, 6046,

---

[1] See ten Brink, § 260, η.

foure 1000; fyvë 5481; six 5532; sevene 274, 426, 752, 1676; nynë 276; twelvë 428; hundred 423; thousand 2142; many thousand 2185; thousand folde 2174, 3861, etc.

Cardinals are treated like weak adjectives: first[e] 4999, 5418, 5448, 6160, 6931, or firthë 186; but ll. 697 and 1029 [?] we find *the first*, used as a substantive, without the final *-e*; sĕcoúndĕ 1284, 2004, in l. 5457, 5489, 6203, 6953 we might as well read *sécoŭnde* (*sécŏnde*); thriddë 1434, 6253, thryd[e] 5491, 6969, thirddë 3636; fourthë 5464, 5493, 6273; fyfthë, fythë, fyftë 5468 [?], 5497, 6315 [?]; sixtë 6375; seveneth 6433.

V. PRONOUNS.

I touch only on those points which are noteworthy in regard to the final *-e*:

(a) Personal pronouns:

Forms like *oure, youre, hire, here* are in Chaucer always monosyllabic. Comp. ten Brink, l. c. § 250, Anmerk 4. In ll. 11 and 2277 of our text, however, I think, we must read hir[e].

(β) Relatives:

which, Plural *whiche*, but also *whichë*: see 1022, 1882, 4815, 4132; comp. also l. 2533 and 6701.

The whichë is treated differently: we always have to read *the whichë* when a subst. follows, 918, 1169, 1631; *the whiche*, standing alone, sometimes drops the final *-e*: 56, 531, 2545, 5009, but, as a rule, *e* is sounded as a distinct syllable: 528, 861, 985, 1002, 1091, 1289, 1301, 1342, 1658.

Other pronouns:

allë: 1, 75, 235, 268 [?], 503, 821, 851, 857, 867, 1025, 1707, 1814, 1831, 1890, 1968, 1989, 2064, 2431, 2658, 3147, 3152, 3329, 3336, etc.

We find *allë* especially in connection with other pronouns or numerals: allë tho 857, 867, 3152, 3336; allë thre 1968, 1989, 2064, 3329; but, on the other hand, we find *al tho* 1545.

bothë (mostly dissyllabic) 86, 642, 685, 700 (bothën), 930, 1369, 1702; fewë 1324.

self is, in connection with my, thy, our, your, him, hire, hem, mostly monosyllabic; but compare: my selvë (twelve) 427, thy selvë 2310, hym selven 3885, hem selven 5044, hir selven 4334, hem self[e] 5235—swichë (plural) 3395, 4002 adj., 6130 adj.— some (in Chaucer always monosyllabic, see ten Brink § 255,[1])

---

[1] Ten Brink is wrong. Comp. *Wif of Bathe's Tale*, 79.

Ch. III. Inflexions. The final -e. 6. Compounds. 33

appears in plural partly with, partly without, the final -*e*: som (some, somme) 28 adj., 76, 941, 943, 1069, 5317; sommë 621, 3833 adj., 3428, 5309, 5325, 5379, 6126, 6174 adj., some (dat. sing.) 469 might perhaps be read as a dissyllable.—eche 165, 1949, 1991.

VI. COMPOSITION.

Romance words in -*ment* generally retain the *e* between the two parts of the compounds: com̄maundëment, comandement, 829, 1790, 2191? (At thyw ovne comaundement'), 2376, 4588, 4690, 5959, 5976; entendëment 757, 880; awysëment 3476, 4938; enchauntëment 3550, 3591, 3757, 6394, 6406; amendëment 5192; Iugëment, 1854, 1868, 2070, 2093, 3298, 3304, 3305, 3310, 3327; but in l. 2089 we certainly have to read *Iugement*. There are other instances enough in Lydgate's works, where compounds in -*ment*, although commonly read with -*ë*, sometimes appear without it. Compare: *Pilgr.* 1540 oynement [?], but 1591 oynëment, 1901 oynëmentys; comp. also l. 14792; enténdement: *Pilgr.* 10926, but entendëment in l. 10918 and numerous other cases; in l. 2191 of our text, I think, we must read: Ăt thýw ŏvnĕ cŏmaúndĕmént'.

The -*e* before -*nes* seems only to be sounded in words where it originally belonged to the first part of the compound. We find -*ë* in: kyndënesse 1654, 6462; doublënesse 3477, 3880, 6522, 6578 (doubilnesse 6194, etc.); straungënesse 4829, 5069; secrënesse 6362. But there is not one conclusive instance of the -*e* being sounded in compounds the stem-word of which ends in a consonant. In fayrenesse 522, w[h]ittenesse 2816, 3956 the metre, it is true, would permit both ways of reading, but I do not see any reason to sound the -*e* here, which, in all other cases, is suppressed. With regard to ll. 4843 f. see notes. The examples adduced by Schick (p. lxix f.) are in perfect accordance with what our text seems to bear out: kyndënes 747, secrënes 900; but derknes 11, 12, 1357, swetnes (adj. swête but O.E. swêtnes); meknes 76, 621; goodnes 745. I can only point to one decided instance which is contradictory to the rule given above. In *Pilgr.* l. 5113 we certainly have to read boldënesse (but a few lines further down l. 5123 the metre again demands boldnesse).

Adjectives and Adverbs in -*ly* are very frequent. Again it is evident from the instances in our poem that where the -*e* already forms a constituent part of the stem-word, it is sounded in the compound: duëly 538, naturëly 711, truëly 965, bodëly 780, straungëly

1440, humblëly 1838, benyng[e]ly 2237 (see *Temple of Glas* 849), hastëly 3297, disgesëly 3645. Exceptional appears *kindely*, as an adj., twice with -ẹ: l. 121 [?] (comp. *Pilgr.* 4454) and 1465. But the sounding of the -e between the two parts of the compound is not at all confined to such cases. Compare: inwardëly 2339 [?], boldëly 6365.[1] See further in *Pilgr.* 4480 and 13251: boldëly; queyntëly 13096.

Of other groups of compounds we note especially doutëles, rekkëles, causëles, which are always trisyllabic.

VII. VERBS.

In far the most cases the ending of the Infinitive [-e, seldom -en] is sounded as a distinct syllable. The instances in which the final -e is dropped are the following:

give yifẹ, etc., 50, 246, 506, 1870, 4676, 6410; berẹ 122, 1622, 1946; descryvẹ 1395 (comp. *T. of Gl.* 79/80), see also: dryvẹ 4606; contrarie 261 [?]; know 740; put 483; ha, han 543, 1636, 3743, 5017; hauẹ 1383, 1472, 5166; contenẹ 561; levẹ 805; holdẹ 844; be-holdẹ 4969; makẹ 2409, 4232, 4627, 4686, 6682; obey 1522; atteynẹ 1515, 1993; sey (say) 1593, 1670; set 2198; affermẹ 1743; răvýshẹ 1876[?]; bekomẹ 2352; komẹ 4892, comẹ 3498; contunẹ 2335; play 3044, reherse 2435; let 2673; confermẹ 3298; abydẹ 4529; takẹ 4610; sustenẹ 4685; tel 5134; wassh 5727; diffacẹ 6196; gruchchẹ 6795.

More important, of course, than a mere enumeration of all those cases in which the -e of the infinitive becomes silent would be some elucidation of the conditions under which the ending is dropped. But our investigations seem to point rather to the conclusion that there is no rule at all as to when the sounding of the *e* takes place and when not. The dropping of the final -e occurs both in verbs of Romance and in verbs of German origin. In the latter class, it is true, we frequently find that the short-stemmed strong verbs lose their ending: *give* and *come* appear almost exclusively as monosyllables.

Paroxytona end in -ẹ *pe*rseuer 3162, 6173; preseuer 4441; dissever 2162, 2458, 4181, 4442, etc.; cherish 6675.

The Gerundives are treated identically with the Infinitive.

---

[1] *goodly* occurs throughout without -e: 486, 494, 1843. In *Temple of Glas*, l. 851, where Schick reads good[e]ly, we might perhaps also do without the -e.

Forms like to seenë, to doonë, to seynë, which are still retained in Chaucer, are also to be found in our text: comp. l. 6185 to done and 1818 to fleene.

Indicative Present, first person:—*ë* in far the most cases; but there is a tolerably fair number of examples in -*ẹ*:

pray (prey) 6772; menẹ 1295, 1745; hauẹ 766, 882, 885, 2986; ha 609, 1348, 2811, 2914, 2924, etc.; takẹ 2283 [?], makẹ 2294; ŏrdéyn 2295; berẹ 2996; know 3293; thinkẹ 4736 [?], menẹ 5113, 5907; hopẹ 6679.

Second person: -*ëst*: herëst 457; hauëst 2056; felÿst 1867; comëst 2667; stondëst 3522; callÿst 4648. In an almost equal number of instances we have to read -*ẹst*: hast 514, 2157, 4231; lyst 607; gest 892, 4767, gettẹst 2700; standest 3530; seyst 4638; yivẹst 4650. No example of the ending -*es*.

Third person: The ending is -*eth*, which generally counts as a distinct syllable. Examples of -*ẹth* or such forms in which the -*th* of the ending is absorbed in the dental consonant at the end of the stems are the following:

lyst 33, 77, 164, 649, etc.; hath 51, 187, 258, 267, etc.; hayth 574; perséuerẹth 4386; séverẹth 290, 292; seth 303, 1360, 2857, 4251, 5380; set 679, 6998; seith 1030, 1129; yivẹth 1059; writ 1130; halt 1457; berẹth 1812, 2872, 6780; stant 2416, 3518, 5397; comẹth 2617; semẹth 4759; fleeth 3050; drinkẹth 3868; abyt 3912, 6386; takẹth 4370 [?]; acordẹth 4490 [?]; ĕxcéllẹth 4557; slethe 5496; syt 5564, 6972; last 6231; fret 6483; fleeth 7006, 7015.

Examples of the northern form in -*ës* (ÿs): obeyës 359; tellys 933. Compare Schick, l. c. lxxi.

Plural. Besides the usual form in -*ë*, -*ën* occurs not infrequently: springën 106; stondën 1494; exceedën 1705; longën 2428; duellën 2658; folwën 3077; drawen 3337; makën 4599; writën 4410; Ianglën 5382, 6314; knowën 5864; suffrën 6263; delytën 6495; hatën 6565; expressën 6723.

In the following instances the *n* stands before a consonant: writen 1755, longen 6656, taken 6225, maken 3647.

Monosyllables: han 1141, 1442, 1651, 3274, 5174; seyn 1342, 1775, 3308; sen 5021. Forms without any ending occur even in the rhyme (see again Schick, l. c. lxii): lovẹ 3, 6559; make 278; lyst 1038; ha 3135, 4241, 4805; berẹ 3879, 3898, 4380, 6722, 6807; feyn 1615; play 5861; herë 6412; let 6412; farẹ 6815.

The old ending is retained in *hath* 454, and *discernëth* 1039. The northern form -*ës* (ys) appears in *duellys* 5046.

Subjunctive, singular in -*ë*. Cases in which the ending is dropped:

haue 64, 589; look 1327 [?]; bere 2674; yive 3483, 3485; marke 4117, turne 4134, happe 4735; ley 3671. Monosyllabic are also: goo 518, 616, 626; do 1474, 2564; fle 4185. Dissyllables assume no -*e*.

Save some auxiliary verbs there are, as far as I can see, no good examples of the plural.

Imperative, singular, second person: no ending:

arys 466; take 466, 520, 659, 823, 2054, 4080; draw 469; begynne 608, 817; ha 3500; cast 628; sey 633; fle 819; se 2064, 4512; love 836; lat 827; set 830, 2188; dred 2298, 2353; make 842, 856, 4127; kepe 854, 4127, 4131, 4136; thinke 3427; stoppe 4128; far 6865. The final -*e* must be sounded in: sey[e] 2065; reysë 820; trustë 2172, 2511; wey[e] 6616 [?].

Romance words generally have -*ë*:

considrë 2057; dispisë 832; remembrë 2698; enclynë 871; voydë 2065; applië 2067; refusë 2308; varië 2697; entrë 4107. The ending -*eth* (*th*) appears in doutëth 2332; hath 632, 2333; trustëth 4471.

Participle Present, in -*ing*. Numerous examples; but there is no instance of -*ingë*. In the adjectival use, we find, of course, the -*ë* of the weak form: ravysshingë 5212.

Gower's form in -*ende* is not found in our text.

Strong Preterite, sing.: without ending. We classify the examples according to the change of the root-vowel:

saugh (sawgh) 206, 427, 949, 4939, 4949, 5232; yaf, gaf, gafe 486, 907, 1004, 1644, 2154; quod 514, 581, 631, etc.; sat 341, 1175, 2793, 2796; bad 909, 1986, 3721; spake 1452, 2894, 2906, etc.; be-gat 1616; stake 2088; gat 4316, 5656; forgat 5886; lay 88, 1974, 1979; came (kam) 848, 1918, 1935, bekam 2840; bar, bare 1744, 2759, 2904, 3528, 5412, 6163, 6610; bere (vowel of the plural *bæron*), 4985; brake 2905, 4775; gan 143, 209, 440, 489, 638, 1848, 2076, 2208, etc.; began 444, 2351; wan 3544, 3584; ranne 3970, ran 4932; fonde 4823, 4825, 4833, 5092; sauge 5255; roos (aroos) 90, 904, 1458, 1943; shoon 411, 1576; abood 477, 991, 1553; roof 3980; rood 4400; ches 918, 6004, 6830; took (toke) 192, 994, 1581, 1620, etc.; vndertook 1279; drough 211, 1545,

Ch. III. Inflexions. 7. Verbs. 37

1751, with-drough 4096; stood 224, 476, 1367, 1732, 3266, etc.; vnderstood 2074, 4702; awook 1834; slough 3575, 3987, 4337, 4724; forsooke̞ 4781; shoop 5873; knyw (knew) 86, 990, 1165, etc.; fil 183, 2236, 4308, 4875; helde̞ (held) 1308, 1422, 1577, 1590, etc.; behelde̞ 212, 969, 1421, etc.; wex 1127, 4275; threwe̞ 1920; bet 2104; heng 4334; lete 4831, 4989, 5625.

Plural: Forms without an ending seem to predominate: 3218; kam 3044; gan 2134, 2478; bare̞ 6730; but, on the other hand, we have: ronnë 940; setën) 1915; wexën 2736, 3942.

Subjunctive, singular: only monosyllabic forms: tooke̞ 1015; stood 2940. In l. 3489 the metre would demand *knywë*. Compare, however, ten Brink, 2608.

Weak Preterit, ending

(α) in *-ëd*: enspirëd 136;. enforcëd 146; forcëd 226'; causëd 528; resemblede̞ 1116; pe*r*sëd 1131; sŭrmóu*n*tĕde̞ 1222, 5839, 5661; sú*r*moŭ*n*téde̞ 3153 ?; corownëd 1230; nedëd 1368; passëde (passÿde) 3529, 5834; semëd 1831; espyëd 1839; flourëde 1874; descendëd 1883; co*m*mandëd 1967; grauntëde 1997, 2009, 2129, 3302; attamede̞ 2460; entrëde 2720; excellëd 2815 [?], 5820; ordeynëd 4100; sparëd 4788; neghëd 4792; pretendëd 4977; walkëd 5628; declarëd 5686; deyëd 5704; lykëd 5722, 6106; rekordëd 5926; cursëd 6635.

(β) in *-dë, -të*: haddë 318, 1379, 2167, 2530, etc.; broght*e* 84, 1644; madë 1626, 1980 [cp. ten Brink, 260 ε]; wrou̇ghte 172, 532; thought*e* 203, 965, 1000, etc.; raughtë 418; seydë 639, 1850, 1912, 2106, 3542; seydyst 3303; clad[de] 906; went[e] 912; toldë 1098, 2116; semptë 974, 1414, 1837, 2112; hyght*e* 1881; kept[e] 1974; demptë 2053, 3308; answerdë 2082; castë 2782, 5701, 6151; durst[e] 3089; feltë 4789, 4836; sent[e] 4903.

(γ) in *-d, -t*: had 49, 78, 473, 1575, etc.; sprad 134; made̞ 3573; caste̞ 215; went 224, 1385, 1419, etc.; felt 228; sempte̞ 329, 334; lyst 1849, 1953, 2046; put 5650; hight' 1971, wroght' 4267; lovede̞ 4303; estáblýsshede̞ 5055; seyde̞ 5920; mérvĕled 6114.

Plural. In most cases we have *-ten, -den*: brentën 1117, 3555; fleddën 3114; madën 3437; mettën 3966; seydën 4571; ouerspreddën 5182; we have also *haddën* and *love̞dën*.

Examples in *-ëd*: conceyvëde̞ 1924; purposëde̞ 2453. See further the forms: had 1806, 3964; lovëde̞ 3180. Quite exceptional appear: shéwëd[e] (Sing.) 1654 [?], and sérvëdén (Plural) 946.

38   Ch. III.   Inflexions.   7. Verbs.

Subjunctive. Only a few instances Sing: hadde̤ 2098 [?]; haddë 231, 3742, 5220, 5350; considerëd 1013; studyed (dissyllabic) 1395; deyëd 5708. Plural: soughtën) 2362.

Strong Past Participle.

ten Brink, § 196. The full ending is -ën; it is retained before a vowel in the following instances:

yoven) 585, 3299, yiven) 759; wonen) 2160; getyn) 1611, geten) 1650; spoken) 3548; dronken) 3973; graven) 5685.

The e of the ending is suppressed: (a) in short-stemmed verbs ending in -r: lorne̤ 610, 3990 (rhyming with aforne); also y-lorne̤ 1322; borne̤ 1623, 5139, 6668 (rhyming with to forn¹);

(β) in the following verbs: sen 1737, seyn 1137, 1570, 2779, 2832, etc.; slayn 1810, but slay[e]n) 3692, 5688;

(γ) in yiven) 1790.

The n has been dropped: be-gonnë 49, foundë 191, 346, 1283, 4111; brokë 3286; takë 3776; I-bode 5977; wonnë 6921 (rhyming with tonne).

The adduced examples are by no means confined to the rhyme.

Cases in which the ending has been dropped altogether are not only confined to originally short-stemmed verbs: yove̤ 574, 718; wove̤ 1397; y-founde̤ 749 (profounde̤); wonne̤ 6707.

Weak Past Participle.

(a) in Romance words.

The ending, as a rule, is -ëd. Polysyllables, with the accent thrown back, end in e̤d: norysshe̤d 107; conquere̤d 2164; exilled 2530; purtreyd 4943, 5549; enamowre̤d 4286; envenymyd 5492; seuere̤d 5665. The other instances, where the ending does not count as an extra-syllable, are the following: apayde̤ 2320, apaye̤d 513, paye̤d 3036; ĕxcélle̤d 2815; rewle̤d 2337; past 4832; atteynt 4257; enoynt 5504; depeynt 6119; feynt 6120; kaught 6087;

(β) in words of Teutonic origin. Syncope takes place:

1 a. in many of the irregular verbs of the first class. The examples of our text are: brought 187, 1072, 2155; wrought 352, 357, 361, etc.; sought 524, 4822; tolde̤ 882, 1050, 1391, 1624, etc.; bought⁺ 3100; solde̤ 3100; y-taught⁺ 3713.

1 b. in verbs ending in -d and -t: set, sette 426, 781, 827, 1261, 6023, etc.; y-set 2366; knet 3288, 4169, etc.; vnknet 3202; knyt 2035, 2289; y-shet 4984; fret 141, 1400, 3756, 5490.

Ch. III. Inflexions. Anomala.

1 c. in verbs of the third class: seyde 609, 4572; fet 5305; had 5731.

2. as a rule in the ending of the long stems: ouersprad 109; sprad 4186; [y]-shent 807, 3758, 4116, 5960; left 899, 3065; [y]-meynt 982, 3320, 3368, 4145; herd 1141, 1437, 1442, etc.; gyrt 1566; sent 6625; rent 1583, 4866; to-rent 1934, 3684; afferde 3104; blent 3449; y-blent 3659; kept 3545, 3743, etc.; brent 3557, 3802, 4115, 4295, ybrent 5188; dreynt 4146, 4258; lad 6325, 6978; y-whet 6500; queynt 6637. Of long-stemmed verbs which originally followed the strong conjugation, I add the following examples: drad 3406, 5453; yrad 4335; rad 4851, 5691.

3. the words of the second class, usually ending in *-ëd*, exhibit syncope or contraction only in a few instances: clad 120, 910; mad 541, 1886, 2311 etc.; y-made 1559, but also makëd 1191, 1563, 1682; called 698 [?], 863; but callÿd, callëd 254, 921, 1683, 1904, etc.; y-callëd, y-callÿd 248, 1582, etc.; wont 3023, 3140.

There are still some contracted forms of verbs, borrowed from other German dialects. I mention: cast 2900, vp-cast 399, and put (the origin of which is rather doubtful) 1238, 1362, 1983, etc.

The very frequently-occurring Anomala and Praeterito-Praesentia are contained in the following lists. I thought it more advisable to put them together in a table of conjugation which I subjoin.

Anomala.

go. Pres. Ind. Sg. go, gost, goth; Pl. go—goon; Subj. Sg. go; Imp. Sg. go; Plur. ———; Pres. Part. going; Past Part. goon, agoo —a-goon.

do. Pres. Ind. Sg. do, dost, doth; Plur. do—doth; Subj. Sg. ———; Imp. Sg. do; Pres. Part. doing; Past Part. do—doon; Pret. didë— did, didest—dist—dest (comp. l. 3505, and further 3323), didë—did.

be. Pres. Ind. Sg. am, art, is; Plur. ben—be—ar; Subj. Sg. be; Plur. be; Imp. Sg. be; Plur. beth; Pres. Part. being; Past Part. ben; Pret. was, wer, was; wer—wern—wer[e]n; Subj. wer, wer.

wil. Pres. Ind. Sg. wil [wol], wilt, wil [wol]; Plur. wil; Pret. woldë [wild], woldëst—woldest, woldë; wolde.

Praeterito-Praesentia.

can. Pres. Ind. can, canst, kan; Pret. koude—koudë; Plur. koudë.

dar. Pres. Ind. dar, darst, dar; Pret. durst—durstë—durst[e].
shal. Pres. Ind. shal, shalt, shal; Plur. shall; Pret. shuldë—
    sholdë, shuldëst—sholdëst, sholdë—shoold; Plur. sholdë—
    shold—shuld.
may. Pres. Ind. may, maist; Plur. may; Pret. might[e]—might;
    Plur. might[e]—might.
mot. Pres. Ind. mot, must, mot; Plur. Pret. moste.
wot. Pres. Ind. ——; Plur. woot.
owe. Pres. Ind. ——, owëst; Pret. ought—ought[e].

CHAPTER IV.

THE RHYME.

FROM the works of Lydgate which have been edited before this poem, we already know as to the quality of the rhyme-vowel, that the monk makes no difference between open and close sounds. To enlarge upon this would mean a mere repetition of what has been clearly enough pointed out by Schick, Krausser and others. All the instances adduced in the works of these editors occur, to a greater or lesser extent, also in our poem.

But I should like to dwell a little longer on the question, how matters stand with regard to the number of syllables that form the rhyme. The settlement of this question is in our case of special importance, as there is no external evidence for the date of this poem. In fact, it is a ground upon which to base our opinion as to the date of composition.

I start at once by adducing instances of such rhymes which would be inadmissible in Chaucer's system:

solace : gracë 887–88, 6351–52;
    : placë 2515–16, 2645–46, 4141–42, 5891–92, 6865–66;
    : chacë, v. 2859–60, 2997–98;
    : facë 5821–22.
trespace : gracë 1787–88, 6771–72;
    : placë 2895–96, 5077–78;
tracë, v : case 2107–8;
ryff (O.E. rife) : wyff 1287–88;
ryfe : wyf 1879–80;
lyve, acc. sing. : descryvë inf. 1395–96, 5131–32;
hede, acc. (n.) sing. [O.E. heâfod] : dredë 1809–10;
    : hedë 5461–62;

Ch. IV. Lydgate's Rhymes in this Poem. 41

fyne, s. (O.F. fin) : lynë, s. 1881-82;
: declynë, inf. 6243-44;
contenë, inf. : sene, inf. 561-62;
quenë : sen, inf., 1343-44, 6143-44;
: flem, inf. 6251-52;
acorde, s. : discordë, s. 877-78, 1493-4, 2155-56, etc. With reard to *acorde*, comp. Chaucer V, 197-99, where we have the rhyme acord : lord, nom. sing. and B 4069 : " In swete acorde ' my lief is faren in londe.' "

In O.F., however, appears the form *acordë*, rhyming with *misericordë*, *se bordë*, 3 ps. sing., etc. See Godefroy, where the word is adduced as acc. s. f.

cherë : messagere 1721-22;
: leysere 1839-40;
: clere adj. sing. 4935-36, 5383-48.

roosë : cloose 4839-40 (*cloose* in Chaucer monosyllabic; comp. B. 4521-22 : toos : cloos).

faire adj. : contrayrë 4957-58 (comp. ten Brink, § 231).

how : drow, 3 p. plur. 5787-88.

maner : chekker [O.F. eschekier] 6017-18; Chaucer (III, 659-60) rhymes the word with *here*, adv.

I add some examples, which strictly speaking do not come under this head:

In the rime *lyche*, adj. sing. : *rychë*—cp. 1309-10, 1407-8, 1591-92, etc., I think *lychë* (O.E. gelîca) is the right form to read. I am almost beginning to believe that *lychë* is the normal form. Again in *square* (esquarre) : *ware* adj. 6117-18, *ware* may be a weak form; cp. Modern English *aware*. In ll. 1451-52 I think we must read *wrake* : *spake*; the form *wrake* might be due to an influence from the Old English *wræc*, neuter. In regard to *wele*, adv. : *felë*, inf. (1401-2) see Bülbring, *Literaturblatt für germ. und rom. Philologie*, 1894, p. 261. More frequently occur feminine forms without the *e* : youthe : kouth, adj. sing. 6161-62. In *al my lyvë* : 1395, 5132, *lyve* might be explained as dative; in this case the phrase would mean as much as *on my lyve*.

These examples suffice to corroborate Schick's conclusion that there is in Lydgate a considerable advance beyond Chaucer in the dropping of the final -*e* in Romance words; but, as far as our poem is concerned, this advance is not only limited to Romance words. In general it can be observed that, with regard to the final -*e*,

Ch. IV. Lydgate's Rhymes in this Poem.

Lydgate is less careful in this work than in the *Temple of Glas* and other earlier poems. Thus the rhyme y : ye, which in the *Temple of Glas* is avoided throughout, is here to be met with in a fair number of cases:

maistry : yvory 2995–96 (comp. in ll. 5421–22 the rhyme *yvory : craftyly*);
lusty : company 5543–44;
specialy : companye 6445–46;
frequently *partyë* rhymes with words in *-y* :
feythfully : party 2121–22;
lowly : party 6007–8;
partye : sodenly 5697–98.

Such rhymes as: partye : chaunpartye 3227–28, iuparty : lye 11–12, magnyfye : iupartye 3183–84, iupartye : maistrie 5867–68, are here out of consideration, for, as has been pointed out by Schick in his review of Kaluza's work on the *Roman de la Rose*, forms like *chaunpartyë* are in Chaucer, too, generally used.

In connection with these last remarks, I should like to adduce a series of rhymes where the *common* Middle-English usage of rhyming employs words assuming a final *-e*, which general etymological considerations would not lead us to expect:

apparayle [O.F. apparail] : faylë 95–96; 155–56, 1021–22, 1895–96; —— : entayllë 349–50; 4269–70 (comp. entaylle : faylle 2823–30); —— : mervayllë inf. 1411–12; —— : countrevaylle inf. 1540–41;
fayllë inf. : travaylle s. [O.F. travail] 2955–56;
skye : eyë 1007–8; —— : wryë inf. 1413–14 (comp. Chaucer, *Hous of Fame* 1599–1600, hyë, adv. : skye);
eterne, adj. sing. : governë 1087–88; —— : discerne, inf. 1275–76 (comp. Chaucer A 1989–90, 3003–4).

At last I may be allowed to touch once more upon the question how Romance words with an especial form for the fem. are treated in English. Ten Brink (l. c. § 242) says with regard to this: "Zweifelhaft erscheint es, ob von einer Motion des französischen Adjectivs die Rede sein kann."

Do the rhymes of our poem offer any material which may be of value in elucidating the disputed point?

Before making general remarks, I put together all the instances which come into consideration:

entere, adj. f. : derë 1617–18; —— : herë, inf. 5817–18;

entere, adj. m. : y-ferë 2527–28 ;
(of hert) entere : materë 41–42, 4991–92 ; —— : derë 873–74 ;
dyuerse, adj. f. : reversë, inf. 59–60 ;
enclynë, inf. : dyvyne, adj. f. 259–60 ; —— : dyvyne, adj. m. 1499–1500 ; dyvyne, adj. plur. 773–44, 1081–82 ;
dyffynë, inf. : dyvyne, adj. sing. n. 5103–4 ;
souereyne, adj. f. : reynë, s. 2263–64 ; —— : peynᴅ 4835–36 ; —— : ordeynᴅ, inf. 5955–56 ;
souereyne, adj. m. : tweynë 825–26 ; —— : treynë, s. 6733–34 ;
cytryne, adj. m. : fynë, inf. 3853–54 ;
femynyne, adj. m. : enclynë, inf. 3871–72 ; —— adj. f. : shynë 6541–42 ;
shynë, inf. : (venym) serpentyne 4037–38.

These examples seem to point to the conclusion that, whenever one of the adjectives under consideration occurs as a rhyming word—no matter whether masc. or fem.—the form with -e is employed. A case like *herbere* : *entere* does not contradict this. Compare O.F. herbiere, erbiere, arbiere, s. f. pré. There are only two instances inconsistent with the above given examples :

kalender : enter adj. plur. f. 6191–92 ;
chekker : enter adj. m. 5999–6000 (comp. Chaucer III, 659 f.).

In other works Lydgate often rhymes words ending in *-ire* with those in *-ere*. See Sauerstein, *Lydgate's Æsopübersetzung*, p. 17 ; Zupitza, *Deutsche Litteraturzeitung*, 1886, p. 850 ; Koeppel, *Mitteilungen zur Anglia* 1890, p. 92, and Schick, *Temple of Glas*, lxi. But this peculiarity does not appear so frequently in *Reson and Sensuallyte*; as far as I can see there are only two instances : 483 f. fere : enquire and 1839 f. chere : leysere.

There is likewise no proof that Lydgate used the Kentish *e* for O.E. *y*. See Schick, l. c. lxi.

I should not like to attach too much importance to these facts. It is only too natural that, when building up stanzas where the difficulties of rhyme were much greater than in rhyme-couplets, our monk should indulge in make-shifts, which he otherwise tried to avoid as much as possible.

CHAPTER V.
ON LYDGATE'S STYLE.

In his Introduction to the *Temple of Glas*, Schick has given us a graphic picture of the peculiarities of style to be found in our monk's works :

"Drawled-out and incompact, are the first epithets which one would most readily apply to the style of the monk's productions. His sentences run on aimlessly, without definite stop, and it is often difficult to say where a particular idea begins or ends. One certainly has the impression that the monk never knew himself, when he began a sentence, how the end of it would turn out. He knows little of logic connection, or distinct limitation of his sentences, and the notion of artistic structure, by which all ideas form, in mutual interdependence, an organic whole, is entirely foreign to him : what is uppermost in his mind comes to the surface without further consideration of the context; for a moment he may lose sight of the first idea when something fresh turns up, to resume it again as soon as his new thought leaves him. . . .

"He is especially in his own element whenever he can bring in long sermons and moralizations. Then showers of commonplaces, proverbs, and admonitions rain down upon us, the fruits of extensive reading swelling the vast store of his own commonplaces. In our poem, this natural propensity of the monk is most apparent in the speeches of Venus, who, in this character of a pedantic moralizer, occasionally appears to us in a very philistine aspect. More commendable, however, is the zeal with which our monk allows his pen free flight, when he comes to a passage which inspires him with unusual fervour. Then he lets loose the floodgates of his eloquence, and a whole deluge of epithets and images is showered down upon us."[1]

This description so exactly suits the facts that I have nothing to subtract from it and very little to add. I would only venture to remark that the natural prolixity of the monk and the inconsistency of his syntactical constructions are less prominent in our poem than in some of his other works. The French original clips the wings of his partiality for overlengthened description.

If I have set before myself in this chapter a task to carry out, it is that of pointing out the various tricks of style which the monk employs in his works :

Reson and Sensuallyte is perhaps more suitable for the purpose than any of his other poems, since a comparison with the original will throw into strongest relief the translator's own peculiarities of style.

The unprejudiced reader who takes into his hands for the first

---

[1] Schick, *Temple of Glas*, p. cxxxiv ff.

time a copy of Lydgate's works, cannot fail to be struck at the outset with a tendency which I should like to denominate " reduplication of expression." The author is rarely, indeed, content with a single expression to denote what he wishes to say, but associates with it a second expression equivalent or similar in meaning to the first. Accordingly we meet frequently with synonymous words and phrases connected together by an *and* or an *or*, e. g. : " synge and make melodye," " for verray joye and gladnesse," " the resemblaunce and the figure," " intellect or entendement."

Occasionally of the two expressions thus conjoined, the one is a word of Teutonic origin, and the other simply its Romance equivalent, *e. g.* :

" to here the briddes chaunte and synge," " no man may contrarie nor withseye," " touching the beaute and fayrenesse," " touching the clothing and vesture," " hool and entere."

Naturally it is not always the case that the two words used to denote the same thing are strictly synonymous. Frequently the two combine to form together a single higher conception, *e. g.* :

" They shal fynde and seen," " disposen and devise," " of malyce and envye," " of slouthe and negligence," " who can mesure yt or compasse," " ye be unworthy and unhable."

In this place may be mentioned such conjunctions as : " hert and body," " al my hert and al my might," " herte and thought," " my thouht and my corage," " bothe mynde and sight," " mynd and thought," etc.

Sometimes the one expression represents a more general idea, under which the other falls under relation of " species " to " genus."

In this case the narrower expression specifies the particular application in which the wider term is intended to be employed, *e. g.* : " in the fourthe was wryte and grave," " which was to me ful profitable and right holsom douteless," " right softe and right deliciouse," " to shewen and exemplyfye."

It must not be supposed that any of these combinations are merely fortuitous, flowing, as it were, by chance from the good monk's pen in moments when he is more than usually slipshod. We have to deal for the most part with constantly recurring expressions having a stereotyped, formalistic character.[1] Thus, for

[1] The following duplicate compound phrases were collected from the first book of *The Falls of Princes* :

in his hert & in his inward sight ; for to know and be put in certayne ; countenannce and chere ; malice and enuy ; fishe and find out ; gather and instance, the first example we have given occurs so often that, given a similar occasion, we may always predict with safety that it will be made to do duty again.

The effort of creating these "double-barrelled" expressions sometimes leads to a curious circumlocution. The adverb *always* is in most cases denoted by some such periphrasis as :

"day and nyght," "night and day," "erly and ek late," "both eve and prime."

Instead of *never* we find "nouther in slombre nor aslepe," "day nor nyght," "ffor never wakyng nor a-slepe."

Nowhere, everywhere, throughout, under all circumstances, have also each their definite forms of expression :

(α) "not in borgh nor toun," "withinne nor withoute," "nygh nor ferre,"

(β) "in every cite and every toun," "to forne and eke behinde," "bothe fer and ner," "high and lowe," "in foul or fayr,"

(γ) "in colde and hete," "for lyf and deth," "each hour and space," "in special and in general."

The combinations collected in the last section, together with many others like them, occur frequently in dependent sentences of a concessive kind introduced by the word *wherso*, e. g. :

"Wherso that I go or ryde," "wherso that thou slepe or wake," "wherso thow go in se or land," "wherso thou gost in foul or ffayr," "wherso she do hem lyve or deye," "wherso that thou be glad or lyght," "wherso that thow be dul or ffresh," "wherso that he be glad or wroth."

The manner in which the adjectival ideas *many, various, all*, find expression is also curious. This is effected mostly by two adjectives related to one another as contraries and following the noun, sometimes introduced by *bothe . . . and* or by *somme . . . somme*, and other times without any introductory expression, *e. g.* : "Weyes somme freysh and feyre—And somme also that be contreyre," "Thinges bothen high and lowe," "All mankynde both high & lowe," "Thynges newe or old," "servantes foule and faire," "fishes

---

compile ; tolde and affirmed ; as lord and kyng ; refourme and redresse ; for shame and feare ; clepe and crie ; doubt and ambiguite ; he list no lenger tarien ne abide ; demure of looke and of visage ; beholde and rede ; of his hoost leader and gouernoure ; ayeinst law, and ayeinst all ryght ; to punishe & to purge ; for helpe & for succours ; flatter & fage ; slain his father and make his sydes blede ; their puissaunce and their might ; tender and yong of age ; of force and might ; was it not routh, was it not pitie ; benigne of loke & face.

gret and smale," "Toknys bothe high and lowe," "Ech estate both young and old," "Of verray ryght both hygh and lowe."

Nor is it only simple ideas capable of being expressed by a single word which are thus represented in duplicate compound phrases, longer or shorter as the case may be, nay, sometimes whole sentences are to be found which are repeated a second time in other words and with the closest possible correspondence of construction. We have selected a few examples only which lay near at hand:

Reson and Sensuallyte 188 f.:
"Whan every hert ys glad and lyght,
And him reioysseth with plesaunce."

446 f.: "Thou art to blame,
And vn-to the yt is gret shame."

910 f.: "In al hast whan I was clad
And redy eke in myn array."

Pilgrimage 6344 f.:
"Yt lyth in thyn ellecc̈ioun
And in thy fre choys yt shal be."

7257 f.: "Pertynent to thy vyáge
And nedful to thy pylgrimage."

8225 f.: "Ma dame, quod I, ne greff yow nouht
Thogh I dyscure to yow my thouht;
And lat yt yow no thyng dysplese
Thogh I declare myn gret vnhese."

Falls of Princes I, 10 D VI:
"And with þe worde John Bochas stil stode
Full soberly to yeue hym audience,
and in the place demurely he abode
To heare þe substaunce of his mortal offence."

further I, 7 C I b.:
"Thus of Cadmus the sorowes to discriue,
and his mischiefe to put in remembraunce."

I, ii E II.: "For there is none more dredeful auenture,
than in kynred to fynd frowardnes,
Nor no damage more perilous to endure,
than in frendship when ther is strangenes."

In some cases the repetition of a thought is effected by means of two sentences, one of which expresses it positively and the other negatively, *R. and S.* l. 381: "She wirketh ay, and cesseth noght"; further 537 f.: "Duely hem for to vse
and nat destroyen hem in veyn";
and 637 f.: "And she ne lyst no lenger duelle,
But in all hast[e] gan me telle."

Pilgr. 6494 : "Iustly to deme, & errë nouht;"
6561 :   " To demë trouthe, and no-thyng erre."

In these cases also it must not be thought that we are dealing with a mere chance occurrence. We are dealing with a principle of art consciously employed and systematically carried through. This becomes clear for the first time when we turn our eyes to the longer instances of combination. Everywhere we see clearly the results of an effort to find for every sentence, and even for every phrase within the sentence, a corresponding counterpart in a parallel construction. Comp. 665 ff. :

"Thorient, {which ys so bryght'
 and casteth forth so clere a lyght',
 Betokeneth in especiall
 {Thinges that be celestiall
 And thinges, as I kaw diffyne,
 That be verrely dyvyne."

1625 ff. :

"Iuno, Iubiter[e]s Wyfe, {{Made quarel non nor stryf,
 Nor was wrothe for this offence,
 But took hyt al in pacience."

5691 ff. :

"And whaw I had the l*ett*res rad, } {Wer profoundely and depe y-grave,
Which in the stonys hard and sad} The scripture for to save
 Wryte of olde antyquyte,
 To conserve the beaute."

For further and more detailed examples see ll. : 765–775, 803–814, [Original 829–836], 817–822, 823–835, 875–879, 974–982, 1103–1111, 1402–5, 2004–2017, 2018–2029, 2209–2226, 3118–3136 etc.

In regard to these instances of compound sentences, constructed of parallel phrases, it is very instructive to compare them with the constructions of the French original. The example last quoted is merely a translation of the following lines :

"Quant joz leu celle merveille,
 Qui me sambla la non p*a*reille."

To our taste Lydgate's style of translation seems anything but elegant. In his own day, however, it must have doubtless appeared a great accomplishment. And that the good monk, though elsewhere he speaks of his art in very modest tones, certainly prided himself no little upon it, is apparent from the ardour and naïve satisfaction with which he resorts again and again to such construc-

Ch. V. Lydgate's Style. His use of Synonyms.

tions. With the reader's permission we will give some further examples with the corresponding text of the French:

520 ff.
" And considre, and take
good hede,
{ "Yf ther fayle in my wirkynge of fairenesse any thynge
Or of beaute ther wanteth ought¹
And of wyssdome that may be sought¹."

" Et que tu consideres bien
Sa beaulte ou Il ne fault rien "

613 ff.: "And fyrst considre well in thy syght
Too go the wey[e] that is ryght¹,
And haue in mynde euer amonge { In thy passage thou go nat wronge,
Nor erre nat in thyn entent."

"Mais garde bien comment quil aille
Que le droit chemin ne te faille."

683 ff.: "God the which of hys goodnesse,
As to forne y dyd expresse,
As he that bothe may and kaɲ),
Hath yove and graunted unto maɲ),
Many vertu in substaunce,
Throgh hys myghty purveyaunce,
Twoo maners of knowlychynge,
As he that is most souereyɲ) kynge."

"DIeux qui a fait maint bien a homme
Si com Je tay· dit en brief somme,
Ly donna par sa pourueance,
Deux manieres de congnoissance."

It is to be noticed especially in the last example how remarkably the two phrases correspond to one another in each case:

"of hys goodnesse"—"throgh hys myghty purveyaunce,"

"as he that bothe may and kaɲ)"—"as he that is most souereyɲ) kynge,
many vertu in substaunce—twoo maners of knowlychynge."

Naturally some of these features which we have above described as peculiarities of Lydgate, are occasionally met with also in Chaucer and other poets of the period. The employment of synonyms plays indeed not a small part in all forms of poetical representation. But the distinctive trait of Lydgate is that he employs consistently and with full consciousness a means of poetical diction which is resorted to in Chaucer only occasionally. If the reader would appreciate Lydgate's uniqueness in this respect, let him first read Chaucer's *Book of the Duchesse*, and then turn to this poem, or still better, after enjoying the simple and smooth flowing verse of Lyndsay's *Monarchy* let him take up the *Pilgrimage of Man*.

Wide indeed though the gulf is which separates his vapid verse, betraying in every line the traces of decadence, from the inimitable creations of Israel's golden youth, Lydgate is, in point of fact, not so far removed from a mere parallelism such as meets us in the poetry of the Hebrews.

It is indispensable that the *reduplication of expression* which we have described, is not developed in an equal manner in the various writings of the prolific monk. It appears more constantly in the four-beat verse than in those works which are written in five-foot iambics. The four-beat line falling as it naturally does into two equal halves separated by the caesura, appears to have been found especially favourable for the parallelism. A considerable difference is however observed also in works written in the same metre. The tendency is more noticeable in the *Pilgrimage of Man* than in our poem. In the *Temple of Glas* it is kept remarkably in the background. It is more apparent in the *Troy-Book* and in the *Story of Thebes*, but in the *Falls of Princes* and the *Secrees of old Philisoffres* it has grown to enormous proportions. Here is traceable a development of usage which it would be interesting indeed to follow out in greater detail. The research would contribute a fresh witness in favour of Cicero's maxim "Senectus loquacior est." Indeed there can be no doubt that this straining after parallelism of expression is ultimately to be explained by the growing tendency of prolixity which is the natural accompaniment of advanced age. In his latest works the monk, often enough, is not content with a simple reduplication of expression; he uses three and even more synonymous words to denote what he wishes to say. Comp., for instance, *Falls of Princes*, I, 19 G iii:

"she could wel flatter, forge and faine";
"though Dalilah complain, cry *and* wepe."

Lydgate's prolixity reveals itself in other directions also. Everything is painted with the strongest possible colouring. When the French original in a running narrative employs the personal pronoun, Lydgate generally casts about him for a heavy substantial periphrasis. Comp. l. 242: "Thys hevenly emperesse"; 773: "that lady debonaire"; 691: "thys myghty lorde." A plain *dame* of the French is promoted by him to the dignity of *emperesse*, the simple *raisons* becomes *reson, the mighty quene*.

Especially at the turning points of his story when the goddesses

Ch. V. Lydgate's Style. His Reduplications. 51

appear, does he seem insatiate in his straining after titles, epithets and apostrophisings. Compare the following examples:[1]

l. 437 ff.: " This *noble* goddesse *honurable*,
Debonayre, and amiable,
Fressh of hewe as eny Rose."

l. 473 ff.: " Whan she had shewyd hir sentence,
This lady most of excellence,
As she that was bothe fair and good."

l. 481 ff.: " But tho in hast[e] this goddesse,
Oonly of her gentilesse,
To put me out of drede and fere,
Of al that me lyst enquire,
Or what that me lyst devyse
Yaf me answere in goodly wyse,
Benyg[n]e of chere and eke of face."

l. 513: "*This lady tho, ful wel apayed*."

l. 581 ff.: " Lady, quod I, *and maistresse
And vnder god cheffe goddesse
Of al this worlde, as semeth me*."

l. 824 f.: " Both to love him and to drede
As thy lorde most souereyne."

Compare further l. 603–691, 1095–97, 2209–10, 2887–89, 1074–76 with the corresponding passages of the French poem.

Frequently also we find that Lydgate has substituted for the simple pronoun of the person addressed a descriptive, abstract noun, e. g. l. 494 ff.:

" Which so goodly lyst appere
And shewe yow *to my symplesse*,
I thanke vn-*to your high noblesse*
And eke to your magnificence."

In the original text:

" Si vous Regraci bonnement
De ce que si benignement
Vous maues voulu visiter."

l. 508 ff.: " I wil in euery thyng obeye,
With al my hert and al [my] myght,
To your plesaunce."

In the French poem:

" Je veuil obeir et cest drois
A vous madame en tous endrois."

l. 925 ff.: " *To my plesaunce* most covenable."

---

[1] We have italicized in these examples all that the monk has added to the original from his own workshop. The exaggeration of his style stands out here in especial prominence.

Naturally intensifying adverbs also play a great part in the monk's vocabulary. At every possible opportunity the simple adjective appears thus strengthened. The goddess which appears to him, is "passing" or "inly faire," and often "faire above al mesure."

She addresses him "in ryght wonder frendly wyse" (1845), so that he, "ful wel apayed," or even "ryght wonder wel apayde" (2320), breaks into tokens of overflowing gratitude.

The following instances from our poem may give some idea of the frequency of the commonest adverbs of this kind:

wel: 43, 498, 505, 513, 514, 571, 613, 1041, etc.
passing: 1097, 1216, 1411, 1538, 2063, 3558, etc.
passingly: 264, 1302, 1352, 2405, 2440, 2748, 3345, etc.
inly: 951, 1796, 1978, etc.
fully: 35, 2266, etc.
pleynly: 153, 413, 504, 750, 1034, 1433, 1560, 1575, 1645, 1853, 2162, etc.
sothely: 79, 558, 1019, 1478, 1539, 1658, 1725, etc.
trewly: 760, 864, 965, 1028, 1214, 1234, etc.

"The more, the merrier," seems indeed to have been Lydgate's principle. Even where the additional meaning given by the adverb contributes nothing to heighten or fix more definitely and fully the thought which he is expressing, he does not on that account fail to drag it in:

R. and S. 3309: "Me semeth in my syght."
Pilgr. 879: "Me semeth in my thouht."
Pilgr. 13665: "I gan consydren in my mynde."
R. and S. 3464 f.: "For, pleynly, to my fantasye—
　　　　　　She is benigne."
„　　3487: "Of entent thou maist declyne."
Pilgr. 14099: "I hate also, in myn entent."
„　971 f.: "Feble in my devis—of wisdam."

Often enough the monk does not content himself with a simple adverbial of so secondary a kind.. Then with a pleonastic munificence two or three are employed together:

l. 79 f.:　　　"To knowe sothely, in sentence,
　　　　　　　The verray trewe difference."

Pleonasm plays generally a great part in Lydgate's works. The astonishing frequency of such expressions as: "Enowgh suffise," "togedirr yfere," "aprochen or neghen nere" is pointed out in the corresponding notes, where this has not already been done by others.

The same appears nearly always strengthened in some way, e. g.:

"Thys ylke same weye,"
"the sylue same place,"
"the sylue same tre."

The connection of two things or persons with one another is generally signified by "both tweyne" as in the following instances:

Pilgr. 4990 ff.: "And bothë tweynë be mortal;
The Ton, the tother, in certeyne
They be but vermës bothe tweyne."

Expressions containing a downright tautology will hardly be found in the present work. In Lydgate's later poems, however, they are frequent: see the following examples from the *Pilgrimage:*

5255: "The trouthë trewly to concyve."
5316: "ffor profyt off thyn ownë speed."

Note also expressions like: "clad in cloth," "worth off valu," "knelynge on his knees."

In agreement with the poet's love of strong effects in positive statements is the tendency which we shall find almost constantly to strengthen his negatives also. Here also—and this is a point we would lay stress on throughout—we have to deal with a feature common to all Middle English literature. See J. Hein, *Ueber die bildliche Verneinung in der mittel-englischen Poesie.* Anglia 15, p. 42 ff., and especially Chapter II.

The peculiarity of Lydgate's position here again consists in the frequency with which he indulges in this practice. The simple negation is generally emphasized and supplemented by a second clause as: "For no chaunce," "in no degre," "in no wyse," "in no cas," "in no manere"; or not seldom by more complicated expressions such as: "in no maner wyse." *Nothing* appears as "no maner thing," *nobody* as "no maner wight."

The simple *not* is very often ousted by the more pretentious "neveradel."

We have been concerned hitherto with the peculiarities of Lydgate's style in respect of its *matter*, i. e. what he says. The question now follows: what are we to say of his poetry in regard to its *form*, i. e. how does he build up his sentence and how connect it with the other sentences? The answer to this question would involve an exhaustive account of our author's syntax, such as lies neither in our purpose nor in our power to give at this place. We must content ourselves here with touching merely on the most salient points.

Let us take once more the standpoint of the uninitiated reader, who takes the verses of our poet in his hands for the first time. The first thing which, I think, will strike his notice is the great number of stop-gap expressions which stand, for the most part, in no syntactical connection with the context. Naturally Lydgate does not stand alone in this respect. Often enough, as Schick, l. c. p. cxxxvii, notices, has a poet like Chaucer recourse to such means, and the original of our poem also exhibits not a few of these "aids to metre."

But in the thoroughness with which he develops this system of makeshifts, Lydgate far outstrips all rivals. They do not occur merely sporadically, but sometimes the poet finds himself reduced to resort to them for two or three consecutive lines. Comp. the following lines of our poem: 1056-57, 1153-55, 1216-20, 1348-51, 1414-16. In ll. 1029-43 we are referred to the original no less than seven times by little reminders parenthetically thrown in.

In spite of the great frequency with which sentences inserted solely to fill up a space occur, the number available for selection is by no means large. The same old stop-gaps, varied a little to suit the necessities of the metre, are dished up again and again. Most frequent are the expressions appealing to the reader and expressing a judgment in which he will concur if he have diligence and insight or a good faith:

Cp. "Who that can espye" (1056); "Who took good hede[1]" (1153); "Who that kan wel vnderstande" (1160); "Who that vnderstood" (1173); "Who vnderstood" (5505); "Who that truly kan espye" (1234); "Who lyst assay[e], he shal fynde" (1337); "As men may se" (1647); "As ye may se" (1655); "As thou maist see" (4337, 4385); "Who that koude looke aryght'" (5760); "Yif ye Lyst heren of entencion" (5796 f.); "Yf ye lyst to lere" (5793).

Often too the inserted stop-gap connects the thoughts already expressed or about to be expressed with the poet's power of observation or insight:

"As me dide seme" (1214); "As sempte me" (1414); "And as I coude espye and knowe" (1415); "Me thought" (1416); "So

---

[1] This is one of the most frequently repeated stop-gaps, which turns up again and again with many variations:
"Yif you take hede" (4264, 4347); "who lyst take hede" (5911); "who so lyst aright' take hede" (5138); "who taketh hede" (4579, 5443), etc.

Ch. V. Lydgate's Style. His Padding. 55

as I kan) devise" (1419); "As I behelde" (1421); "So I koude knowe" (5754).

In close connection with these stand the formulae relating to the poet's own activity or the progress and advance of the recital:

"Yif I shal nat tarye" (1057); "As I kan) telle" (1093); "Lyche to forn) as I yow tolde" (1098); "As hyt was seyn)" (1137); "As ye han herd aforn) declare" (1141); "As I reherse shal" (1316); "As ye aforn) han) herd deuyse" (1442); "Lych as I haue tolde to forn)" (1624); "And also eke I dar expresse" (1634); "I dar expresse" (5607); "And to reherse hem oon) by oon)" (5451); "Thus I mene" (4679); "To declare yt and expresse" (4889); "Shortly to telle" (5009); "And to conclude in lytill space" (5050); "To make iust comparison)" (5108); "As I kan dyffyne" (5103).

To these should be added the formulae of asseveration which the poet thinks right to repeat again and again:

"This no fable" (1147); "This no fayle" (1895); "This noo tale" (1149); "It is no Iape" (1259); "Also god me save, and spede,—And me defende from all damage" (1154 f.); "I knew yt wel, me lyst nat lye" (1165); "out of drede" (1203); "Wythout[e] were" (1263); "Sooth to sey" (1357); "I yow ensure" (1217, 1366); "But of Reson) I dar wel seyn),—And afferme hyt in certeyn)" (1219 f.).

Unusually common also are references to the original. I do not mean those by no means unimportant passages so welcome especially to the student, in which an author is cited by name, but those expressions repeated *ad nauseam* which refer either to the writer's immediate source or quite generally to poets' books, writings, etc.:

"As seith my boke," "as I rede," "the booke seyth thus," "as clerkes write—And in her bookes lyst endyte," "So as they discerneth," "lyke as they lere."

All these examples occur in the passage 1029–43 above-mentioned. Compare further:

"Rede poetis, and ye shal se" (1051); "And as myn) Auctour seyth certeyn),—The which ne writ no thing in veyn)" (1129–30); "Bookys seyn) so" (1253); "As bookes telle" (1306); "As hyt ys founde" (1283); "As yt is ryff" (1287); "so as I rede" (1301).

But it would be useless to heap up further examples. If we recollect, however, that the part of the poem from which this last group of examples is quoted covers hardly more than 150 lines, it becomes clear what a part these literary "acknowledgments"—if we may use the expression—play in the poetic art of our monk.[1]

We should like to point out also that the list of such phrases as given above is not exhaustive: for instance, it does not include a formula which stands almost next to none in frequency of application, viz. "to reknen alle." We need only mention here some of the many variations under which this phrase is found: "To reckene hem oon) by oon)" (4717); "to reherse hem oon) by oon)" (5451); "for to rekene al the Route" (5279); "for to rekne hem euerychon)" (1488).

We might mention also phrases referring to a moral judgment, e. g.:
"As yt ys skylle" (4590); "Which was nouther good nor faire" (1448).

A somewhat curious instance of this kind is found in the Pilgrimage, 17571 ff.:
"Thys hand ful hih vp-on A tre
Maketh many on enhangyd be;
And with hys ffeet (wych ys nat fayr),
Ffor to waggen in the hayr."

But we had better stop here. Naturally more important than a comprehensive analysis of these quite meaningless parentheses is the question, how are they worked into the sentence in such a way as to fulfil their purpose as make-shifts?

As a rule, the stop-gaps constitute the second half of the verse. Their selection is then determined by the exigencies of rhyme. They occur less often in the first half of the verse where one or two feet of the line have to be supplied. In *Reson and Sensuallyte* I find not a single example of their occurrence in the middle of the line; but there are occasional instances of this in the *Pilgrimage*, where phrases like "I mene," etc., are inserted between the two halves of the verse.

A poet whose style is concise, and whose rules of syntactical connection are strict, would scarcely find himself able to use stop-gap phrases to such an extent.

And in reality the extent to which he indulges himself in this

---

[1] In truth, our poem is more beautifully blessed with them than any other of Lydgate's works. And the cause lies near at hand. The author of the French poem, a learned and deeply read man, seldom forgets to acknowledge his source. Besides, in the part of his work relating to the rose-garden he lay under a natural necessity to point again and again to his original. Thus it happened that the French poem satisfied in the completest manner Lydgate's partiality for inserting clauses of a similar kind.

usage is typical of Lydgate's syntactical constructions. Without troubling himself to express manifold shades of logical connection which exist between the parts of a syntactical whole, he produces verse after verse in haphazard order. He starts with any part of the sentence—often the subject or the object. If there is anything in the way of apposition, adjectival attributes or adjectival sentences to be found, they are made to do duty; then follow relative sentences broken up by adverbial qualifications or clauses and infinitive phrases of all kinds, until finally the object which occasioned all this eloquence becomes invisible to our syntactical consciousness. Then the poet picks it up again by means of a pronoun, often introduced with a "I mene," or some such expression; again his pen spreads its wings on its blythe career, and once more he drops into a tangled skein of countless qualifying clauses and dependent sentences. See, for example, the following passages: ll. 1265-74, 1464 ff., 4094 ff., 4233 ff. Especially typical are ll. 4200-4218: After "How, through vnhappy aventure" we expect for certain the end of the sentence, but the poet finds it convenient first to insert a number of explanatory clauses. Then he takes up the broken thread again in the words "For which, throgh hys vnhappy chaunce." But again he disappoints our expectation. First there stands in the way a stop-gap clause, then a causal sentence introduced with a "for," the connection of which with the rest we are left to conjecture; then this in its turn suggests a further independent sentence. At last he loses himself entirely in his construction: for the words "For which al the worlde they brent," etc., are only the close of the preceding interpolation.

However, as regards the syntax all parts of our poem are not of equal quality. The middle part, especially the description of Diana and the rose-garden, exhibits in places a remarkable want of continuity in the construction. I should not like to impute this to a greater carelessness on the part of the author. I believe the fact is to be traced rather to the following circumstance: Instead of relating quietly in epic style the many tales brought forward to illustrate the adventures of Venus, the poet falls into the error of investing *en passant* the separate details of a history which is sometimes spun out rather long. The last-mentioned quotation is typical in this connection also. It is, however, not possible to arrange so much material *en passant* in grammatically dependent sentences without ruining the style even of the best writer.

It is not to be wondered at that amidst such looseness of construction it often happens that a sentence is not properly rounded off, and it is often difficult to say for certain where one sentence ends and the next begins (see Schick, *l. c.* p. cxxxiv).

It is not until we have recourse to comparison with the original that we are able to punctuate in all cases with precision, a new conception generally ushered in with an *and*. In the same way examples are not wanting of cases in which the sentence is not completed at all, but breaks off in the middle, *e. g.* 940 and 3543.

Schick has also noticed that *oratio recta* often passes into *oratio obliqua* and *vice versâ*. In the present work this occurs sometimes within the compass of a single line. It speaks little, moreover, for the poet's carefulness, that sometimes even his own *oratio recta* is introduced with "quod he," cp. 2637, 3019.

So much for the point to be noticed concerning the structure of the lengthier grammatical constructions and the method of their connection. Let us now for a minute consider the single elements of the syntax one by one. Here also we meet with a large amount of licence, if we are to refrain from calling it carelessness. This is especially the case as regards the position of the words. The rule that the conjunction must introduce the dependent sentence seems to have no existence for Lydgate. The conjunction is very often itself preceded by an adverbial phrase which qualifies the dependent sentence, *e. g.* "In-to Colchos whan he went" (3525). The object too is often placed at the head of such dependent sentences, *e. g. Pilgr.* 13769 " The trouthë, yiff I shal the telle," and again 14252 " The wychë, whan the ffox beheld."

In principal sentences also Lydgate does not hesitate to place the object at the beginning, and picks it up again later on by a pronoun, *e. g.*:

"Hys honour gold, hys goode fame—Al I tourned yt . . ."
"Thys lessoun I forgete yt nouht."

Such inversions of the order, if prudently and sparingly employed, are indeed by no means to be condemned : on the contrary, they are perhaps in view of certain desired effects deserving of commendation. In Lydgate, however, they are not the outcome of a balanced and delicate insight. They are concessions, and their frequent recurrence cannot fail to strike us as such.

The same is true of the arbitrary manner in which he splits up and separates words which should naturally go together. A qualifying genitive, for instance, is cut off from its noun by a longer or shorter clause, e. g. 3836 f.:

> "By clere refleccion),
> In the watir *of his face.*"

Here might be mentioned, l. 4265 f. :

> "The *crafty* man) Pigmalion)
> *To grave* in metal and in ston)."

Note also in the following instance the startling connection of the abbreviated relative clause with the preceding *hir* :

> "To make *hir* fre from) al servage
> *Inly fair of hir) visage*" (1795-96).

See another example in which a single continuous phrase is broken up into a chiasmus which is quite artistic :

> "In-to Colchos whan) he went
> There to conquere of entent,
> In-to that Ile famous and olde,
> *The Ram)*" (3524 ff.).

CHAPTER VI.

THE SOURCE OF LYDGATE'S POEM.

1. THE source of the English poem is the still-unprinted Early-French love-romance, *Les Échecs amoureux*, whose first 4873 lines Lydgate has spun out into 7042. Of the contents of this work I have given some account in my book bearing the same name, to which I have referred in Part I. And as the reader of *Reson and Sensuallyte* may naturally desire to know how Lydgate's poem should have ended, I will sketch concisely the French continuation.

The author first describes the chess-board and then the game. He is checkmated by his fair opponent, and the defeat greatly grieves him, but Deduit comforts him with kindly words, and then leads him to Amor, who is ready to take him as a retainer, and prepares him for that office by appropriate instructions. He shows him the right art to serve Love. Lady Nature, in wise care for the conservation of her works, knew how to unite love and sensual delight. Amor presides over love. Venus is the goddess of sensual delight. Both are aided by Oiseuse and Deduit (Idleness and Pleasure).

We next come to the grave considerations which lay hold of the Poet after Amor has left him. He ardently wishes to conquer the fair maid at chess, but ever doubts whether he be fitted for the task. The state of his heart is that painted in Goethe's verse:

"Hangen und bangen
In schwebender Pein."

Once more Amor approaches the dispirited one and comforts him. He blames the lover's unsteadiness of spirit, and exhorts him to keep his mind right. He must learn to bridle his impatience. Venus, he assures the lover, would be sure to keep her word, and let him win the maid she has promised him. Only little-spiritedness could induce a doubt of the power of Venus. No one can resist her fire.

Strengthened and encouraged, the Poet now asks for instructions for his farther bearing. Amor first lays stress on the necessity of the author believing in the power of the goddess of love, and in his own power. Hope and Self-confidence are represented as the most indispensable conditions of success; and unconditional obedience must be yielded to the decrees of Amor.

These decrees are now formulated; they are:

1. Be loyal. Attempt no unlawful manœuvre, no violence and no magic. Nor can any buying or selling take place in the commerce of love.

2. Be discreet. You must be on your guard against Jalousie and Malebouche; cause for attack too easily is given to these enemies. Nor is it advisable to employ the aid of strangers or any sort of mediators.

3. Be zealous. Your wooing must be cleverly adapted to the character of the woman. You must be able to laugh or to weep, as the nature of the lady requires. The metamorphoses of Jupiter show how, by skilful contrivance, one always reaches the goal. And zeal must be connected with persistency, which is manifested in firmness and patience. Only by persistence does a man succeed, who wishes to undertake some great task. Only the brave are aided by the gods. Use, too, only gentle and flattering words. The advantages of the *doulʒ-parler* are incalculable. The form of prayer, also, must be used to obtain one's end.

Amor's words do not fail to have the expected effect on the poet. All hesitation seems to have gone from his heart, and he bravely longs -to turn Amor's theory into practice. At once his imagination leads him into the presence of the lady. In a rather long speech he invites her to a new battle of chess. To checkmate her in it, is the thought which occupies him exclusively.

Ch. VI. The Source of Lydgate's Poem. Its Continuation. 61

At this moment Pallas appears before our meditating poet. She admonishes him to struggle manfully against his lamentable condition of mind, and to devote his life to some useful aim.

In his reply the poet seeks to show that, by following Amor as his liege-lord, he commits no wrong. But Pallas, in reply, insists that it is unworthy of a man to waste his time in the service of Venus. Only by resisting sensual feelings, and submitting to the commands of Reason, does man rise above the animals, and become his own master. But if, on the contrary, he pays no heed to Reason, he withdraws from his proper vocation, and commits a wrong against Lady Nature.

With manifold arguments Pallas seeks to confirm her judgments. A lover's life injures the body, and brings about disturbances of health, cares and grief. At every step the lover sees himself exposed to jealousy and evil report. The delight which Venus grants, ends with the power of enjoying it. Moreover it is manifest that Amor fulfils his office so unjustly. Love itself is inconstant and faithless. Its sweet joy is soon mingled with sad bitterness.

Further, a lover's life is not worthy of a human being; it is of an animal nature; it tends towards idleness, from whence arise neither utility nor fruits. Virtue and wisdom can be obtained only by trouble and work.

With a renewed and urgent exhortation to flee under all circumstances from a lover's life, Pallas closes this part of her discourse.

The poem then passes on to the question of how the passion of love can be cured. Pallas gives the author thirty-five remedial rules, which are drawn up in tolerably close similarity with Ovid's *Remedia amoris*. To him who has overcome the malady of Love, we are further told, two roads offer themselves towards a useful way of spending his life and finding true happiness. This highest happiness is offered by a contemplative life. The best school for preparing oneself for such a life is offered by the city of Paris. The praises of this wonderful place are sung in sonorous words. Its university is a school of Christianity, a source of Wisdom, and the mother of Philosophy.

Still, not every one feels that he has a calling towards philosophical contemplation. But to him stands open the way to an active practical life. This practical life embraces four stations of life: 1. the King, 2. his Councillors, 3. the Judges, and 4. the People. The people again contains the Clergy, the Nobles, Artists,

Craftsmen, Merchants and Peasants. Then the Author proceeds to enlarge on the essence of the position of these different stations of life, and on the duties of each, as follows—

1. Princes and lords must direct their eyes and their heart wholly towards God, in order to be able to govern well, *i. e.* in accordance with the precepts of sound reason; they must possess all the qualities —Courage, Wisdom, Affability—which we still to-day consider the necessary virtues of a good prince. But they could not have a complete survey of a State nor govern it wisely, unless they were supported by 2. Councillors, whose task it is to consider and advise, —without falseness or deceit, without flattery, and with proper foresight,—the ways and means which appear calculated to obtain a great and worthy aim. 3. The third rank or station in life belongs to the judges. They must judge, above all, in accordance with the orders of the government and conformably to the existing laws, more especially in accordance with the spirit, rather than the letter, of these laws, but never arbitrarily. The judge moreover must not allow the lawyers to indulge in fine words, or to overwhelm the opposing party with insults. Yet, adds the author, I am speaking of judges as they ought to be, not as they are. 4. The fourth rank, the People, must lead a virtuous and good life: so much is demanded by nature. To render this possible, towns have been established; however, the instinct of sociability—as evidenced by marriage, formerly by love, now often for the sake of money—has had a part in the foundation of towns. However that be, we may regard that town as the best, in which the inhabitants possess but moderate riches; for in it prevails neither arrogance, nor envy, nor covetousness, but constant peace and quietness, as well as reverence and obedience to princes. A strong column of political order is the rank of Knights, which opposes enemies, supports the Right, and punishes the ill-disposed. But only the worthiest men in the nation may become knights; thus the Ancients chose, from each thousand men, only one to be a Knight (the word appears formed from *mille*, hence *miles*). After an ample account of the education of an Esquire, and the accomplishments and qualities of a worthy knight, our poet touches with surprising brevity upon the clerical ranks. In the towns this rank is very much required, in order that the people may love, fear, and serve God. The Clerics must have a dignified exterior and high mind; above all, they must not come from among bondsmen. The House of Worship must be worthily

Ch. VI. *The Source of Lydgate's Poem. Its Continuation.* 63

and splendidly furnished with paintings, gold, silver, and precious stones. But your inclinations do not lie in the direction of this station of life. I prefer therefore to speak to you of the married state. Marriage is required on various grounds; but not on those only: it is also the noblest form of friendship, and comprises within itself every kind of love. The books which speak ill of it, one must look on with suspicion, for rationally no one can speak ill of it. One ought not to marry too early, nor on the other hand too late. The right age is 18 for the woman, and 24 to 30 for the man. The wife one choses must not be chosen from among one's relations. She must have some fortune, as well as good qualities of body and soul. Both husband and wife must be devoted to one another in esteem and faithfulness, and must try to mend each other's failings. Whilst the wife, in propriety and decency attends to the house, the sewing, spinning, embroidery, with but little visiting, and not being much seen in the street, simpleness in dress, and without rouging or otherwise painting, the husband must go out into general life, to carry on his business, yet not lose sight of the affairs of the house.

The children are to be fed by the mother herself; yet, if a wet-nurse be necessary, one should be chosen between the age of 24 and 36, in good bodily health, and of sound normal mind. The weaning of the child must take place in winter, with boys at the age of $2\frac{1}{2}$ to 3 years, with girls between 2 to $2\frac{1}{2}$. The child must not be allowed to walk before it is a year old. The process of teething may be rendered easier to the child by the gums being rubbed with honey, or the blood of fowls, or the brain of hares.

As the child grows into knowledge, it is to learn the Creed and the Commandments, and is to live honestly and with good breeding. The children of the rich are to study Philosophy, Divinity, or Medicine. Their teachers must be honest men of deep science and great knowledge of the world, so that they may be able to influence their pupils, both by word and example. The children are to be brought up in moderate ways; they are not to drink any wine, nor eat too much, and then only at fixed hours and in a proper way; above all, they must chew their food well. Their habiliments are to be warm in winter, light in summer; at no time luxurious. In speaking, the child must only use its mouth, not its arms and legs. Their games are to be decent, and appropriate to their age. One of the noblest among them is music, which invigorates men, and brings peace to a troubled heart, leading, moreover, the way to speculative meditation. For everything in Nature is, according to Pythagoras, ordered by the laws of Music, and is by them well proportioned, as the music of the Spheres, etc. Bodily exercises make a child healthy, keep the medical man away, and call forth the sense and the understanding of the beauty of Nature. Walking tours through beautiful parts of the country, riding on horseback, hunting, going in a vehicle or in a boat, throwing stones at a mark, running, leaping, fighting with a friend with staff or lance, amusing themselves with nine-pins or balls, swinging by a rope, singing—these are games for both children and grown-ups. The education of girls has to be still more careful than that of boys, that they may grow up respectably, and worthy of a good marriage. The good father of the family has to pay heed, too, to the servants, that they do their proper work, lead good lives, and receive appropriate wages. The house you inhabit must be both fine and healthy, and fit to protect your property. It must be situated in a healthy neighbourhood and in good air; it must contain a hall, a kitchen with appurtenances, good bedrooms, a room for praying, a wardrobe, a bath-room, a closet, a loft, a granary and cellarage. All round the house are to be gardens and stables, also pigeon and peacock houses. The water must not contain any metallic admixture, or trace of a marsh; it must be clear, and without any smell, and must come from a well or a cistern. The best water, however, is that which flows over gravel, more especially in an easterly or northerly direction, and is subject to sun and wind. The house must be situated so as to be cool in summer, warm in winter; the wine-cellar should face the north; the barns must open to the north, but the stables must be closed.

Man is meant to strive for making a fortune, and this is possible in various ways. It can best be attained by dealing in letters of exchange, and earning interest on money. It is necessary to invest money, it must not root in its strong-box. The art of exchange is a very fine one, for the conclusions one has to come to in that line sharpens the intellect. Thus, too, we become familiar with the different sorts of coin, and to distinguish them, by comparison: 1 *mars fin d'or* is always equal to as many *livres*, as 1 carate 10 *deniers* is worth; *e.g.* if 1 carate is equal to 100 times 10 *deniers*, then 1 *mars fin* = 100 livres.

2. In my book on the *Échecs amoureux* I have treated at some length the sources of this early French Romance. I have

Ch. VI. The Source of Lydgate's Poem and of its Original. 65

shown that a number of classical and mediaeval authors have furnished the poet with the material of his work. The book *de Planctu Naturae* by Alanus ab Insulis, the Latin Mythographers, the *Roman de la Rose*, books on Chess (*libri Scaccorum*), the books on Love by Andreas Capellanus, Ovid's *Remedia amoris*, and other writings: such are the principal sources, whose confluence has produced the stream of the French poem. As to the less interesting and more didactic second part of the *Échecs amoureux* I had omitted it in my inquiry about the sources. A pupil of mine, however, Mr. H. Höfler, induced by me, has examined more fully into the relation of this second part to the mediaeval cyclopaedias, and has thus arrived at the following results which, with his kind permission, I here publish.

In the introductory observations on the three ways of life and the different manners of obtaining happiness, there appears a close connection with the *Spec. Doctr.* of Vincent of Beauvais. Cf. lib. 5, cap. 34. An agreement with Brunetto Latini is apparent in the chapter on the position of princes. Cf. iii, 2, 25 and iii, 2, 3, also iii, 2, 24. Further, what is said here on the rank and offices of Councillors, reminds one of Brunetto. Cf. ii, 1, 17. The discussion of the duty of monogamy is in complete harmony with the views of Vincent of Beauvais. Cf. *Spec. Nat.* lib. 30, cap. 32 and 33. The notion that one is not to marry a relation[1] is laid down in Vincent, 1. c. 30, 17. Especially close is the parallelism with Vincent in that part which treats of the feeding of the infant, and the necessity of choosing a wet-nurse. The prudential measures to be taken in the choice of one appear to be a translation of the chapter *de eligenda nutrice et eius regimine* (*Spec. Doctr.* lib. 12, cap. 29). Many details are likewise borrowed from Vincent as to the treatment of a child in its first years.

I had already indicated in my *Échecs amoureux*, how the far-digressing *excursus* of our author on Music becomes intelligible by a survey of the literature of that time, which was fond of such digressions. I would here further and specially refer to the Anticlaudianus of Albanus (lib. 3, cap. 5). It has now been found that this *excursus*, in almost all its parts, is in Vincent of Beauvais. There we find at once the introductory musings on the delicious and befooling influence of sounds (*Spec. Doctr.* lib. 18, cap. 10). There, too,

---

[1] This is part of the doctrine of the Church as to prohibited degrees in Marriage.

we find the treatise on the cosmic system of Pythagoras; cf. lib. 18, cap. 24. The immediately preceding chapter of the same book, and especially chap. 21 have also left their traces on the French poet. The theory of the music of the spheres, on which our author dwells rather at length, is touched on by Vincent in several passages. Cf. lib. 18, cap. 10 and 16. In the sixteenth chapter we also meet again with the assertion laid down by our author concerning the existence of certain musical harmonies and relations in the four elements, the four seasons, and in the constitution of man himself.

Our author's general view of physical recreation coincides with what Vincent says in *Spec. Doctr.* lib. 15, cap. 62. The advice to take all bodily exercise before breaking one's fast is found in Vincent, l. c. lib. 15, cap. 63.

In the last section of our poem, which treats of the house, the following traits occur in Vincent also: (*a*) indications as to the situation of the house, *Spec. Doctr.* lib. 6, cap. 16, 17 and 39; (*b*) the stress laid on the necessity of having good drinking water, lib. 6, cap. 39; (*c*) rules as to cellar, loft and stables, lib. 6, cap. 21–23. The part-coincidence with Brunetto Latini, in some places, is accidental. It arises from the fact that both Brunetto and Vincent point back to the same source, viz. the Roman author Rutilius Taurus Aemilianus Palladius, who in the fourth century wrote in fourteen books his work *de re rustica*.[1] Compare also *Spec. Nat.* lib. 5, cap. 45 ff., 49, 54, and 56.

What is said about the order and position of Councillors, is taken from Brunetto, cf. ii, 1, 17. As to his information on the class of knights, our author, beside the corresponding portions of Jacobus a Cessolis, has used, according to his own statement (fol. 102 *a* and *b*), a Roman author of the fourth and fifth century, Flavius Vegetius Renatus. The latter wrote his work *Epitome rei militaris* in four books, of which the first treats on levying and drilling of recruits, the second on discipline, the third on campaigning and strategy, the fourth on the war of sieges. The work of Frontius, *de re militari*, which our author likewise cites, is now lost.

In the foregoing, the relation of the French poem to mediaeval cyclopaedias seems, without too much detail, clearly established.

But it has now become patent that, in a much larger proportion than Vincent of Beauvais and Brunetto Latini, another mediaeval author has furnished our poet with the material for the second and

---

[1] Comp. Teuffel-Schwabe, *Geschichte der röm. Literatur*, § 410.

Ch. VI. The Source of Lydgate's Poem and of its Original. 67

extensive part of his poem. This is Guido da Colonna. Guido's book, *De regimine principum*, was the authority on which the poet of the *Échecs amoureux* depends, in giving so exhaustive a picture of life, of its rank and duties. Of this point Höfler's essay, which we may hope to see soon in print, may give more complete elucidation.

3. In still one more direction do I feel impelled to extend what I said in my essay on the *Échecs amoureux*. The chess-poem has called forth a lengthy and interesting commentary. As to the contents and disposition of this commentary cf. p. 89 ff. of my essay. Now it has been found that, beside the two MSS. mentioned by me, of this commentary (*Fonds français*, 1508 and 143) there are three others in the *Bibliothèque nationale*. These are the Codices, which in the *Catalogue des Manuscrits français* are entered as Nos. 19114, 24295, and 9197. With the exception of No. 143, which dates from the 16th century, all the MSS. have been written in the 15th century.

As to the contents and plan of the commentary, the reader, I think, will get an idea from the following remarks.[1] The quotations are taken from No. 143 of the above-mentioned MSS.

The first heading at once informs us of the origin and aim of this commentary: Ce livre present fut fact et ordonné principalment à l'instance d'ung aultre fact en ryme, nagueres et de novel venu à cognoissance qui est intitulé des Eschez amoureux et des eschez d'amours aussi comme pour declairer aucunes choses que la ryme contient, qui semblent estre obscures et estranges de premiere face. Et pour ce fut il fait en prose, pour ce que prose est plus clere à entendre par raison que n'est ryme.

As regards the plan and general intentions of the poem which we are explaining, we find the following remarks: Fol. 1. r°· c. 2. Pour ce que la matiere d'amours est delictable en soy et joyeuse, et plaisant a plusieurs escoutans, et par especial aux jeunes gens du monde ausquelz le fait d'amours aussi est plus appartenant, pour ce voult cilz qui fist le livre des eschez amoureux monstrer comment il fut amoureux en sa jeunesse, espris et esmeuz de l'amour d'une jeune damoiselle. Et ce voult il signiffier couvertement par le jeu des eschez plus que par aultre voye par aventure: Fol. 1. v°· c. l. pour ce que c'est le plus beau jeu, et le plus merveilleux, et le plus proprement a amours comparable, qui soit quant à present en nostre usaige. Et pour ce dient les astronomiens a ce propos mesmes que

[1] Comp. *Échecs amoureux*, p. 97 ff.

ce jeu est de la signification de Venus, qui estoit des anciens poetes deesse d'amours appellée sans faille, pour ce que ce livre plus agreablement et plus generalment feust de tous receu jeunes et anciens. L'acteur, avec l'amoureuse matiere entremesla, et adjousta plusieurs choses estranges qui proffitent aux meurs très grandement et au gouvernement de nostre vie humaine, affin que ceulx qui y regarderont, avec la recreacion et le delit qu'ilz pourroyent prendre, aucun proffit aussi rapporter en peussent. Et quant a ce aussi ressemble il aux poetes anciens qui, en leurs faitz et en leurs escriptures, quirent tousjours proffit ou delectacion. Car le delit que on a et la plaisance en lire ou en ouyr les anciennes escriptures recree moult et resjoyst nature, dont grandement vault mieulx la corporelle disposition, et le proffit aussi que on en rapporte parfait l'ame et amende. Finablement l'entente principal *de l'acteur dessusdit et la fin de son livre, c'est de tendre a vertu et a bonne oeuvre et de fuyr tout mal et toute folle oiseuse.*[1] Il ressemble aux peres anciens, en tant qu'il parle aucunes foiz aussi comme en faignant et fabuleusement en disant moult de choses qui ne sont pas du tout a entendre a la lectre ainsi come elles gisent de premiere venue, ains ont mestier d'aucune declaracion a ceulx qui ne sont pas apris ne acoustumez, Fol. 1. v°· c. 2. de la fainte maniere de parler des poetes, car elles ne sont pas sans raison ainsi faictes, ains contiennent en elles aucune grant sentence secrete moult souvent. Item, il ressemble aux poetes a ce qu'il fact son livre par rymes et par vers, car de ceste maniere de parler par rymes et par metres usent communement en leur faitz les poetes pour plus subtillement et plus plaisamment dire ce qu'ilz veulent ; car en rymes et en metres est la parolle assise et mesuree par musical mesure, c'est a dire par nombres ressemblables a ceulx dont les consonances musicaulx deppendent, en laquelle musical consonance se delicte moult l'ame humaine naturelment, si comme dit Aristote aillures.

Here the commentator attempts to show, in connection with the title of the poem, how the game of chess has been conceived as a picture of the commonwealth of the state, further how it has been compared to a battle, to events which are represented in the vault of the heavens, and lastly, how it can be made to refer to the game of Love. The headings of the chapters in question run as follows:

1. Fol. 1. v°· c. 2. Cy nous monstre l'acteur comment le jeu des eschez a esté et peult estre a plusieurs choses comparez.

2. Fol. 2. v°· c. 1. De bataille commune.

---

[1] The lines in italics are underlined in the MS.

Ch. VI. The Source of Lydgate's Poem.

3. Fol. 3. v°· c. 2. Comment ce jeu est d'aucuns comparé au ciel et aux estoilles et a police du ciel.

4. Fol. 4. r°· c. 2. Comment le jeu des eschez est ou peult estre aussi comparez a amours.

As to the contents of these headings, the reader may compare my remarks on the battle of chess in the garden of Deduit: *Échecs amoureux*, p. 161 ff.

The commentator wishes to have the observations, which have been so far only given in outline, considered as a sort of prologue, which is to prepare for the actual discussion of the poem. This discussion, upon which he now enters, follows the plot closely. This is shown by the sequence of the headings, which may be given here for the sake of the general review.

Fol. 5. r°· c. 2. Cy commence lacteur de ce livre a declerer aucunement la ryme dessus dicte et premierement parle de fortune.

Fol. 6. r°· c. 1. Encores de ce et monstre l'acteur comment aucuns ont ramené fortune a la vertu du ciel.

Fol. 7. r°· c. 1. Come les anciens figuroient fortune.

Fol. 7. v°· c. 2. Cy applicque l'acteur a son propos ce qu'il a cy devant dit de fortune.

Fol. 9. r°· c. 1. Cy parle l'acteur de ce livre de nature comment elle se vint monstrer a l'acteur dessusdit et que ce signifie. Et premierement il monstre que on ne doit pas les parolles entendre a la lettre du tout et que on peult faindre aucunes fois pour plusieurs causes.

Fol. 10. r°· c. 1. De diverses manieres de faindre.

Fol. 10. v°· c. 2. De nature et de son ordre.

Fol. 11. v°· c. 1. Encores de nature et de sa beaulté.

Fol. 12. r°· c. 1. De la principalité que Dieu a en l'ordre de nature.

Fol. 13. v°· c. 2. De l'aage de nature et de ses vestemens.

Fol. 14. v°· c. 1. De troys deesses fees lesquelles scelon le poete ont a ordonner de la vie humaine.

Fol. 15. v°· c. 1. Cy parle l'acteur de ce livre de l'attour du chief de nature et en descoevre la signification pour l'occasion de laquelle matiere il parle de la composition de ce monde premierement.

Fol. 16. v°· c. 2. Cy parle l'acteur dessusdit du ciel et des estoilles.

Fol. 18. r°· c. 2. Des IX esperes que les philozophes mettent communement ou ciel et des deux mouvements dont elles se meuvent.

Fol. 18. v°· c. 2.   Encores de ce mesmes.
Fol. 19. v°· c. 2.   Ce chapitre parle des cercles ymaginaires ou ciel en la IXe espere qui est premiere.
Fol. 20. r°· c. 2.   Encores de ce mesmes.
Fol. 21. r°· c. 2.   Des planetes et de l'excellence et grandeur du soleil.
Fol. 22. r°· c. 2.   Des cheveulx de nature.
Fol. 23. r°· c. 1.   Comment nature introduit l'amant de fuyr oysivete.
Fol. 23. v°· c. 2.   Encores de ce mesmes.
Fol. 24. v°· c. 2.   Encores de ce mesmes propos.
Fol. 26. v°· c. 2.   Cy apres s'ensuyt la declaration des troys deesses qui a luy se monstrerent et de Mercure qui les y admena pour laquelle cause il parla premier des figures des dieux, et des deesses scelon les anciens poetes.
Fol. 27. v°· c. 2.   Ce chapitre est des ymages et des figures que les anciens assignoyent aux dieux, et des deesses selon les aultres poetes.
Fol. 29. r°· c. 2.   De ce mesmes.
Fol. 30. r°· c. 1.   Exposition de Saturne.
Fol. 31. v°· c. 1.   Encor de ce mesmes.
Fol. 32. v°· c. 1.   Aultre exposition de Saturne.
Fol. 33. r°· c. 1.   Comment Jupiter est figuré.
Fol. 34. r°· c. 1.   De ce mesmes encores.
Fol. 36. r°· c. 1.   Comment Mars est figuré des anciens.
Fol. 36. v°. c. 2.   Comment Appolo, c'est a dire le souleil estoit figuré et fait.
Fol. 38. r°· c. 1.   Encores de ce mesmes.
Fol. 39. r°· c. 1.   Du monstre terrible de Appolo.
Fol. 40. r°· c. 2.   De ce mesmes.
Fol. 40. v°· c. 1.   Du lozier et du corbel.
Fol. 41. r°· c. 2.   Cy parle des IX muses.
Fol. 42. v°· c. 1.   Encore de ce mesmes.
Fol. 44. r°· c. 1.   Comment par les IX muses on en peult entendre IX sciences notables.
Fol. 45. v°. c. 2.   De geometrie.
Fol. 47. r°· c. 2.   De astronomie.
Fol. 49. r°· c. 1.   Encores de astronomie.
Fol. 50. v°. c. 1.   De la mutation de l'an.
Fol. 50. v°· c. 2.   Des nativitez.

Ch. VI. The Source of Lydgate's Poem.

Fol. 52. v°. c. 1. Des interrogations.
Fol. 53. r°. c. 2. Des elections.
Fol. 56. r°. c. 2. Encores de ce.
As far as here the headings are written out in red ink. There are three more headings in black:
Fol. 57. v°. c. 2. La VIIe partie.
Fol. 59. r°. c. 1. La VIIIe.
Fol. 59. v°. c. 1. La VIIe [!] des.

The commentator follows the thread of the plot to the game of chess in the garden of Deduit, the allegorical meaning of which he describes in detail, through the different stages of the fight. With the check-mate of the author his commentary breaks off. He confines himself to giving the further course of the poem in shortened form.

Fol. 357. v°. c. 1. Apres le mat s'ensuyt comment le dieu d'amours, qui du mat ot grant joye, se fist cognoistre a luy. Comment il luy parla de son estat et de quoy ilz servoyent luy et sa Venus mere, et de deduyt et oyseuse, et comment celluy luy fist finablement hommage. C'est a dire qu'il se donna du tout entierement cueur et corps a amours et comment celluy dieu luy bailla ses commandemens et ses reigles et luy monstra comment on se devoit maintenir en amours. Et comment oultre apres la deesse Pallas, C'est a dire sapience ou prudence ou raison, le vint en fin reprendre, et blasmer sa folye et luy monstra premierement comment Fol. 357. v°. c. 2 la vie delectable que Venus et amours et deduyt et oyseuse enseignent a ensuyvre, est une vie decevable et perilleuse et quelle n'est pas seullement a raison ennemye, ains est nuysant mesmes et contraire a nature. Elle luy monstre aussi secondement comment il se pourroit de ceste vie folle retraire s'il vouloit, et comment oultre aussi il pourroit myeulx sa jeunesce employer en vie raisonnable, et luy parla de la vie contemplative et de la vie aussi active moult longuement; laquelle en soy comprent moult de divers estatz qui tous sont bons honnourables et licites a tenir, qui en scet bien user. Et luy dist dame Pallas et monstra moult d'enseignemens beaulx, et moult de belles choses proffitables a meurs et a honneste vie et qui seroyent belles a declairer, mais pour certaine cause je m'en tairay a tant, quant a present. Amen.

The commentary ends with the following verses:

> Je layray donc ceste matere,
> Tant soit elle de grant mistere.

> Je n'y puis briefment plus entendre
> Ne ma nef plus avant estendre ;
> Car je nay pas vent avenant.
> Face qui veult le remanant.
> Il me convient ailleurs deduyre
> Et Dieu vueille ma nef conduyre.
> Amen.

These verses are not, as I was inclined to believe,[1] the work of the commentator himself, but the last verses of the commentated poem. This is proved by No. 9197 of the Paris MSS., where we read: Ces vers estoient en la fin de loriginal.

So much for the outward plan of the Codex. The reader is not offered any complete and clear picture of the way in which the commentator has conceived and carried out his task in detail. He would not receive it at all, unless he could form an opinion for himself, as to how the commentator works, by means of a concrete example. Therefore I hope we may be permitted to give here a longer, connected extract from the manuscript. We choose those portions which concern the introduction of the poem, and which, therefore, attempt to explain the fiction of Dame Fortune.

Pour la declaration donc du chapitre premier ou il fait mention de fortune il nous convient premierement considerer quelle chose ce peult estre de fortune. Fol. 5. v°· c. 1. Pourquoy nous devons scavoir que des choses que nous veons advenir entre nous. Les unes sont et se font par nature qui en est cause come les choses naturelles. Les aultres sont faictes par art et par raison humaine qui en est aussi cause come les choses artificielles. Et aucunes aultres aussi sont faictes et adviennent par fortune, si come toutes manieres de gens communement confessent et accordent. Et pour ce convient il confesser que fortune soit aucune chose reele et vraye et non pas chose du tout simplement fainte, et qu'elle soit aucunement aussi cause des choses qui ainsi adviennent fortunement. Car ce seroit bien grant frivolle a dire que de ce qui seroit tout purement neant peust advenir aucun notable effect.

Pour veoir doncques quelle chose fortune est et aussi de quelle chose elle est cause. Nous devons oultre apresent aussi scavoir que fortune proprement prise n'a lieu fors en l'espece humaine seulement, et mesmement en ceulx qui ont usaige de raison, et qui font, ce que ilz font, par deliberation et de certain propos. Car nous ne disons point que les enfans et ceulx qui sont folz de nature, ne les bestes aussi, ne

---

[1] Comp. *Échecs amoureux*, p. 105.

Ch. VI. *The Source of Lydgate's Poem.* 73

les aultres choses communes qui n'ont point d'ame, soyent ne bien ne mal fortunées pour chose que elles facent ne pour chose qui leur advieigne, combien qu'il leur advieigne moult de choses casuelles et moult d'aventures senestres.

Sans faille nous disons bien aucunesfoiz, scelon le commun usage de parler de fortune, que les enfans sont fortunez ou bien ou mal pour la fortune bonne ou malle aussi de leurs parens et de leurs amys, et mesmes fol. 5. v^o c. 2. les bestes, disons nous, estre aussi aucunesfoiz bien ou mal fortunées selon ce qu'elles vivent soubz seigneur qui bien ou mal les nourrist ou gouverne, mais ce n'est pas bien proprement de fortune parlé. Et pour ce devons nous encores aussi sçavoir que des effectz qui adviennent par nous et par noz oeuvres ou qui a ce s'ensuyvent. Les aucuns sont de nous advisés par devant et entenduz et pour eulx sommes nous esmeuz à oeuvre et de certain propos, et telz esfectz ne sont point a fortune attribuez, ne nous ne devons point aussi par eulx estre ditz bien ne mal fortunés. Les aultres ne sont point en riens de nous advisez par devant, ne par nous entenduz, ne nous ne mectons point a oeuvres pour eulx, ains nous esmerveillons quant ilz adviennent et sont proprement les effectz de fortune et pour lesquelz nous sommes ditz bien ou mal fortunez scelon leur qualité mauvaise ou bonne. Exemple :

Quant aucun va fouyr en sa vigne ou en son champ pour avoir plus de fruit et plus, il n'est pour ce dit, quant à ce, bien ou mal fortunez ne ne doit estre dit combien qu'il luy en viengne bien ou mal. Mais s'il trouvoit, en ce faisant, ung grant tresor mucié, ceste chose seroit lors a fortune attribuée et diroit on qu'il seroit, quant a ce, bien fortunez, et ainsi peult on dire de toutes aultres semblables aventures bonnes ou malles.

Fortune donc, a proprement parler, n'est aultre chose que ce qui nous esmeult a aucune oeuvre faire, a laquelle s'ensuyt aucun esfect inoppi[na]ble et ce n'est aultre chose que nostre volunté ou nostre entendement, auquel les philozophes finablement ramainent ceste fol. 6. 1° c. 1. fortune, car l'entendement nous esmeult et adrece aux oeuvres dessusdictes, ausquelles l'esfect inoppinable dessusdit aulcunesfoiz s'ensuyt.

· Et pour ce appert il que l'entendement, qui, au regard des effectz dessusdits, est appellé fortune, n'en est pas proprement ne directement cause, ains en est seullement cause par accident ; mais il est proprement et directement cause des oeuvres principaux de certain propos faictes et des esfectz que nous y entendons. Et pour ce, quant a ce, ne doit pas ainsi estre appellez fortune. Il ne doit pas aussi estre oblié que les esfectz inoppinables dessusdits, qui a fortune sont aussi attribuez, doivent estre notablement bons ou mauvais. Car se c'estoyent choses de petite valeur ou de petit malice, on n'en serait ja, pour ce, appellez ne repputé pour eureux ne pour malfortuné. Car de petite chose qui bien ou mal ne fait, on n'en doit tenir compte. Aussi come se aucun en fouant en sa vigne trouvait ung faulx denier ou ung charbon, il n'en serait pour ce bien ne mal fortunez.

In connection with this the commentator explains how the good or evil decrees of fate were ascribed to the influence of the stars, and later, in another chapter, how Dame Fortune was represented by the ancients. Then he continues as follows:

Fol. 7. v$^{o.}$ c. 2. Cy applicque l'acteur a son propos ce qu'il a cy devant dit de fortune.

L'acteur donc dessusdit en son premier chapitre veult ainsi dire que le premier commencement de son aventure et le premier mouvement qu'il nous veult recorder secretement par le jeu des eschez se fist en sa jeunesse, ou il le faint ainsi, des lors, ou assez tost apres quil se veit hors d'enfance et qu'il ot commencé a sentir que c'estoit de joye et de tristesse et de bien et de mal suffisamment; si Fol. 8. r$^{o.}$ c. 1. qu'il scavoit ja mectre prestement difference entre la licqueur doulce et la licqueur amere des tonneaulx dessusdits dont fortune nous sert, de laquelle chose la simplesce de enfance ne se donne garde.

Et oultre il dit que ce fut en printemps pour ce que cilz printemps est le plus doulx et le plus gracieux, et le plus attrempez par nature de tous, et cilz aussi ouquel amours monstre myeulx sa puissance et sa vertu, et a la verité toute creature terrestre s'en resjoyst, et aucunement lors se mue et se renovelle pour la doulceur du temps et l'actrempance, si come les elemens monstrent evidamment et auques toutes les choses de nature. Et pour ce, loe il, et recommande si en tant qu'il compare la terre au ciel et aux estoilles et ce n'est mye sans aucune raison. Car tout aussi que les estoilles cleres et lumineuses embellissent le ciel et le grant monde, tout aussi la verdure des herbes et les plantes et les belles florettes de diverses couleurs qui ou printemps habondent et qui dessus le terre sont aussi, come les estoilles l'embellissent et parent plaisamment et font tresgrant confort en ce bas monde et par especial a humaine nature.

Pour ce aussi le compare il a la jeune espousée, qui le jour que on l'espose se cointoye et se pare au plus bel quelle peult et le plus noblement.

Briefment aussi semble il que la terre lors faicte qui adonc semble estre au ciel maryée nouvellement pour la grant influence de sa vertu qui lors aussi, come soubdainement, se monstre et plus notablement que en nulz des aultres temps; et ceste comparaison fut prinse ou livre Aristote du gouvernement des princes, a la recommandation du printemps dessusdit.

Fol. 8. r°· c. 2. Pour l'occasion de ceste matiere nous devons scavoir que l'an fut party et divisé des saiges anciens en quatre temps ou en quatre parties pour la diversite et la grant difference de leurs natures.

L'ung est le printemps, come dit est, qui aultrement est appellé ver selon le latin, lequel est chault et moite actrempeement.

Le second est esté qui est chault et sec.

Le tiers est autompne, qui est froid et sec. Et le quart est yver qui est froid et moite. Nous devons oultre aussi secondement entendre que les quatre temps dessusdits se pevent commencer ou pevent estre prins en troys manieres, scelon troys diverses considerations. Premierement scelon la consideration des medicins qui voulentiers se arrestent et se tiennent au sens et a l'experience. Car la medicinal consideration ne se doit point de experience ne du sens descorder. Les medecins donc considerent en l'assignation des quatre temps leurs esfectz et regardent ce que sensiblement on voit de leur nature et scelon ce les partissent et prennent. Pour ce dit Avicennes que le printemps commence quant les arbres se commencent a fueillir et que les neges des montaignes se fondent et degastent et que nous n'avons pas aussi trop grant mestier de nous vestir ne couvrir pour le froid ne de eventation aussi trop grant pour la chaleur, et ce, dit il, pour la bonne attrempance de sa nature. Et scelon ce que auptonne au contraire est le temps que les fueilles des arbres commencent a muer leur couleur naturelle et les aultres deux te[m]ps esté et yver sont entre ces Fol. 8. v°· c. 1. deux, et est esté le temps qui habonde en chaleur et yver d'aultre part qui habonde en froidure.

Secondement les quatre temps sont prins scelon les astronomiens qui au soleil regardent et a son mouvement, pource qu'il en est cause principal scelon la verité. Et pource dient ilz que scelon ce que le soleil se meult ou sodiaque et que il passe parmy les quatre poincts principaulx de son cercle, selon ce s'en ensuyvent les quatre temps divers aussi, dont nous parlons, et scelon ce aussi les quatre temps de l'an sont aussi come egaulx, et contient chascun d'eulx le temps que le soleil mect a passer troys signes qui contiennent la quarte partie du sodiaque dessusdit.

Le printemps donques, scelon ceste maniere, se commence quant le soleil par son mouvement entre ou signe du mouston et dure tant qu'il vient en la fin des jumeaulx, et pour ce sont en son commencement les jours egaulx aux nuytz, sicome dit la ryme, laquelle chose fait moult a sa bonne attrempance.

In the same way the duration of the other seasons is settled. In connection with this we are instructed about a third manner of dividing the seasons. But it would lead us too far to give these explanations also. They are only in so far instructive, in that they show forth to us the pedagogic aim of the commentary, which, as we know, was destined for a distinguished brother and sister, and therefore justified to give some general explanations.

We see, from this fragment, how painfully accurately the commentator did his work. His first and principal task is, to reveal to us the deeper intentions of his author, and to make clear to us the real meaning of the allegorical poem. In doing this he does not disdain to go into the details of the poem. Certain expressions, allegories and parables, which the poet uses, are shown up by him and expounded.

We may be sure that, in his effort to explain everything, the commentator often overshoots the mark, and that therefore the common fate of all commentators devolves upon him.

Thus, the motive of the seasons, at the beginning of the poem, is certainly nothing more than a concession to the prevailing taste of the time. And certain features of the description of spring, over which the commentator thinks it necessary to linger, the author has simply copied from his prototypes.

The commentary is uncommonly precious by reason of the number of literary references which it contains. But here also the investigator must not allow himself to be led, without criticism, by the assertions of the commentator. Certainly the latter had at his command a much larger number of the sources of classical antiquity, brought to light by the Renaissance, than his author, who did not know all the works to which he refers.

NOTES.

1–6. COMPARE with these opening lines the following passage from the preface of the MSS. 7390 (now Lat. 10286) and 7391 (now French 1173) of the National Library at Paris (quoted from *Palamède* ii, p. 82):
"Pour les beautés de ce jeu, doivent désirer les savoir tous les gens gentils, qui veulent se récréer honnêtement et éviter l'oisiveté, et specialement les amants par amour, car il est venu premièrement de l'amour d'un chevalier et de sa dame."

12. *iupartye*] O.F. *iu parti*, later *ieu parti*, lit. *divided play or game*, chiefly employed, from the very beginning of its use, as an expression in chess. The word occurs, with the same meaning, also in other writings of Lydgate. Comp. *Troy-Book* ii, 11, F. ii f:
"Of the chesse the playe moste gloryous, . . .
For though a man studyed al his lyue
He shal ay fynde dyverse fantasyes
Of wardes makynge and newe Iupartyes."
See also Chaucer, *Book of the Duchesse*, l. 666. On the *jeux partis* (prov. *jocs partitz*) as a literary genre see Gaston Paris, La littérature française au moyen âge, § 126.

23. *hyndring of my name*] In Gower's *Conf. Am.* the expression occurs several times: ii, p. 64, 24 and p. 130, 10. Comp. Tiete's *Dissertation*, p. 30. In *Myrr. our Lady* 241 we hear of "the hendrynge of her sowle."

27. *at prime face*] See further, l. 3366, 3905, 3950. Comp. also *Troy-Book* i, 407; *Assembly of Gods* 157. Triggs, in his note on this line, has pointed out that the date of the first instance of the English usage of this phrase, as given in the *Stanford Dict.* (1406), is wrong. In this case the phrase renders the French "de première face," instead of which the original of our poem sometimes has "prime face."

32–41. Lydgate when recommending his book seldom forgets to bring in the request to correct "al that ys mys." Comp. *Temple of Glas*, p. cxli, and Schick's note on l. 1400. This, as is already apparent from Schick's note, is not only a peculiarity of Lydgate's. In those of his works for which we have the French source at hand, it is also found in the original. The passage in question reads in the French:
"Mais qui par bonne diligence
Ceste escripture aura leu
Et bien la sentence esleu
Lors vueil Je bien quil me Reprende
Sil y voit riens ou Je mesprende
Ou quil lamende a son vouloir
On ne men verra Ja douloir."

For instances in other French works see Deguileville, *Le Pelerinage de Vie Humaine*, 13517 ff. (ed. Stürzinger):
"Se ce songe n'ai bien songie,
Je pri qu'a droit soit corrigie
De ceuz qui songier miex saront
Ou qui miex faire le pourront."

See further the preface of the above-mentioned Paris MSS. which wind up with the following words: "Comme nulle chose ne peut être parfaite, je demande à mes seigneurs, à mes compagnons, à mes amis, à tous ceux à qui parviendra ce livre, de vouloir bien le rectifier et le corriger." Comp. also Schmid, *Literatur des Schachspiels*, p. 86.

47 ff. *Fortune and her two tons*] The direct model of this passage is *Le Roman de la Rose* 7097 ff. (see Marteau ii, p. 178), where Homer is referred to as the source of the fiction. The poet has in mind the 24th book of the *Iliad*, where Achilles tells his story to King Priamus in order to console him of the death of his son Hector. Comp. Marteau's note. See also Schick's note on l. 198 of the *Compleynt*, which gives a collection of allusions to the casks of Fortune or Jupiter containing sweet and bitter liquor. Especially noticeable is Gower's detailed account (see Pauli iii, p. 12, etc.). The author of the *Confessio Amantis* says in a marginal note: "qualiter in suo cellario Iupiter duo dolia habet, quorum primum liquoris dulcissimi, secundum amarissimi plenum consistit, ita quod ille, cui fatata est prosperitas, de dulci potabit, alter vero, cui adversabitur, poculum gustabit amarum." I may be allowed to add a few more instances to Schick's list: *Troy-Book* II, 10 E iv b:

    "To some sugre and hony she distylleth
    And of some she the botell fylleth
    With bytter galle myrte and ales
    And thus this lady wylfull and recheles
    As she that is frowarde and peruers
    Hath in her seler drynkes of dyuers
    For she to some of fraude and of fallas
    Mynystreth pyment bawme and ypocras
    And sodeynly whan the soote is paste
    She of custome can gyue hym a caste
    For to conclude falsly in the fyne
    Of bytter eysell and of egre wyne
    And corrosynes that fret and perce depe
    And Narcotykes that cause men to slepe."

In *Secrees of old Philisophres* 249 "the licour of Citheroes tonne" is mentioned, which gives rise to the following note of the editor: "Is this a reference to the vats of sweet and bitter, of which each of us may take one?" In the *Pilgrimage of the Life of Man* Fortune speaks of the "sour and swete" of her gifts. There is another allusion to Jupiter's two tons in *Le Roman de la Rose* 11009 ff. The passage refers to the other Jean who is to continue the romance, and reads as follows:

    "Et quant après à ce vendra
    Que Jupiter vif le tendra,
    Et qu'il devra estre abevrés,
    Dès ains néis qu'il soit sevrés,
    Des tonneaus qu'il a tous jors dobles,
    Dont l'ung est cler et l'autre trobles,
    Li uns est dous, et l'autre amer
    Plus que n'est suie, ne la mer," etc.

48. *Which ofter changeth as the mone*] Comp. *Pilgrimage* 19549 f.:
    "Than y, lykned to the mone,
    ffolk wyl chaunge my namë sone."
Chaucer, *Romaunt* 3777 f.:
    "Aftir the calm the trouble sone
    Mot folowe, and chaunge as the mone."

and again 5331 ff. :
"[This] love cometh of dame Fortune,
That litel whyle wol contune ;
For it shal chaungen wonder sone,
And take eclips right as the mone."

Compleynt of Mars 234 f. :
"Algates he that hath with love to done
Hath ofter wo than changed is the mone."

Hous of Fame 2115 f. :
"to wexe and wane sone,
As dooth the faire whyte mone."

51. *with-oute wer*] The phrase occurs again l. 326, 1263, etc. It appears very frequently in Lydgate. See Schick's note on l. 651 of the *Temple of Glas* and Triggs's note on l. 1872 of the *Assembly of Gods*.

52. *Couched tweyn in hir celler*] Similar expressions occur in *Pilgrimage* 176 f. :
"the sugryd tonne
Off Iubiter, couchyd in hys celer."

and 20433 ff :
"no taverner
That couchyd hath in hys celer
So many wynes."

67. *ydropyke*] = having an insatiable thirst, like a dropsical person. Comp. E. Mätzner, *Altengl. Sprachproben. Wörterbuch*, p. 22, and Murray, *Engl. Dict.* under *hy*. There we find another instance from Lydgate's *Falls of Princes* (vii, 8) :
"This excessif Glotoun
Moste Idropik drank ofte ageyn lust."

The word is rather rare in Middle English. The Old French equivalent is found more frequently. See *Roman de la Rose* 6263 f. :
"Car l'écherie si les pique,
Qu'il en sunt tretuit ydropique."

These lines, which likewise refer to the insatiability of those who once have tasted the sweet liquor of Fortuna, were perhaps in Lydgate's mind, when he chose the word "ydropyke." Another passage which closely resembles Lydgate s lines is found in Gower's *Conf. Am.* ii, p. 135, 25 ff. The author having pointed out the greediness of King Midas continues :

"Men tellen, that the malady,
Which cleped is ydropesy
Resembled is unto this vice
By way of kinde of avarice,
The more ydropesy drinketh,
The more him thursteth, for him thinketh,
That he may never drink his fille.
So that there may no thing fulfille
The lustes of his appetite."

With the whole of Lydgate's description of the delicious drink may be compared *Roman de la Rose* 6245–64. In E. Ballerstedt, *Über Chaucers Naturschilderungen*, p. 32, we find printed the lines from Anticlaudianus corresponding to this passage.

101–200. The season-motive is one of the conventional traits of mediaeval poetry. For the text of the French original see Vol. I, Appendix and *Échecs Amoureux* p. 230, 32, 34 and 36. How much Lydgate borrows from Chaucer is pointed out on p. 224 ff. Especially noticeable is the accordance of our passage with the introduction to the *Book of the Duchesse* iii, 291 ff. and the *Romaunt* 49 ff. See also note on l. 112–14 and 145–48.

Lydgate's dependency upon his great master is also evident from the following list: to almost every line may be found similar passages from Chaucer. For shortness' sake I initialize the works referred to in accordance with Skeat, *Students' Chaucer:*

90–91 : III, 336–37.	147–48 : III, 410–12 ; R. 58, 61–62.
92–93 : A. 11; R. 82–84.	155–56 : R. 63–68.
95–98 : R. 68 ; T. I, 159.	158–59 : R. 63–65.
104 f.: R. 1433 ; T. I, 158.	161–64 : R. 71–77 ; III, 313–14
105–106 : R. 1433–34 (rhyme) ; R. 128.	(rhyme).
	165 : IV, 17.
107–8 : R. 57, A. 1509, R. 127–28 (rhyme).	170–172 : R. 57 ff. ; III, 410–12.
	173–75 : R. 82–86 ; 90–91.
109 : R. 1436–37.	177 : R. 107.
110 : R. 60 ; A. 1 ; III, 414.	186–87 : T. I, 154–56.
112–14: III, 406 ; R. 59, 63.	188–89 : R. 82–83.
130–32 : R. 130–31 ; V, 204–5 ; III, 340–42.	196–97 : R. 101-2.
	Comp. also with ll. 449–54 : A. 1493 ff.
133 : III, 336–37 ; R. 74.	
135–37 : III, 402 ; A. 5–7.	

Other spring-descriptions in Lydgate show perhaps still more what an extensive use the good monk makes of Chaucerian formulas. Thus the description in his *Troy-Book* I, 8, E I, is nothing but a poor paraphrase of the introductory lines to the *Canterbury Tales*, A 1 ff.

112–114. These lines run in the original as follows :

. . " la terre est si orgueilleuse
Et si se cointoye *et* se pare
Quil samble quelle se compare
Au ciel destre mieulx estellee."

With regard to this imagery comp. Ballerstedt l. c. p. 19 f. Ballerstedt's statement that the *Roman de la Rose* did not contain a metaphor of that kind is incorrect, for the lines quoted are borrowed directly from that work. Comp. l. 8741–47. I have already stated this fact in my *Échecs Amoureux* p. 139. Similar passages are to be found in Chaucer. See the *Book of the Duchesse* 405 f. :

" For hit was, on to beholde,
As thogh the erthe envye wolde
To be gayer than the heven,
To have mo floures, swiche seven
As in the welken sterres be."

125. *veynes*] Comp. Gower, *Conf. Am.* iii, 92 f. :
" For right as veines ben of blood
In man, right so the water flood
Therth of his cours maketh ful of veines. . . ."

141. *fret*] I do not feel sure whether *fret* is here a p.p. =set, adorned. Perhaps it might be explained as 3 pres. plur. either of *fret*, O.E. fretan = 'to waste away' or 'to move in agitation' (comp. *New Engl. Dict.*, fret v.[1]), or of *fret*, O.F. freter = to form a pattern upon. (*New Engl. Dict.*, fret v.[2].) In l. 1400, 3576 and 5490 the word is certainly a

p.p., meaning as much as 'furnished,' 'supplied.' For similar instances see *Pilgrimage* 587 f.:
> "cordys rovnd & long¹,
> All yffret with knottys strong¹,"

and l. 14800, *Troy-Book* II, 11, F i b: "A crowne of golde with ryche stones frette." Chaucer, *Romaunt* 4705: "A trouthe, fret full of falshede." *Legend of Good Women* 1117 "juwel, fretted ful of riche stones."

145–148. Comp. *Book of the Duchesse* 410 ff.:
> "Hit had forgete the povertee
> That winter, through his colde morwes,
> Had mad hit suffre[n], and his sorwes."

Romaunt 59 ff.:
> "And th'erthe wexeth proud withalle,
> For swote dewes that on it falle,
> And [al] the pore estat forget
> In which that winter hadde it set."

Legend, Prologue A, 112 ff.:
> "Forgeten had the erthe his pore estat
> Of winter, that him naked made and mat,
> And with his swerd of cold so sore had greved."

In a similar way, birds and trees and flowers are said to rejoice, and to forget
> "the harmys and gret damage
> That wynter wroughte with his rage."

203 ff. Dame Nature appears more frequently than any other personification in mediaeval poems, with the exception perhaps of Dame Resoun. Alanus ab Insulis gave her form and figure in *De Planctu Naturae*. See Migne, *Patr. Lat.* 210, p. 431 ff. The fiction was employed *in extenso* by the poet of the second part of the *Roman de la Rose* 16553 ff. We find it again in Lydgate's *Pilgrimage* 3344, and, of course, in the French original of this poem. A very original use of this fiction was made by Chaucer in his *Parlement of Foules* 368 ff., 379 ff. Comp. further III, 871. In Langland's dream Nature appears and shows the wonders of the world: p. xi, l. 311–25. Our poet's description is borrowed from Alanus but considerably influenced by the *Roman de la Rose*. Lydgate again introduces Dame Nature in *Pur Le Roy*. See J. O. Halliwell, *A Selection from the Minor Poems of Dan John Lydgate*, p. 2 ff. There are many allusions to this "lady and godesse" in the other writings of Lydgate. Comp. *Troy-Book*, I, 5, C I a: "kynde whiche is so hye a quene;" further C I b, where the unchangeable laws of Nature are pointed out:
> "the godesse that called is nature
> Whiche next hir lorde [hath] all thynge in cure
> Hath vertue gyue to herbe gras and stone
> Whiche no man knoweth but her selfe alone
> The causis hyd be closed in her hande
> That wytte of man can not vnderstande
> Openly the myght of her workynge."

In the *Assembly of Gods* 452 ff. Attropos asks Nature to testify that she got the office of death-bringing. 1268 ff.: Nature protests that her servant Sensuality should be set at liberty. 1325 ff.: The patent which the gods have granted to Attropos is only legal in the jurisdiction of Nature. In 1380 ff. the "carnall myght" of Nature is alluded to. As to the *Ballad on the Forked Head Dresses*, see the above quoted *Minor Poems*, p. 47: "clad al in flours and blosmes of a tre—He sauhe nature." See also

Ballad gyuen vnto þe kyng Henry st. 10 (see Add. MS. 29279 fol. 145 *b*) :
"the lady which is called nature satt in her see lych as a presydente."
Of later descriptions of Dame Nature the most beautiful is that of Dunbar in the *Thrissil and the Rois*.

209–10 and 221–23. Comp. *Troy-Book* IV, 30 S vi :
"hym thought he myght nat endure
To beholde the bryghtnesse of hir face
For he felte thorugh his herte pace
The persyng stremys of hir eyen two."

213–216. Verses of this kind are rather frequent with Lydgate. Comp. 1. 1004 f. :
"For they yaf as gret a lyght
As sterris in the frosty nyght."

Pilgrimage 691 f. :
"a rechë sterre,
Wych that cast hys bemys ferre
Round abovten al the place."

and 700 ff. :
"a crowne of gold
Wrouht of sterrys shene & bryht,
That cast aboute a ful cler lyht."

A close remblance to the lines of our poem is also seen in the following passage from Chaucer's *Anelida and Arcite* 40 f. :
"al the ground aboute hir char she spradde
With brightnesse of the beautee in hir face."

243 *Moste digne to vere corovne*] Comp. *Pilgrimage* 14151 :
"Worthy for to were a Crowne."

276. *mevyng of the speres nyne*] Since it was deemed impossible in ancient times, that the planets could move freely in space, the theory arose of a system of planets of which each was fixed to a sphere. These spheres were concentric and fitted into one another like a series of round boxes. Each planet was fastened to its own sphere, and it followed that there should be the same number of spheres as there were heavenly bodies having different motions and periods of revolution. Plato considered the earth as resting and motionless on its axis in the centre of the universe. Then followed, in seven circles, the seven planets (the sun and moon being included). The utmost sphere, enclosing all the others held the fixed stars. Comp. *Somnium Scipionis* iv, 9, where the different planets are enumerated in the following order : Saturnus, Jupiter, Mars, Sol, Venus, Mercurius, Luna. Meissner, *Somn. Scip.* p. 21, note l. 9.

277–282. The music of the spheres is a hypothesis of the Pythagoreans who supposed that the then known seven planets, as they rotated in space, called forth a melody too delicate to be heard by the ear of man. The Pythagoreans, led by the idea that the entire universe was composed of harmony, considered the seven planets as the seven strings of the heptachord, and supposed that their rotation about the centre produced a series of musical notes. These notes, taken together, formed an octave, or, which was the same thing to the Pythagoreans, a harmony. The pitch of each note corresponded to the rapidity of rotation of its planet, and the distance between the planets was determined by the interval of the octave. The heptachord of that time was the seven-stringed Terpandros (named after the poet, about 644 B.C.). How far the author of Lydgate's source was acquainted with these facts appears from his work later on where he treats on music in the following chapters—fol. 130 *b* :—Cy commence pallas pour loccasion des Jeux et des Recreacions a parler de musique qui vault a cest propos.—fol. 131: Encore de ce et monst*re* comment Musique vault a III choses.—fol. 131 *b*: Encore de ce et parle de la seconde chose a quoy musique vault pour le occasion de laquelle Il commence a *pa*rler comme*nt* pithagoras trouua premierement musique.—fol. 132 *b*: Encore de ce et monstre comme*nt* Les proporcionz de musique sont trouuez es chosez de nature.—fol. 133: Comment armonie est entendue ou ciel.—fol. 133 *b*: Comment ceste celestre musique est ce samble segnefie par les muses que li poete anchijen metoient ou ciel. Encore de ce & pa*r*le du songe du Roy cipion.—fol. 134: Comment musique selon lez Anchijens est aussy es IIII elemens & es chosez de nature trouuee. Encore de ce et des IIII temps.—fol. 134 *b*: Encore de ce et parle des mutacions du monde.—fol. 135: Comment les proporcions de musique se monstrent et sont de grant efficace en pluiseurs chosez.

In *Somnium Scipionis*, to which the author of the *Échecs amoureux* refers, the harmony of the spheres is spoken of at great length in V, § 10–11. Comp. the reference to this passage in Chaucer's *Parlement of Foules* 59–63:

"And after shewed he him the nyne speres,
And after that the melodye herde he
That cometh of thilke speres thryes three,
That welle is of musyke and melodye
In this world heer, and cause of armonye."

In the *Roman de la Rose* the harmony of the spheres is touched upon in the following lines—17631 ff.:

". . cors du ciel reflamboians
Parmi l'air obscurci raians,
Qui tornoient en lor esperes,
Si cum l'establi Diex li peres.
Là font entr 'eus lor armonies,
Qui sunt causes des melodies
Et des diversités de tons,
Que par acordance metons
En toutes manieres de chant :
N'est riens qui par celes ne chant,
Et muent par lor influences
Les accidens et les sustances
Des choses qui sunt souz la lune ;

Par lor diversité commune
Séspoissent li cler élement,
Cler font les espés ensement ;
Et froit, et chaut, et sec, et moiste,
Tout ainsinc cum en une boiste,
Font-il à chascuns cors venir,
Par lor pez ensemble tenir ;
Tout soient-il contrariant,
Les vont-il ensemble liant ;
Si font pez de quatre anemis,
Quant si les ont ensemble mis
Par atrempance covenable
A compelexion raisonnable."

Marteau appends a long note to this passage in which Plato's ideas on the subject are set forth. Allusions to the music of the spheres in modern English poetry are innumerable. I give only the instances which I collected from Shakespeare, *Twelfth Night* III. 1. 105 ff.:

"But would you undertake another suit,
I had rather hear you to solicit that
Than music from the spheres."

Antony and Cleop. V. 2. 83 f.:

"his voice was propertied
As all the tuned spheres."

Pericles V. 1. 227:

"The music of the spheres! List."

and 231 ff.:

"Most heavenly music
It nips me unto listening, and thick slumber
Hangs upon mine eyes."

Merchant of Venice V. 1. 60 ff.:
"There's not the smallest orb which thou behold'st
But in his motion like an angel sings,
Still quiring to the young-eyed cherubins."

Henry VIII. IV. 2. 19:
"I sit meditating
On that celestial harmony I go to."

282. *crop and roote*] In the hyperbolical language of Lydgate we meet metaphors of this kind very frequently. Comp. the following lines from our poem: 324, 2169, 2599–2600, 5990.

For instances in other Lydgate works see *Pilgrimage*, 5015 f.:
"To ha pes wiþ hys neihëbour,
As roote off al perfeccioun."

7992 f.: "lownesse and humylyte,
Ground and rote of eche good werk."

8011 ff.: "ffor perseueraunce (I dar seye)
Ys the verray parfyt keye
And lok also (I dar assure)
Off perfeccioun off armure."

8044: "he that was off wysdom flour."

Troy-Book, Prologue A, I c:
"of knyghthod welle & sprynge."

I, 5 B v b: "this noble worthy kynge
As he that was of fredam a myroure."

C, I a: "he of poetes was the sprynge & welle."

C, VI a: "of bounte sprynge and welle." (11,10.)

E, V c: "Roote and stocke of chyualrye
And of knyghthod very soueraygne floure
The sours and welle of worshyp & honoure
And of manhod I dar it wel expresse
Example and myroure and of hye prowesse
Gynnynge and grounde" (*i. e.* Hector).

Temple of Glas 307:
"she was rote of womanly plesaunce."

410: "Dorigene, flour of al Britagne."

1207: "þe floure of womanhede."

455: "of trouth crop & rote." (Comp. Schick's note.)

751 f.: "roote of al plesaunce
And examplaire to al þat wil be stable."

754: "Mirrour of wit, ground of gouernaunce."

758: "A welle of fredome."

970–73: "Princes of iouþe & flour of gentilesse,
Ensaumple of vertue, ground of curtesie,
Of beaute rote, quene & eke maistres
To al women."

981: "o wel of goodlihed."

1208–10: "þis wor[l]dis sonne & liȝt,
The sterre of beaute, flour eke of fairnes—
Boþe crop and rote—and eke þe rubie briȝt."

Assembly of Gods 620: "vnhappy capteyns of myschyef croppe and roote." Comp. Triggs's note.

Tretis of the kynges coronacion (Add. MS. 29729, fol. 84 a), st. 12, 6 : "myrrour of manhed ;" st. 13, 1–2 : "of resoun croppe and root."
Ordonaunce of a prosesyon (Add. MS. 29729, fol. 166 a), st. 2, 4–8 : "frut celestyall honge on þe trees of lyffe — þe frute of frutes for shorte conclusyon—our helthe our foode and our restoratyffe—and cheffe repast of our redempcyon." st. 10, 1 : "myrrour of sapience." st. 15, 1 : "blessed baptist of clennesse locke and keye."

Falls of Princes, Prologue A, II, where Lydgate says of Chaucer : " of our language he was þe lodesterre," and Tullius is called "chefe wel of eloquence"; I, 10 D v Adrastus is praised as "floure of chiualrye," and in the next chapter, D vi, Atreus is styled "roote of vnkindnes," "of treason sours and well," "ground of falsenes." From the great number of praising metaphors showered down upon Hector I give the following : I, 16 F vi, " of prowesse the lanterne & the light"; the same image is applied to Athens which is called, I, 12 E ii : " Sonne of al sciences of Grece the lanterne and the light."

In Chaucer, too, such metaphors are frequently met with. Here are the instances I gathered from *Troilus*.

Comp. II, 178 : " of worthinesse welle."

II, 348 : "of beautee crop and rote."

II, 841 ff. : "the welle of worthinesse,
Of trouthe ground, mirour of goodliheed,
Of wit Appollo, stoon of sikernesse,
Of vertu rote, of lust findere and heed."

III, 1472 f. : "of my wele or woo
The welle and rote."

V, 25 f. : "she that was the soothfast crop and more,
Of al his lust, or joyes."

V, 1245 : "now knowe I crop and rote."
V, 1330 : "of wele and wo my welle."

V, 1590 f. : "ensample of goodlihede,
O swerd of knighthod, sours of gentilesse."

How different does it sound, when Shakespeare adopts expressions of this kind. Comp. *Troilus* III. 1. 30 f., where a servant calls Helen "the mortal Venus, the heart-blood of beauty, love's invisible soul."

Sober Gower comparatively seldom indulges in this kind of figures. From his *Confessio Amantis* I collected the following examples : I, p. 46 :
"she (viz. Venus) whiche is the source and welle
Of wele or wo."

II, p. 186 : "he, (viz. God) which is the welle of helth,
The highe creatour of life."

p. 214 : "She is pure hede and welle
And mirrour and ensample of good."

III, p. 291 : "the lusty floure of youth."

p. 338 : "Here cometh the welle
Of alle womanishe grace."

307. *The forge of Dame Nature* again mentioned 4521. For similar allusions comp. *Roman de la Rose* 16553–66, 16671–78, 20137–40. These passages are suggested by Alanus ab Insulis, who in his *De Planctu Naturae* represented Dame Nature as working at a forge.

314. Plato, and especially Aristotle, are frequently referred to as authorities in mediaeval writings. See again 340. The "philisophre" in

l. 6279 is likewise Aristotle. Comp. also *Pilgrimage* 621 f. 5536 ff.: Nature sends her clerk "Arystotyles the wyse, In dyffence off hyr fraunchyse," to Wisdom. Plato together with Aristotle is named in *Hous of Fame* 757 ff.:

" Lo, this sentence is knowen couthe
Of every philosophres mouthe,
As Aristotle and dan Platon."

Comp. also l. 931, *Prologue* 295 and 741. *Chan. Yem. Tale* 895; *Maunc. Tale* 103 f.; *Squieres Tale* 225; and the numerous references in *Boetius*.

315. *Touching the beaute*] The word *touching* occurs very frequently in Lydgate's translations; it is, of course, the equivalent of the French *quant à*; as an easy way of getting started it is often to be found at the beginning of a chapter. See l. 347, 407, 1464, 1539, 2091, 4094, 4102, 4233 of our poem. Comp. further *Secrees* 974, 979, 1022, 1234. *Pilgrimage* 17442, 17763, 19751, 20027. There are instances, but only comparatively few, where *touching* has the signification of " coming (or being) in contact with." Comp. *Falls of Princes* I, 14 T ii: as they [viz. Hercules and Antheus] wrestled Hercules found

"touching the earth, this Giant it is true,
his force, his might did alway renewe."

315-328. Comp. the lines from the *Book of the Duchesse*, in which the lover describes the beauty of his lady: 895-917.

317 f. Lydgate again and again asserts that he has no "kunning to descryue," whatever he is about to write upon. See further 355, 410, 981, 1001, 1394 ff., 2552, 2811, 3382. Comp. also *Temple of Glas* 951, 1289 ff.; *Pilgrimage* 401 f.; *Troy-Book*, Prol. A i c; I, 5, B vi b; II, 11 F i. In other writers of that time we find similar lines. Comp. Hoccleve, *Regiment of Princes* 3788-90:

" O wommanhode! in the regneþ vertu
So excellent, þat to feble is my witt
To expresse it."

Chaucer, *Book of the Duchesse* 895-903.

336. *fer y-ronne in age*] Comp. l. 343 "to be fal[le] fer in age"; *Pilgrimage* 904: "folk that ben on age ronne"; *Secrees* 53: " whanne he was falle in Age"; 1090-92: "And greet Recours of ffemynynyte ... makith hem falle in Age"; *Falls of Princes* I, 1 A iv b, where we hear of the things in Paradise that they " Euer endure and neuer fall in age"; II, 2 B ii b: "Nembroth gan feble and fal into gret age"; *Troy-Book* IV, 30 S iv b: "hym that was so ferre ronne in age."

361 f. Comp. Chaucer, *Legend of Good Women* 2228 f.:

"Thou yiver of the formes, that hast wroght
The faire world, and bare hit in thy thoght
Eternally, or thou thy werk began," etc.

369-379. In the *Roman de la Rose*, too, the destructive powers in Nature are touched upon several times. Comp. l. 16631 ff.:

" Ainsinc Mort qui j'à n'iert saoule,
Glotement les pieces engoule :
Tant les sieut par mer et par terre,
Qu'en la fin toutes les enserre."

16672 ff: " el (viz. Nature) voit que Mort l'envieuse
Entre li et corrupcion
Vuelent metre a destruccion
Quanqu'el trueve dedens sa forge."

Comp. further 20475-84 and 20508-39. The three sisters are often named in contemporaneous writers. Especially Antropos is often alluded to. In *Story of Thebes* Atropos is one of the Fates, in *Assembly of Gods* Atropos, a male figure, is identified with Death. Comp. also *Temple of Glas* 782 f. :

> "Riȝt so shal I, til Antropos me sleiþe,
> For wele or wo, hir faithful man be found."

Gower, *Conf. Am.* II p. 94 :

> "For whan my moder was with childe
> And I lay in her wombe clos,
> I wolde rather Atropos,
> Which is goddesse of alle deth,
> Anone as I had any breth,
> Me hadde fro my moder cast.
> But now I am nothing agast,
> I thanke god, for Lachesis
> Ne Cloto, which her felaw is,
> Me shopen no such destine."

Falls of Princes I, 1 A vi. :

> "Antropos, which afore shall gone
> For tuntwie his lyues threde anone."

I, 9 D v b :   "he endured mischiefe sorow and drede
tyl Atropos vntwined his liues threde."

I, 11 E ii :   "our fatall end, in sorrow and mischiefe fyned
when Atropos our liues threde hath twined."

Read also what is said in I, 14 about Antropos and her sisters.

377–79. The French reads :

> "Cerberus qui tout engoule
> Qan quil happe a sa tripple goule
> Riens ne len pouroit saouler
> Ains vouldroit tres bien engouler
> A vn cop par sa desmesure
> Toute la cotte de nature."

The French poet evidently bore in mind what is said about Cerberus in *Roman de la Rose* 20517 ff. and 21027 : "The porter infernal" in our text is Lydgate's addition. Comp. *Assembly of Gods* 37, where Cerberus likewise appears as "the porter of hell," and *Story of Thebes*, fol. 375, where he is called "chief porter of hell." In our poem there are two more allusions to the cruel and monstrous beast : 1382 ff. and 1746 ff. With this last allusion is to be compared *Testament*, p. 236 :

> ". . . Ihesu
> Took out of helle soulys many a peyre
> Mawgre Cerberus and al his cruelte."

In the *Troy-Book*, too, Cerberus is mentioned. Comp. Prologue, A i, "Cerberus so cruell founde at all." See also Triggs's note on l. 37 of the *Assembly of Gods*.

393 ff. Comp. Boetius, *Philos. Cons.* V, metr. 5 :

> "Prona tamen facies hebetes ualet ingrauare sensus.
> Vnica gens hominum celsum leuat altius cacumen,
> Atque leuis recto stat corpore despicitque terras.
> Haec, nisi terrenus male desipis, ammonet figura,
> Qui recto caelum uultu petes exeresque frontem,
> In sublime feras animum quoque, ne grauata pessum
> Inferior sidat mens corpore celsius leuato."

The marginal note is taken from Ovid, *Metam.* I, 84 ff. :
"Pronaque cum spectent animalia cetera terram
Os homini sublime dedit: celumque tueri
Iussit, et erectos ad sidera tollere vultus."

417 f. Things very great are said "to reche up to the sterres," or "above the sterres." Comp. *Falls of Princes* I, 1 A vi, "their renoun recheth aboue þe sterres clere"; II, 2 B ii b, "whose (viz. Nembroth) pomp raught above þe sterres clere."

422–24. Comp. Chaucer, *Book of the Duchesse* 434 ff. :
"Shortly, hit was so ful of bestes,
That thogh Argus, the noble countour,
Sete to rekene in his countour,
And rekene[d] with his figures ten...
Yet shulde he fayle to rekene even
The wondres."

Further, *Roman de la Rose* 13378–84.
The story of Io guarded by Argus is told in l. 1780 ff. of our poem. See also *Roman* 14983–96.

442. Comp. *Falls of Princes* I, 7 B iv b : "þe fine of his entent"; *Fabula Duor. Mercat.* 361: "the somme of your desyre."

449–54. Comp. *Troy-Book* I, 6, D ii b :
"Whan that Tytan had *with* his feruent hete
Drawe up þe dewe from the levis wete."

Chaucer, *Knightes Tale* 635 ff. :
"And fyry Phebus ryseth up so brighte,
That al the orient laugheth of the lighte,
And with his stremes dryeth in the greves
The silver dropes, hanging on the leves."

The Legend of Good Women 773 ff. :
"Whan Phebus gan to clere
Aurora with the stremes of hir hete
Had dryed up the dew of herbes wete."

l. 455–56. Comp. Gower, *Conf. Am.* III, p. 94 :
"The moist droppes of the rein,
Descenden into middel erthe
And tempreth it to sede and erthe,
And doth to springe gras and floure."

See however Add. MS. 29729, fol. 140 b, where we find the following lines of Lydgate :
"the freshe floures glad
on ther stalkes he dothe fade."

In most cases the *to* after *do* is wanting. See l. 1474 and 1504 of our poem, l. 587 of the *Temple of Glas*, etc.

ll. 463–65. Gower, *Conf. Am.* II, p. 38 :
"Among these other of slouthes kinde,
Whiche alle labour set behinde,
And hateth alle besinesse,
There is yet one, whiche idelnesse
Is cleped, and is the norice
In mannes kinde of every vice."

p. 80 :   "For he that wit and reson can,
It sit him wel, that he travaile
Upon such thing, which might availe,

>   For idelship is nought comended,
>   But every law it hath defended."

p. 115: "slouthe, whiche as moder is,
The forth drawer and the norice
To man of many a dredful vice."

Comp. further *Falls of Princes* I, 13 E iv *b*, where idlenesse is called "mother of vices." I might also refer to the poem *Le Dit de Perece* in A. Jubinal, *Nouveau Recueil de Contes* II, p. 58 ff.

513–28. According to the doctrines of stoicism, it is the duty of man to comprehend the marvellous structure of the world in order to adapt his will and actions to the laws of reason in operation throughout the universe.

Comp. *Somnium Scipionis*, iii, 7 : "Homines enim sunt hac lege generati, qui tuerentur illum globum, quem in hoc templo medium vides, quere terra dicitur." See C. Meissner, *Somn. Scip.* p. 19, where is quoted the following passage from Cat. m. 77 : " credo deos immortales sparsisse animos in corpora humana, ut essent, qui terras tuerentur, quique caelestium ordinem contemplantes imitarentur eum vitae modo atque constantia."

531 etc. Gower, *Conf. Am.* iii, p. 101 : "All erthely thing, which god began,—Was only made to serve man." The whole passage from which these lines are taken (iii, p. 100, 28—p. 102, 4) may be compared with the next chapters of *R. and S.* to which it bears a striking likeness. I am inclined to believe that Gower's dissertation, too, is to be traced back to Alanus.

552. The idea of a man being a microcosm is Platonic. It is very frequently to be met with in the literature of the Middle Ages. Comp. Baumgartner, *Die Philosophie des Alanus ab Insulis*, p. 88, note 2; further Müllenhoff-Scherer, *Denkmäler* II. Bd. (3. Ausg.), p. 171. With regard to the fructification of the idea in Lydgate's writings, I adduce Triggs's note on l. 932 of the *Assembly of Gods*. A certain likeness to the passage in question is seen in the following lines from *Secrees* 2313–17 :

>   "in beeste nor thyng vegitable,
>   No thyng may be vnyuersally
>   But yif it be founde naturally
>   In mannys nature. Wherfore of Ooon Accoord
>   Oold philisoffres Called hym the litel woord."

[*woord* ought, of course, to be the *worlde* of all other MSS.] Note further the following passages from the *Pilgrimage* 12370 ff. :

>   "'Mycrocosme' men the calle;
>   And microcosme ys a word
>   Wych clerkys calle 'the lassë world.'"

15637 ff. : "phylosoffres Alle
'The lasse world' a ma*n* they calle."

·21165 ff. Sorcerye puts this question to the pilgrim :

>   "Herdystow neuere (off aventure)
>   That a man, in scrypture,
>   Off thys phylosofres alle,
>   How Mycrocosme they hym calle
>   (Shortly to tellen, at o word)
>   Nat ellys but 'the lassë world.'"

The answer of the pilgrim is :

>   "I haue herd yt in scolys offte,
>   Ther yrad, bothe loude and softe."

The direct source of the ideas here set forth is, of course, *Alanus ab Insulis*, who repeatedly points out the frequent agreement between the regulation of the world and of man. See *De Planctu Naturae* (Migne 210, p. 443, etc.); *Dist. Dict. Theol.* (p. 866); *Anticlaud.* (p. 517). Comp. also the *Roman de la Rose* 19715 ff. Gower, too, touches upon the idea; see *Conf. Am.* i, p. 35:

"Gregoire in his morall
Saith, that a man in speciall
The lasse worlde is properly,
And that he proveth redily."

Regarding the expression "the lesse world," see Triggs's note on l. 1829 of the *Assembly of Gods*.

565-66. *God* or *the gods* very frequently have the attribute *celestial*, comp. l. 1894 and 3768, "goddys celestial." In general, *celestial* seems to signify a thing which is in heaven or has some claim to heaven. Comp. *Pilgr.* 21237 f. "a man .. callyd celestyal"; *Ballad made for Queen Katherine*, Envoy (Add. MS. 29729 fol. 129 b.):

"ye cite
Which is a-bove celestiall."

610. not in the original. A line which in a similar form frequently occurs in Lydgate. Comp. the following examples from the *Pilgrimage*:

9936 :   "that your tymë be nat lorn."

12223 ff. :   "Be wel exspleyted (in certeyn),
And ellys thy labour ys in veyn,
Lesynge thy travaylt euerydel."

12443 f. :   "My labour may me nat avaylle;
I do but lesë my travaylle."

12460 :   "My tyme I lese, *and* my sesoun."

Comp. also the French quotation in Chaucer's *Fortune*:
"Iay tout perdu mon temps et mon labour."

637 ff. The two opposite rotations of the firmament seem to have given rise to mystical speculation even in ancient times. Comp. *Somn. Scip.* IV, 9, and further *Macrob. in Somn. Scip. Libri* i, xvi, etc. Note especially what Macrobius says on the "extimus globus," conceived as the soul of the universe which includes all virtues, and on its relation to the human soul which comes from that utmost sphere and, after having wandered though the exile of this world, finally returns to its origin. To a certain extent these remarks already contain the elements of Alanus's description, which is the primary source of our text. If the last sphere encircling all the others was identified with the essence of all virtues, viz. reason, the other spheres could only signify the sensual inclinations of man striving against the godlike quality of reason. Thus Alanus, being always anxious to prove that everything in nature is symbolic of the organization of man, uses the opposite rotations of the celestial bodies as a kind of simile for the illustration of the antagonistic inclinations of the human soul.

Lydgate as well as the French author plainly identify the two opposite courses of the rotating stars as the conflicting inclinations in man. The rotations of the celestial bodies are also described in the *Roman de la Rose* 17486 ff., but without any reference to man. In the *Pilgrimage* 12208 ff. we find a discourse which, in many parts, resembles the account of our poem, and may have been known to the author of the French original. The opposite rotations of the firmament are illustrated by means of two concentric wheels. Comp. with the whole note my remarks in *Échecs Amoureux*, p. 134–136. With the marginal note may be compared Isidor, *Etym.* vii, 2, 27 : "Oriens, quia luminis fons, et illustrator est rerum, et quod oriri nos faciat at vitam aeternam." See also Alanus, *Distinct.* (Migne, l. c. p. 866) : "sicut in mundo majori firmamentum movetur ab oriente in occidentem et revertitur in orientem, sic ratio in homine movetur a contemplatione orientalium, id est coelestium, primo considerando Deum et divina, consequenter descendit ad occidentalia, id est ad considerationem terrenorum, ut per visibilia contempletur invisibilia, deinde revertetur ad orientem iterum considerando coelestia. Et sicut planetae moventur contra firmamentum et retardant eius motum, sic quinque sensus moventur contra rationem et impediunt eius motum, ratio tamen eos fert secum et servire cogit." With regard to *oriens* and *occidens* comp. Pitra, *Spicilegium Solesmense* ii, 81, and iii, 480.

680–682. Comp. l. 1237 "worldly thing most transitorie"; *Tretis of the Kynges coronacion* (Add. MS. 29729), st. 3, 7 : "to fore all thynges that been transitorye—love god ! "
Pilgr. 9667 f. :   "thynges off veynglorye
       That be passynge & transytórye."

683–816. With the whole dissertation may be compared what Boetius says about the different qualities of man in *Philos. Cons.* V, pros. and metr. 5.

729–764. Similar ideas we find expressed in *Falls of Princes* I, 1 A vi *b* and B i. :
"And of his grace here in this mortall life,
as we precell in wisdome and reason,
and of his gift han a prerogatife,
toforne al beastes by discrecion,
therfore let vs of whole intencion :
as we of reason beastes farre excede,
let vs aforn them be by word, example and dede."

Men are often called "reasonable beasts," in M.E. poetry. See Hoccleve, *The Regiment of Princes* 3895.

731–740. Comp. *Romaunt of the Rose*, 7168 ff. :
"Now have I you declared right
The mening of the bark and rinde.
That maketh the entencions blinde.
But now at erst I wol biginne
To expowne you the pith withinne."

The imagery may have been suggested by Alanus ab Insulis, *De Planctu Naturae* (Migne 210, p. 451 c) : "At, in superficiali litterae cortice falsum resonat lyra poetica, sed interius, auditoribus secretum intelligentiae altioris eloquitur, ut exteriore falsitatis abjecto putamine, dulciorem nucleum veritatis secrete intus lector inveniat."

760–64. Comp. with this passage *Pilgr.* 2033 ff. where Dame Resoun says :
"And pleinly, ek, I kan yow telle,
All the whyl that I dwelle
With you, A-mongys hyh *and* lowe,
ffor verray men ye shal be knowe,
Thorgh wysdom & thorgh prouydence,
And haue A verray dyfference
ffrom other bestys to dyscerne
How ye shal your sylff gouerne.
Al the whyle that ye me holde

With your tabyde, as I tolde,
'Ye shal be men, & ellys naught
And yiff the trouthë be wel souht,
Whan that I am fro yow gon,
Ye may avaunte (& that a-noon,)
That ye be (thys, no fable)
Bestys and vnresownable,
Dyspurveyed of al Resoun.'"

Secrees, 655-56, Aristotle advises Alexander:
"To leve al manerys that be bestial,
Vertues to folwe that been Inperyal."

    Caxton, *Game and Playe of the Chesse*, p. 104: "And man that is callyd a beste resonable and doth not his werke after reson and truthe Is more bestyall than any beste brute"; further, p. 171: "woman whyche ought to be a best Raysonable." See also Cicero, *De Off.* 1, 4; Boetius, *Phil. Cons.* IV, pros. 3 and V, metr. 5.

    781. Comp. further 830:
"Set thy desire and thyn entent
To thinges that be celestiall."

4587:
" I ha set myn entent
To ben at his comandement."

Pilgr. 17876: "Myn hertë on malys ys so set."
20953 f: " And that hys hertë was so set
To worshepë A Marmoset."

Temple of Glas 430–32:
"Because I cnowe your entencion
Is truli set, in parti and in al,
To loue him."

1061: "as ȝoure entent is sette
Oonli in vertu."

Gower, *Conf. Amant.* iii, 161:
"But all his hertes besinesse
He sette to be vertuous."

    Examples from Chaucer are *Prologue* 132: "In curteisye was set ful muche hir lest"; *Prioresses Tale* 98: "On Cristes moder set was his entente"; *Clerkes Tale* 117: "Ther as myn herte is set, ther wol I wyve."

    817 ff. The admonition which Dame Nature winds up with is to be compared with Gower, *Conf. Am.* iii, p. 342, 14–343, 6, and p. 344, 11–347, 6. Lines which in an especially striking manner recall the sentences of our text are the following:

p. 342-43: "But certes it is for to rewe
To se love ayein kinde falle, . . .
Forthy my sone, I wolde rede
To let all other love awey,
But if it be through such a wey
As love and reson wolde accorde."

p. 346: "Set thin hert under that lawe,
The which of reson is governed
And nought of will."

p. 347: "For I can do to the no more,
But teche the the righte way.
Now chese, if thou wilt live or deie."

1. 817 ff. The passages hinted at in the marginal note are taken from *Somnium Scipionis* (ed. Meissner) III, 8 : " Sed sic, Scipio, ut avus hic tuus, ut ego, qui te genui, institiam cole et pietatem, quae cum magna in parentibus et propinquis, tum in patria maxima est. Ea vita via est in caelum et in hunc coetum eorum, qui iam vixerunt et corpore laxati illum incolunt locum, quem vides." VI, 12 : " Tum Africanus : Sentio, inquit, te sedem etiam nunc hominum ac domum contemplari. Quae si tibi parva, ut est, ita videtur, haec caelestia semper spectato, illa humana contemnito. Tu enim quam celebritatem sermonis hominum aut quam expetendam gloriam consequi potes ? " VII, 17 : " Quocirca si reditum in hunc locum desperaveris, in quo omnia sunt magnis et praestantibus viris, quanti tandem est ista hominum gloria, quae pertinere vix ad unius anni partem exiguam potest ? Igitur alte spectare si voles atque hanc sedem et aeternam domum contueri, neque te sermonibus vulgi dedideris nec in praemiis humanis spem posueris rerum tuarum. Suis te oportet inlecebris ipsa virtus trahat ad verum decus [quid de te alii loquantur ipsi videant, sed loquentur tamen],sermo autem omnis ille et angustiis cingitur iis regionum, quas vides, nec umquam de ullo perennis fuit : et obruitur hominum interitu et oblivione posteritatis extinguitur."

820–25. The biblical character of these lines is obvious. For scriptural passages which might be adduced as sources see Deuteron. vi. 5, and x. 12 ; Ecclesiast. ii. 7 and 9. For similar lines in other writings of Lydgate comp. *Pilgrim.* 7866 ff. : The Sword Righteousness teacheth man

" To louë god with al hys myght,
A-boue al other Erthly thyng,
As hym that ys most myghty kyng."

Tretis of the kynges coronacion, st. 3, 8 : " love god and hym drede & gyn so thy passage." *Falls of Princes*, I, 1 A vi *b* :

" For vnto a man that perfit is and stable,
by good reason mine auctor doth wel preue
there is nothing more fayre ne agreable,
than finally, his vicious life to leue,
On very God rightfully beleue :
him loue & worship aboue al erthly thinges
this passeth victory of Emperors and kinges."

Hoccleve, *Regiment of Princes* 1332, " god honoure and drede " ; see also 2898.

837–40. Lydgate was evidently thinking of the *regula aurea perfectionis*, Matt. vii. 12 : " Omnia ergo quaecumque vultis ut faciant vobis homines, et vos facite illis." The same thought is expressed in *Roman de la Rose* 5699 ff. :

" Fai tant que tex envers tous soies
Cum tous envers toi les vodroies ;
Ne fai vers autre, ne porchace
Fors ce que tu veus qu'en te face."

There are some more passages in the *Rom. de la Rose*, which remind us of the admonition of Dame Nature, for instance l. 1552 ff. :

" Mes raisonnable créature,
Soit mortex hons, soit divins anges,
Qui tuit doivent à Diex loanges,
S'el se mescongnoist comme nices,
E defaut li vient de ses vices
Qui le sens li troble et enivre :
Car il puet bien Raison ensivre,
Et puet de franc voloir user :
N'est riens que l'en puist escuser."

847–50. Here the thought is expressed that our soul does not begin its existence at the moment of its birth, but that it has already existed before with God, to whom it finally returns. The idea is taken from Plato, and is adapted to Christian doctrine. Again we notice the influence of the *Somn. Scip.*, where we read (iii, 5), "Hinc profecti huc revertuntur," and further (iii, 7), "iisque (*i. e.* hominibus) animus datus est ex illis sempiternis ignibus," and where the purified soul is stated to return "in hanc sedem et domum suam." Comp. Meissner, note 10, p. 17. For similar passages in Lydgate comp. l. 1245–1277 of our poem, and especially *Pilgr.* 12257 ff.:

". . . thow haddest, in allë thyng,
Off hy*m* orygynal begynnyng, . . .
To hy*m*, off verray ryht certeyn,
Thow must resorte and tourne ageyn."

12301 ff :
". . . the spyryt (in hys entent)
Meueth toward the oryent,
Whych thenys kam. & yiff he sholde
Thyder ayeyn, fful ffayn he wolde."

12377 ff. :
"ffor thy lyff (yt ys no doute),
Ys lyk a cercle that goth aboute,
Round and swyfft as any thouht,
Wych in hys course ne cesset nouht
Yiff he go ryht, *and* wel compace
Tyl he kam to hys restyng place
Wych ys in god, yiff he wel go
Hys ownë place wych he kam ffro."

The same idea occurs in the *Roman de la Rose*, comp. l. 18159 f.

856–63. Comp. *Romaunt* 4766–69 :
"Love makith alle to goon miswey,
But it be they of yvel lyf,
Whom Genius cursith, man and wyf,
That wrongly werke ageyn nature."

With regard to Genius, the priest of Nature, see *De Planctu Naturae* (Migne 210, p. 479–82), *Roman de la Rose* 16942 ff. In Gower, *Conf. Am.* i, p. 48 ff., Genius acts as the clerk of Venus.

892–96. The expression "thou gest no more of me" occurs, with slight variations, very frequently ; comp. *Fall. Duor. Mercat.* 852 :
"Ye han that herd, ye gete no mor of me."

Pilgr. 21029 : "Thow gest no mor, as now, for me."

21036 : "Ffor thow gest no mor off me."

Troy-Book, I, 5 B vi *a* :
"Thou gettest no more of me
Do as thou lyste I put the choys in the."

I, 6 D iv *b* : "ye gete no more of me."

Chaucer, *Legend* 1557 :
"Ye gete no more of me."

895. *Lo, this the ende !*] Similar phrases occur l. 4540 and 4628 :
"Lo, here is al ! "

Lydgate uses this "lo, here is al" very often, not only to finish up a speech, but also, as a kind of expletive sentence, in the middle of an oration. Compare, for instance, *Pilgr.* 1979, 2031, 2340, 10552, 10712, 17448, 19661. Chaucer, too, has this phrase ; see *Troilus,* ii. 321.

Now and then we find the variation "here (this) is al." Comp.

Falls of Princes, I, 8 C iv *b* :
"Here is al and some. I can say you no more."

Troy-Book, IV, 29 T ii *b* :
"This all and some and that we hens wende
I can no more my tale is at an ende."

897–902. After the departure of a goddess or one of the other fictitious personages of allegorical poetry, Lydgate and other contemporary poets usually bring in complaining verses of this kind. Comp. *Pilg.* 17113 f., where the poet, after the departure of Tribulation says :
"And as I stood allone, al sool,
Gan compleyne, and makë dool."

19668 f., where we read, after Dame Fortune has gone :
"And also sone as she was gon,
I stood in dred and in gret doute."

Comp. also the following instances from the *Romaunt* 2954–56 :
"He (viz. Cupido) vanished awey al sodeinly,
And I alone lefte, al sole,
So ful of compleynt and of dole."

3167–69 :   "Than Bialacoil is fled and mate,
And I al sole, disconsolate,
Was left aloon in peyne and thought."

3332–35 :   "With that word Resoun wente hir gate . . .
Than dismayed, I lefte al sool."

3359–60 :
"Fro me he (viz. Daunger) made him (viz. Bialacoil) for to go,
And I bilefte aloon in wo."

949 ff. Comp. the enumeration in *Hous of Fame* 896–903.

1007. *skye*] O.E. sky = cloud, nubes. This is the usual meaning in M.E. Comp. *Pilg.* 9600, 9641, 9829, 11032, etc.; *Temple of Glas* 36, 611 ; *F. of Pr.* I, 12 E 11 *b* : "These Centaures . . . wer whilom engendred of a skye." Chaucer's *Hous of Fame* 1600, and Gower's *Conf. Am.* p. 50, 2. But there are instances in which the word undoubtedly has the signification of "sky" or "cloudy sky." See *Pilgr.* 9626, "a clowdy skye" ; 9979, "aboue the skye I was wont to fle" ; *Troy-Book*, Prologue 13 f.: "the leuen that alyghteth lowe Downe by the skye." *F. of Pr.* I, 10 D iv : "some cloudy skye of vnware sorow."

1029 ff. : The quotation in the first marginal note is from *Eccles.* i. 1 : "Omnis sapientia a Domino Deo est, et cum illo fuit semper, et est ante aveum." Comp. first marginal note on p. 33.

1089–94. Comp. *Apocalypsis* xxi. 3 ff.

1107. The expression *out of joint* occurs twice more in our poem : 2939, "Thow art in party out of Ioynt," and 3016, "I stond in partye out of Ioynt." Instances from other works of Lydgate are numerous.

1109–14. In the marginal note we certainly have to read [im]mortales. Apart from the sense, our conjecture is proved by Fulgentius, *Mythol.* II, 1, where we read: "Minerva denique et Athene Grece dicitur, quasi athanate parthene : id est inmortalis virgo, quia sapientia nec mori poterit, nec corrumpi." See Helm's edition.

1115–18. Comp. Albricus, *De Deor. Imag.* lib. viii : "Haec igitur oculos habebat splendidos." Boetius, *Philos. Consol.* pros. I: "mulier reuerendi admodum uultus oculis ardentibus." In the *Roman de la Rose* Dame Raison is likewise gifted with two star-bright eyes. See 3087 f.:

"Li oel qui en son chief estoient,
A deus estoiles resembloient."

With this and the following notes compare my remarks in *Échecs Amoureux*, p. 141 ff.

1123–38. See Boetius, l. c. pros. I: "Nam nunc quidem ad communem sese hominum mensuram cohibebat, nunc uero pulsare caelum summi uerticis cacumine uidebatur: quae cum altius caput extulisset, ipsum etiam caelum penetrabat respicientiumque hominum frustrabatur intuitum."

1147–72. Boetius, l. c. pros. I: "Vestes erant tenuissimis filis subtili artificio indissolubili materia perfectae quas, uti post eadem prodente cognoui, suis manibus ipsa texuerat." With regard to the three colours see Albric. l. c. viii: "triplici colore pallium induebat, distinctum aureo, purpureo et coelesti." Fulgent. l. c. II, 1: "Triplici etiam veste subnixa est, seu quod omnis sapientia sit multiplex, sive etiam quod celata."

1187–93. Fulgent. l. c. II, 1: "Cristam cum galea ponunt, ut sapientis cerebrum & armatum sit & decorum." Albricus has "ipsamque cassis cum crista desuper (de)tegebat."

1188 ff. The allegorical interpretation of the armour of Pallas—"a bryght¹ helme of a-temperaunce," "the egal launce of ryght¹wysnesse," "a myghty shelde of pacience"—is the work of Lydgate. The French only names the three parts of the armour. Lydgate's interpretation reminds us of the *armatura mystica christiani* as it is described by St. Paul in *Ephes.* vi. 14 ff.: "State ergo succincti lumbos vestros in veritate, et induti loricam justitiae, et calceati pedes in preparatione Evangelii pacis: in omnibus sumentes scutum fidei, in quo possitis omnia tela nequissimi ignea extinguere: et galeam salutis assumite et gladium spiritus (quod est verbum Dei")." With regard to the second note on p. 33 comp. *Prov.* xii. 23: "Homo versutus celat scientiam," and x. 14: "Sapientes abscondunt scientiam."

1194–1206. See Albr. l. c. viii: "ipsa autem lanceam tenebat in dextra: in sinistra vero scutum crystallinum habebat, quod caput Gorgonis a cervice serpentibus monstrose continebat." Fulgent. l. c. II, 1: "Gorgonam etiam huic addunt in pectore, quasi terroris imaginem, ut vir sapiens terrorem contra adversarios gestet in pectore."

1207–13. The French for these lines reads (fol. 6 b):

"Touteffois la deesse honneste
Nauoit pas son hayaulme en teste
Quant Je la vis a celle fois
Mais cest mesperance et ma fois
Quelle lauoit fait a cautelle
Pour moy moustrer sa face belle
M Jeulx *et* plus descouuertement
Affin que plus appertement
De sa beaulte Jugier peuisse."

I am inclined to believe that these verses are the result of a misinterpretation of the following faulty passage from Albricus, l. c. lib. viii: "cuius caput viri decinctum circum erat, ipsamque cassis cum crista desuper detegebat."

1214–37. For the primary source of these lines I refer the reader to the *Roman de la Rose* 3089 ff., where Lorris speaks of Dame Raison as follows:

> "Si ot où chief une coronne,
> Bien resembloit haute personne.
> A son semblant et à son vis
> Pert que tu faite en paradis,
> Car Nature ne séust pas
> Ovre faire de tel compas."

1238 ff. The bird of Pallas is the owl. See Fulg. l. c. II, 1: "In hujus etiam tutelam noctuam volunt." Comp. *Échecs Amoureux*, p. 143 and Preface, p. viii.

1245–77. The whole passage is an addition of Lydgate. The French simply reads (fol. 6 *b*):

> "Et sachiez quen tour luy to*us* temps
> Auoit chienettez voletans
> Et tournians entour sa teste
> Aussy com pour luy faire feste."

The marginal note in Lydgate's work refers to the following passage from Alanus ab Insulis, *De Planctu Naturae* (Migne 210, p. 435–36): "Olor sui funeris praeco, mellitae citharizationis organo, vitae vaticinabatur apocham." Chaucer, too, has this passage in mind when, in his *Parlament of Foules*, l. 342, he says: "The jalous swan, ayens his deth that singeth." Comp. also *Legend* 1355:

> "the whyte swan
> Ayeins his deeth beginneth for to singe."

The story of the swan singing before his death is old. There is a proverbial saying in Greek "Τὸ κύκνειον ᾄδειν" = to try the last. Com. *Pol.* xxx, 4, 7 and xxxi, 20, 1. The above-quoted passage from Chaucer's *Legend* is taken from Ovid's *Heroides*, where the letter of Dido begins with these lines:

> "Sic ubi fata vocant, udis abiectus in herbis,
> Ad vada Maeandri concinit albus olor."

The saying of St. Paul referred to we find in *Phil.* i. 23: "desiderium habens dissolvi, et esse cum Christo." Comp. *Joan.* xi. 25 f.

1264 ff. That the soul is placed in the body for a punishment is an idea of Plato. It finds expression in Cicero's *Somnium Scipionis* iii, 6: "Immo vero, inquit, hi vivunt, qui e corporum vinculis tamquam e carcere evolaverunt, vestra vero, quae dicitur, vita mors est." Meissner, in his note to this sentence, mentions a passage from *Oratio pro Scaur.* 4: "Socrates illo ipso die, quo erat ei moriundum, permulta disputat, hanc esse mortem, quam nos vitam putaremus, cum corpore animus tamquam carcere saeptus teneretur, vitam autem esse eam, cum idem animus vinclis corporis liberatus in eum se locum, unde esset ortus, rettulisset." Boetius, too, in his *Philos. Cons.* points out that the soul has its true home in Heaven, living here in a kind of exile; comp. IV, metr. 1. It is only natural that Chaucer, the translator of Boetius, should have similar ideas; comp. *Knightes Tale* 3058:

> "Why have we hevinesse,
> That good ticite, of chivalrye flour,
> Departed is, with duetee and honour,
> Out of this foule prison of this lyf?"

I think it is not out of place here to refer the reader to Wordsworth's beautiful *Ode on Immortality*, further to Byron, *Childe Harold's Pilgr.* iii, st. 73 f.

1276 f. *Fer a-bove the sterrys clere*] Comp. for similar expressions *Secrees* 663:

> "God that sit hihest Above the sterrys cleer."

Pilgr. 4783 f.: "My soule vn-to my Fader dere,
That syt above the sterrys clere."
14579 f.: "Hable to fflen vp to heuene,
ffer aboue the sterrys seuene."

1299 ff. The expulsion of Saturn from Heaven and the happiness reigning in the Golden Age are themes frequently touched upon by classical and mediaeval writers. See *Roman de la Rose* 8671–8712 and 20807–20924; Ovid, *Met.* i, 89–150 and *Eleg.* iii, 8. 35 ff.; Virgil, *Georg.* i, 125 ff.; *Tibullus* i, 3. 35 ff.; Boetius, *Philos. Cons.* II, metr. 5; Lactant. *Fabulae* i, 3; Gower, *Conf. Am.* II, p. 155 f. Comp. my remarks in *Échecs Amoureux*, p. 158 f. With l. 1332 ff. may be compared the long discourse on the development of covetousness and avarice in the *Roman de la Rose* 9843 ff.

1306 f. *With his lokkys hoore and gray*] Comp. 1347, where Saturn is described as "Corbed, croked, feble, and colde," also 3091, where we read: "For he was courbed, gray, and olde"; 1438 where the god appears with a "frosty berd," and 3103 where he has a "siluer berde." These lines remind us of the description of Saturn in Albric., *De Deor. Imag.* I: "pingebatur, ut homo senex, canus, prolixa barba, curvus, tristis et pallidus, tecto capite, colore glauco." For other descriptions of Saturn I refer the reader to *Assembly of Gods* 278–287, *Mirror for Magistrates*, introduction.

1335. *lucre*] The word is not very frequent, but in *Amor vincit omnia*, st. 6 and 7 Lydgate uses it not less than four times. In *F. of Pr.* there are also some instances: I, 13 E iv: "Some for lucre can maintene wel falsness"; I, 18 G i: "Lyf, body, good, al put in auenture, Onely for lucre, great riches to recure"; and again: "Pleters which for lucre and mede Mayntain quarels." As far as I can see, Chaucer has the word twice: *Chanouns Yem. Tale* 849: "Lo! swich a lucre is in this lusty game"; and *Prior. Tale* 39: "foule usure and lucre of vilenye." From Gower's *Conf. Am.* I collected the following instances—I, p. 358: "To make werres and to pille—For lucre"; II, p. 194: "Where he (viz. covetise) purposeth him to fare—Upon his lucre"; p. 217: "For lucre and nought for loves sake"; p. 222: "And marriage is made for lucre;" p. 274: "Such lucre is none above grounde"; III, p. 180: "Withoute lucre of such richesse." More frequently *lucre* occurs in Hoccleve. Comp. *Regiment of Princes* 634, 1544, 3059, 3911.

1359. With regard to Fortune, "the gerful lady with hir whel," see Triggs, note on l. 316 of the *Assembly of Gods*. We have the fiction further *in extenso* in *Pilgr.* 19463 ff. The allusions to the wheel of Fortune are far too numerous to be enumerated here. Comp. only *Conf. Am.* I, p. 8, 7–10; p. 28, 18; III, p. 198, 26 f. p. 295, 3 ff.; p. 333, 14 f.

1368. Comp. *F. of Pr.* I, 19 G iii *b*:
"whan these verkes ferre yrone in age
Within them self hath vaine glory & delite
For to farce and poppe their visage."

Romaunt 1018 ff.:
"No windred browes hadde she,
Ne popped hir, for it neded nought
To windre hir, or to peynte hir ought."

1410–1432. Comp. what is said about the array of Juno with the description of Albr. l. c. xi: "Erat enim foemina in throno sedens, sceptrum regium tenens in dextra. ejus caput nubes tenebant opertum supra diadema, quod capite gestabat, cui & Iris sociata erat, quae ipsam per circuitum cingebant. . . Pavones autem ante pedes ejus lambebant : qui a dextris & a sinistris dominae stabant, avesque Junonis specialiter vocabantur."

1428. *Aungelys fethers bryght*'] Comp. 5244 :
"As an Angel fethred faire."
5358 f. :   "And of fethres he was as bryght'
As an Aungel of paradys."
Chaucer has similar lines : *Romaunt* 741 f. :
"they were lyk, as to my sighte,
To angels, that ben fethered brighte."
Legend 168, A : "And aungellich hes wenges gan he sprede" (Cupido).
1433-64. Comp. what Gower says about the birth of the goddess : *Conf. Am.* ii, p. 156.
1445. *fatal ewre*] In *F. of Pr.* I, 11 E ii we have "vnhappy eure." The contrary is "good ewre." Comp. *Tretis of the kynges coronacion*, lenvoy : "grace and good ewre." The word without any adj. occurs *Pilgr.* 131 : "Swych grace & Eur, God to hym hath sent"; *Troy-Book* I, 5 B ii b : "It was hir vre to konne what hir leste." From *ewre* is formed the adj. *ewrous.* Comp. l. 1084 of our poem: "ewrous and fortunat"; this phrase is frequently met with in Lydgate. A similar expression is "happi and Ewrous," see *T. of Gl.* 562 (comp. Schick's note). There is also a verb *ewre* : *Troy-Book* I, 5 C ii b : "That by assent of fortune and hir whele—J ewred were to stonde in his grace." D ii b : "Right as ferforthe as fortune wyll him eure."
1457. *halt = tenet, holds*] Comp. Lydgate's *F. of Pr.* I, 19 G iii b. "Bochas affirmeth and halt it for no tale." The form is not so very rare as one might conclude from the marginal note. In Hoccleve's *R. of Pr.* it occurs twice : 4608 and 5226 ; in his *Male Regle* once : 53.
1495-1523. The French for this passage is quoted in my *Échecs Amoureux*, p. 218 f. The primary source is Andreas Capellanus, *De amore libri tres* I, 4, as I have already pointed out in *É. A.* p. 145. The text runs as follows (ed. E. Trojel) : "Effectus autem amoris hic est, quia verus amator nulla posset avaritia offuscari, amor horridum et incultum omni facit formositate pollere, infimos natu etiam morum novit nobilitate ditare, superbos quoque solet humilitate beare, obsequia cunctis amorosus multa consvevit decenter parare." Comp. also *Le Bien des Fames* in Jubinal, *Jongleurs et Trouvères*, p. 85 :

"Fames si fet simples et dous   Et esveillier les endormis.
Cels qui mult sont fel et estous,   Mult est fame de grant pooir,
Cels qui sont fels et desdaigneus;   Quar par fame, je sai de voir,
Fames si fet les envieus   Devienent large li aver.
Venir à sens et à mesure ;   Toz li mondes doit fame amer,
Fame si est de tel nature   Quar de fame vient si granz preus
Qu'ele fet les coars hardis,   Qu'ele fet les mauvès preus," etc.

The refining and all-conquering power of Love is a favourite theme of Lydgate and other mediaeval writers. See lines 2026-29 of our poem. See also *Temple of Glas* 321-27, 985, 1171. Gower touches upon the subject several times in his *Conf. Am.* See ii, p. 78 f. :

"For ever yet it hath be so,   It yiveth, so that the verray
That love honest in sondry wey   prowesse
Profiteth, for it doth awey   Is caused upon loves reule
The vice, and as the bokes sain,   To him that can manhode reule,
It maketh curteis of the vilain   And eke toward the womanhede,
And to the coward hardiesse   Who that therof woll taken hede."

III, p. 4 :

"Love is of so great a maine,
  That where he taketh a herte on honde,
There may nothing his might withstonde.
The wise Salomon was nome,
And stronge Sampson overcome,
  The knightly David him ne might Rescoue, that he with the sight Of Bersabe ne was bestade.
Virgile also was overlade,
And Aristotle was put under."

III, p. 149 :

"Through hem (viz. women) men finden out the wey
  To knighthode and to worldes fame,
They make a man to drede shame
And honour for to be desired."

Comp. also *Roman de la Rose* 893–900.

1535–1600. The portrait of Venus is not quite in accordance with the mythographers, as, for instance, Chaucer's picture in *Hous of Fame* I, 131 ff. Comp. Fulg. l. c. II, 4, and Albr. l. c. V. Our poem rather reminds us of the description which Lorris gives of the Goddess of Love. See *R. de la R.* 3546 ff. Comp. my remarks in *É. A.* p. 144 f.

1569–1600 read in the French as follows : (Fol. 7 *b*). :

"Ceste dame en lieu de couronne
Auoit aueuc toutes ces choses
Vn chappel de vermeilles Roses
Qui b*ien* li seoit sur le chief
Ou Jl not point de coeuurechief
Ains estoit assis li chappiaux
Sur les cheueux quelle ot si biaux
Quil sambloient estre dores
Tant estoient bien couloures
SJ ne pourroit pas sceu estre
Quelle tenoit en sa main destre
Vn brandon de feu tout ardant
Qui esbahist le Regardant
Et a la fois hart et esprent
Se bien ad ce garde ne prent
Voire de si faitte maniere
Que se trop fort nest Jamais nyere
Chilz fus ne Rescous ne estains
Car Jl nest Jen suy tous c*er*tains
Feu gregois tant soit m*er*ueilleux
Qui puist estre plus perilleux
Ne qui soit de vertu plus forte
Que li fus est que Venus porte."

1576. Comp. *Troy-Book* iv, 30 S v *b* :

"Hyr heer also resemblynge to gold wyere."

1577–89. With regard to the fire-brand of Venus and its dangerous effects, see *Roman de la Rose* 3548–50 :

"Ele tint ung brandon flamant
En sa maint destre, dont la flame
A eschauffée mainte dame."

Also *Romaunt* 3705 ff. The brond or fire of Venus is frequently mentioned in our poem : 2023, 4117 f., 4285, 4295, 6949 ; "lovys bronde" occurs 5188, "lovys fire" 5466, and 6284 ; in l. 2018 Venus appears with "hir firy cheyne." In *Troy-Book* iv, 29 T iv *b*, this "firy chayne" is given to Cupido. There are many more instances in Lydgate where the brond of Venus or Cupid is mentioned.

T. of G. 436 :

"w*ith* my brond I haue him set afire."

632 f. :   "þe fire
of louis brond is kindled in my brest."

Compleynt 556 "Cupidis bronde" ; *Pilgr.* 8155 "ffyry brond" ; *Troy-Book* i, 5 B v "loues bronde."

C ii *b*: "Loue hathe hir caught so newly in a traunce
And I marked with his fury bronde."

C iii :   "the furyous god Cupyde—
Hath suche a fyre kynled (!) in her syde."

Notes. Lines 1582–1671.

C iii b: "The fyre that love hath in hir brest enclosed."
IV, 30 S vi: "Cupydes bronde hath hym marked so."
F. of Pr. I, 15 T iv. Cupide causes Narcissus to have his part "of Venus bronde and of her fyry dart." Comp. Schick's notes on 1. 436 and 838 f. of the *T. of Gl.* Allegorical expressions of this kind are not only adapted to the passion of love. Comp. *Romaunt* 5706: "So hote he brennith in the fire—Of coveitise;" and 5716: "The fire of gredinesse."

1582. *That fire which is y-callyd greke*] "Greek fire, a combustible composition, the constituents of which are supposed to have been asphalt, niter, and sulphur. It would burn on or under water, and was used with great effect in war by the Greeks of the Eastern Empire who kept its composition secret for several hundred years. Upon the conquest of Constantinople, the secret came into the possession of the Mohammedans to whom it rendered repeated and valuable service." Comp. *Cent. Dict.*

1583. *rage*] So far as I know Chaucer does not use this word as an adj., but it is very frequent in Lydgate. See ll. 4133, 4222, 4365, and 4532 of our poem. Comp. further *Pilgr.* 1657 "floodys raage"; 14757 "rokkys wylde *and* rage"; *Deuyse of a desguysinge* (Add. MS. 29729 fol. 140 b) "a rage fleed;" *F. of Pr.* I, 1 A v b:
"thylke beastes that toforne were mylde
After their sining full rage wexe";
and again, on the same page, "wethers rage;" I, 2 B i b: "his furious yre so mortall was and rage"; I, 4 B v: "waues rage;" on the same page and I, 18 G i we have again "floudes rage."

1607. *my stile dresse*] Comp. *F. of Pr.*, Prologue A iii b: "J gan my stile dresse;"
I, 6 B vi: "J wil . . . vnto Cadmus forth my style dresse;"
I, 8 C iii b: "To whom J must now my style adresse;"

Other expressions—
I, 2 B i b: "myne autor transported hath his stile;"
I, 6 B v: "His stile conueyed . . to;"
I, 10 D v b: "direct his stile;" D vi: "turne thy style."

1643 f. Comp. Martianvs Capella (ed. F. Eyssenhardt), p. 37: "cui lacteam papillam gaudens dedit nouerea."
"Soft as silke" occurs also in *T. of Glas* 540. Comp. Schick's note. In *F. of Pr.* I 23 G vi we find "lippes soft as silke."

1657. I think we must take *facounde* as an adj., although we read in the original: "dieux de faconde." Comp. Horat. *Od.* I, 10:
"Mercuri facunde nepos Atlantis
Qui feros cultus hominum recentum
Voce formasti catus."

With Mercury as "god of eloquence" deals Schick's note on l. 132 of the *T. of Gl.*

1657–71. The French for this passage reads, fol. 8 a:
"Cest chilz qui est dieux de faconde
Car sur tous aultrez Jl habonde
En langaige aourne et bel
Et se luy auient si tres bel
Com ny puet veoir mespresure
Car tous ses mos sont par mesure
Par pois et par nombre ordonne."

Again the influence of Mart. Cap. is clearly visible. That the author of the French poem certainly knew the celebrated book of Mart. Cap. appears later on. On Fol. 44 *a-b* of his work we read:

"Pour ce se dient aucuns saiges
Firent li dieux li mariaiges
Du dieu mercure lautrefie
Et de dame philosophie
Car on ne puet veir ce samble
Deux chosez mieulx seans ensamble
Et cest pour ce que chilz habonde
Dessus tous en belle faconde
Et en biau langaige parfait
Et sapience le parfait."

How much Mart. Cap. was read in the Middle Ages is evident from Schick's note on l. 129–136 of the *T. of Glas*, and from E. Langlois, *Origines et Sources du Roman de la Rose*. See p. 63.

1658. *except* is certainly not to be changed. With our punctuation the lines render the French not at all badly. I can find only one instance where *except* occurs with a similar meaning. *Romaunt* 4291:

"She was except in hir servyse."

Skeat, *Student's Chaucer*, alters *except* into *expert*. "Expert in langage" occurs in *F. of Pr.* Prologue A iii: "no man is more expert in language."

1662–66: Comp. the frequently quoted hexameter:

"Pondere, mensura, numero deus omnia fecit."

1664. *rape = haste, hurry*] Comp. Chaucer, *Wordes unto Adam, his owne Scriveyn:* "And al is through thy negligence and rape."

Gower, *Conf. Am.* I, p. 296:

"that sometime in rape
Him may some light word overscape."

See also *Pilgr.* 13781:

"For haste nor rape,
Thow shalt not fro my daunger skape."

Troy-Book IV, 29 S ii *b*:

"no nelygence
Of hasty speche sothly for to rape
Myght make a worde his lyppes to escape."

1665 f. I do not see how else to arrange these lines. Rhyme and sense require the omission of *reseyved*.

1677–84. As to the relation of Mercury to Phebus, comp. Mart. Cap. Note especially p. 11, 25 ff: "Haec dicente Mercurio 'quin potius' inquit Virtus 'uterque uestrum Iouem uoce conciliet, nam et hic eius consiliorum conscius et tu praeceptionis arcanus. ille mentem nouit, tu verba componis. Phoebo sueuit instanti concedere, tibi pectus [solitus] aperire. addo quod uos numquam conuenit disparari et licet hic cursor Apollinei plerumque axis celeritate uincatur ac remorata statione consistens captet demum festinata praeuertere, tamen dum consequitur ita libratus anteuenit, ut cessim plerumque recursitans gaudeat occupari. una igitur uestrum Iouem pia pignora conuenite."

1699–1708. The textual difficulties disappear by referring to the French which reads (fol. 8 *a*):

Notes. Lines 1701–1723.   103

"Cest chilz quant Jl a pris en main   Que ne peuist estre sceu
Qui dispose lengien humain   Ainsy sont en terre veu
En tel maniere quil habonde   Li Philosophe et li prophete
En soubtillete si parfonde   Qui mainte merueille secrete
Quil perche la terre et les cieulx   Qui excederont par samblance
Et y voit telz choses que cieul⁔   Toute lumaine congnoissance
Qui sa vertu ne sentiroient   Sceuent et voyent clerement
Jamais ne se consentiroient   Ou temps futur meismement."

1701 ff. Comp. Fulgentius, *Virg. Cont.* (Helm 94, 21): "Mercurius enim Deus ponitur ingenii."

Ammiani Marcellini, lib. xvi, 5. 5: "occulte Mercurio supplicabat, quem mundi uelociorem sensum esse, motum mentium suscitantem theologicae prodidere doctrinae: atque in tanto rerum defectu explorate rei publicae *munera* curabat." Comp. *É. A.* p. 146 f.

1708. With regard to our conjecture, comp. *Troy-Book* II, 10 E vi:

"And in eche art hadde experyence
Of thynges futur fully prescyence
To tell afore what that shall betyde;"

further, II, 12 F vi *b*:

. . . "auysed
To caste afore what that schalbe fall
And thynges futur aduertynge from a ferre."

1709–23: The description of the French poem reads as follows (fol. 8 *a*):

"Chilz dieux qui de nature est telle   Par droite mesure parfaitte
Estoit de taille aussi moult belle   Et cest verites que dedens
La face ot par samblant Jonette   Elle estoit garnie de dens
Sestoit sur toute blance et nette   BJaulx et nes et bien arrengies
Et pollie et bien ordonnee   On ne les veist pas mengies
Et bien a son droit aournee   Ors ne pourris mais blans et gens
De membres plaisans et faittis   Plus que nest yuoires ne argens
De verdz yeulx de long nez traittis   Le corps auoit gresle et plaisant
De petite bouche bien faitte   Non pas mal ostru ne pesant
                                              Mais sur tous Jsnel et legier."

I should like to call attention to the conventional character of traits like these: "verdz yeulx," "long nez traittis," "petite bouche bien faitte." Comp. *De Venus la Deesse d'Amor* (ed. W. Foerster), st. 156 ff., where the lover describes his lady in the following manner:

"Les ex uairs et rians, lonc et traitis le nes.
. . . .
La bocete a uermeille, le menton forceles,
Les dens blans con argens, menus et entasses,
Le front blanc et poli con yuoires planes,
Et tos ses autres menbres sont a conpas oures."

Note also the portrait of Chaucer's Prioresse, *Prologue* 118 ff., especially 152–53:

"Hir nose tretys; hir eyen greye as glas;
Hir mouth ful smal."

The *verdz yeulx* of French authors are in English translations usually changed into *yen greye*. Comp. *Romaunt* 822, where it is said of Deduit:

"With metely mouth and yën greye;
His nose by mesure wrought ful right."

The original version of these lines runs thus (833-34):
"Les yex ot vairs, la bouche gente,
Et le nez fait par grand entente."

Gower, *Conf. Am.* ii, p. 210, mentions "eyen grey" as one of those qualities which increase a woman's charms.

1724-33. Comp. Albr. l. c. vi: "De albis vero nigra, *et* de nigris alba faciebat, quod ostenditur per ejus pileum semialbum *et* seminigrum"; further, Ovid, *Met.* xi, 314 f.:
"Qui facere adsuerat, patriae non degener artis,
Candida de nigris, et de candentibus atra."

1735-54. With regard to the *yerde* of Mercury, see Albr. l. c. vi: "in manu autem sua laeva virgam tenebat, quae virtutem habebat soporiferam"; Virg. *Aeneid,* iv, 242 ff.:
"Tum virgam capit: hac animas ille evocat Orco
Pallentes; alias sub Tartara tristia mittit;
Dat somnos adimitque, et lumina morte resignat."

The *yerde of Moyses* is also referred to in other writings of Lydgate. Comp. *Pilgr.* 1656 ff.:
"*with* hys yerdë, thys was he
That passedë the floodys raage,
And made hem haue good passage."

Again, 3576 ff. and 3908. Mercury's "slepy yerde" is also mentioned in Chaucer, *Knightes Tale* 529: "His slepy yerde he (viz. the messenger of the gods appearing before Arcite) bar uprighte."

1746. Comp. *F. of Pr.* I, 12:
"to hell they descend
Duke Pirithous and worthy Theseus
Maugre the daunger of cruel Cerberus."

1760 ff. Comp. Albr. l. c. vi: "Fistulamque de calamo factam Syringe ad os suum ponebat, dextra sonans."

l. 1765. *sugred* is one of the favourite adjectives of Lydgate, see l. 5213, 6398, 6415 of our poem; comp. further *Secrees* 220: "his sugryd Enspyred Elloquence"; 376: "Tullius sugryd Elloquence"; 1309: "sugryd mellodye." *Amor vincit omnia* (Addit. MS. 29729), st. 5, 3: "Homerus w*ith* his sugeryd mouthe." *Troy-Book,* Prol. 56 f., where we read of Calliope:
"that with thyne hony swete
Sugryst tunges of rethoricyens."

277-78: "sugred wordes"; *Pilgr.* 14287: "sugryd galle"; *Chorle and Bird* (Halliwell, p. 182): "the soote sugred armonye"; *Play before Eestfeld* (Add. MS. 29729, fol. 133): "that sugred bawme awreate"; *F. of Pr.* Prol. A iii *b*: "sugred aureat licour" (viz. of the Muses), I, 8 D i:
"fames trumpe blew his name vp loude
with sugred sownes semyng wonder sote."

I, 14 F i *b*: "flattry and sugred faire langages"; I, 15 F v: "sote sugred armonie."

1770-79. Comp. the detailed description in l. 3620-67. These lines and the marginal note refer to Isidor, *Etym.* XI, 3. 30-31 (Migne, *Patr. Lat.* 82): "Sirenas tres fingunt fuisse ex parte virgines, ex parte volucres, habentes alas, et ungulas; quarum una voce, altera tibiis, tertia lyra canebat. Quae illectos navigantes suo cantu in naufragia trahebant." Nearly the same description, and in its wording even more recalling the lines of Lydgate, is found in *Brunetto Latini* I, 5, chap. cxxxvii. See further the

Notes. Lines 1780–1910.   105

Bestiaire of Pierre le Picard (13) who, like Brunetto, follows Isidor's *Etym.* Allusions to the song of the Sirens are very frequent in Lydgate and contemporary writers. See l. 4098, 5257 and 6732 ff. of our poem; *Pilgr.* 14689 ff.; *Nonne Preestes Tale* 449–52; Hoccleve, *Male Regle* 233–258. On the Sirens in the works of Early Christian art see Piper, *Myth. d. christl. Kunst*, p. 377 f.

1780–96. The story of Io is told in Ovid, *Metam.* 1, 588 ff. Comp. also Apollod. *Biblioth* II, i. 3. Lydgate's lines remind me of the *R. de la R.* 14983–96. Comp. also Gower, *Conf. Am.* II, p. 113 f., and E. A fol. 40 *b*–41. Argus is referred to once more in the *R. de la R.* 13378–84.

1788. *Ther was as tho noon*͗ *other grace*] Comp. *F. of Pr.* I, 8 C iii : "there was none other spare"; I, 9 D iii : "there was none help nor other remedye"; "there was none other grace"; the latter phrase occurs also I, 20 G iv *b*; I, 21 G v *b*, and I, 23 G vi : "but of vs tweyn there is none other grace saue onely death." *Troy-Book* IV, 30 S. vi :

> "hym thought he must nedes deye
> But if that he founde in hir some grace
> There was no geyne."

1797 ff. Comp. Albr. l. c. vi : "[Tenebat] et gladium curvum, quem Harpen homo vocabat."

1816 ff. Comp. Albr. l. c. vi : "Erat ipsius signum homo unus, qui in capite & in talis alas habebat."

1847. Expressions of this kind are very frequent in the *Troy-Book.* See I, 8 E i : "Began to lande in all the haste they myghte."

E i *b*:   "in all the haste we may
             Let vs set on."

11, 13 H iv: "in all the hast they may
             They cast anker."

H v: "To the temple anone he hath hym hyed
            Full thryftely in all the haste he myght."

H v *b*:   "To his shyppes he helde the right way
            And than anone in all the haste he may."

II, 14 I i *b*:   "Kynge Pryamus alyghte
             And anone as faste as euer he myghte."

IV, 30 S iv *b*: "euery maner man
             Gan arme hym in all the haste they can."

S v *b*: "forth he went in all the haste he may." For other instances see *F. of Pr.* I, 9 D ii : "This yong childe ... shalbe deliuered in all the hast he may"; I, 14 F ii *b*: "Hercules ... gan to espye in all the hast he may."

Assembly of Gods 958 f. :
           "I commaunde yow all without delay
           Toward felde drawe, in all the haste ye may."

Gower, *Conf. Am.* III, p. 58:
           "And he with all the hast he might
           A spere caught."

p. 255:   "With all the haste that they might,
           They riden to the siege ayein."

1910. *mortal*] = deadly, destructive to life, fatal, causing death, occurs frequently in our text. Comp. l. 2465, 3134, 3406, 3418, 3737, 4013, 4260. The word occurs very often with the same meaning in other works of Lydgate. From the *Pilgr.* I have collected the following instances: 9056 "mortall ffo," 10242 "mortal ennemy," 10525 "mortal stryff," 13679 "mortal ffer," 13959 "mortal lawe," 12485 f. "dedly synne .. The wych ycallyd ys 'mortal.'" In *F. of Pr.* the examples are far too numerous to be enumerated here, comp. only 1 7 B vi "his mortal distres," C i *b* "all his mortall peynes," "the furious mortall heauinesse," I, 8 C iii "the mortal vengeaunce," C iv "his mortal fone." In the *Play before Eestfeld*, st. 3 (Add. MS. 29729, fol. 134 *b*) "mortal" is used in contrast to "heuenly": "gyfftes that be both heuenly and mortale"; in *Pilgr*. 9306 it has a similar signification: "this mortal lyff," also in *F. of Pr.* I, 1 A vi *b*: "this mortall life." In *Pilgr.* 14847 the word seems simply to mean *great, violent,* "mortal rage"; also in *F. of Pr.* I, 1 A v *b*: "manye mortall strife of hote and colde." Characteristic of Lydgate's tendency to tautologize are such phrases as "deadly mortall payne" (*F. of Pr.* I. 1 A iv *b*), "dedly mortal wo" (*Pilgr.* 12157).

1926. Comp. Chaucer, *Knightes Tale* 519 "turned was al up-so-doun"; Gower, *Conf. Am.* I, p. 282: "All up so down my joie it casteth"; II, p. 20: "all the world torne up so down"; III, p. 189: "It maketh a lond torne up so down"; Hoccleve, *R. of Pr.* 5087: "pryue galle all turnyth vp-so-do*u*n." From Lydgate's works comp. *Pilgr.* 17388: "tourne al vp-so-doun"; further *F. of Pr.* 1, 8 C iii:

". . . if it wer by incantacion
·which so wel could turne vp so do*u*n
Sundry thinges of loue and of hatred;"

1, 23 G vi : "losse & fortune hath turned vpso doun our grace."
1934. Comp. the portrait of Envye given in the *Romaunt* 247–300.
1946. *to bere the belle*] to be the first or leader, in allusion either to the bell which was the prize at a horse-race, or to the leading horse of a team or drove, that wears a bell. Comp. *Cent. Dict.* The expression occurs *Troy-Book*, II, 3 B i *b* : "For of connynge he myght bere the bell." Chaucer, *Troilus*, III, 198 :

"lat see which of yow shal bere the belle
To speke of love a-right."

In *Secrees* we have the phrase "to bear away the flour"; see 224: "of Tullius gardyn he bar awey the fflour"; 1176: "Clergye beryth a-wey the fflour"; also in *F. of Pr.* I, 15 F v: "for he (viz. Adones) of fayrenes bare away the floure." Gower prefers the expression "to bear the prize." See *Conf. Am.* I, p. 135: "my lady berth the prise," and III, 298 f. :

"he all other men surmounteth
And bare the prise above hem alle."

Comp. also *F. of Pr.* I, 14, E vi :
"she in hir auice
Of this victory should beare away þ*e* pryce."

And F i *b* : "he bare away the pryse."

1950. *to holde chaunpartye*] This expression is very frequent in Lydgate, as Schick has already pointed out. See note on l. 1164 of the *T. of Gl.* I may be allowed to adduce the following instances from the first book of the *F. of Pr.*

B iii : "and let your power proudely vnderfong
your self with pryde, for to magnifye
against the heauen to holden champartie."

C ii : "Hector .. againe al tilles holdeth champartie."

D i : "Where god aboue holdeth champartee
there mai ayeinst him be made no defence."

1953 f. Comp. *Troy-Book* II, 12 F vi *b* :

"For he desyreth of knyghtly hye prudence
To stynte werre and to norysshe pes
For he is nouther rakel nor rekles."

F. of Pr. 1, 9 D iv *b*: "to stint warre, and to cherish peas."

2071 ff. With the marginal note may be compared Fulgentius, *Mythol.* II, i, and Vincent de Beauvais, *Spec. Doctr.* V, cap. 34.

2232. *dalyaunce*] The word means here as well as in ll. 6576 and 7024 merely conversation. See *F. of Pr.* I, 18 G i *b*, where it is said of Zenocrates that "he was solayne of his daliaunce." Comp. the notes of Schick on l. 291 of the *T. of Gl.* and of Triggs on l. 1509 of the *A. of G.*

There are instances in which the word has a wider signification: *Countenance de table* (Add. MS. 5467, fol. 67 *b*): "All honest myrthe latte be thy daliaunce."

2256. Comp. *F. of Pr.* I, 14 E vi *b*: "Althea gan sore muse and heng in abalaunce"; also 1, 8 D i *b*:

"Al earthly blisse dependeth in a were
in a balaunce vneuenly hanging."

I, 5 C iii *b* : "And thus she stode in Jupardye
Of loue and shame in maner of a traunce
Un-euenly hanged in balaunce."

2316. See also l. 2983. I refer the reader to Schick's note on l. 1026 of the *T. of Gl.* How often Lydgate recurs to such expressions, is evident from the following list containing the instances I have collected from the *Pilgr.* L. 997: "yt shal ynowh suffise"; 2146, "Wych ouhte ynowgh to yow suffyse"; 3009, "Yt ouhte ynowh to the suffyse"; 3378, "Yt outhe ynowgh to yow suffyse—The party that ye han ytake"; 4190, "yt doth nat ynowgh suffyse"; 5178, "A lytel dyde ynowh suffyse"; 5200, "so lytel qua*n*tyte . . Myghte of resou*n* ynowh suffyse"; 6963, "Wych doth nat ynowh suffyse"; 7246, "To me yt doth ynouh suffyse." See further 9895, 10741, 11023, 11784, 12920, 13438, etc. In some cases the pleonasm is already contained in the original : l. 3378 f. reads in the French: "Souffire vous dëust assez—La partie que vous avez." I think it will not be out of place here to add a list of other pleonastic expressions found in Lydgate's works—*Pilgr.* 3931: "The comou*n* good in general"; 4990, "bothë tweynë be mortal;—The Ton, the tother, in certeyne—They be but wermës bothë tweyne"; 5255, "The trouthë trewly to conceyve"; 5279, "verrayly in dede"; 5316, "ffor profyt off thy*n* ownë speed"; 5724, "He that was wysest in bataylle, Off wysdam & dyscrecyou*n*"; 6208 and 6265, "bothë tweyne"; 15969, "bothë two yffere"; 9125, 9938 and 13470, "to-gydre yffere"; 11603, "thys ylkë samë weye"; 12007, "the syluë samë place"; 15184, "the syluë samë Tre"; 14953, "Round aboute*n* envyrou*n*"; 19986, "allone, al sool"; 17770, "worth off valu"; 20447, "Alt folkys ha suffysau*n*ce, Plente ynough." Under the same heading come such expressions as "to neghen nere," "aprochen nere," "aprochen & neghen ner," "avale a-doun," "dedly mortal." From the first book of the *F. of Pr.* I adduce the following instances : 7 C i, "verily in dede"; 8 C ii, "both twaine"; C iii *b*, "Sonne by discent of Jupiter," "He and his wife compelled both two"; 10 D vi *b*, "There is no damage in comparison, that may be likened by no resemblaunce"; 11 E ii, "This tragedy sheweth a figure,—a maner of ymage, and also likenes."

2390–2397. Middle-English poets often try to render descriptions of merry-makings more graphic by a detailed list of the performers and the instruments used. Cp. here l. 5571–5592 of our poem, also Chaucer, *Hous of Fame* 214-26, *Roman de la Rose* 763 ff. A similar enumeration occurs in the *Squyr of Lowe Degre* 1069 ff. (Joseph Ritson, *Ancient Engleish Metrical Romanceës*, III, p. 189-190):

"There was myrth and melody
With harpe, getron and sautry,
With rote, ribible, and clokarde,
With pypes, organs and bumbarde,
With other mynstrelles them amonge,
With sytolphe and with sautry songe

With fydle, recorde, and dowcemere,
With trompette, and with claryon clere,
With dulcet pipes of many cordes,
In chambre revelyng all the lordes,
Unto morne that it was daye."

Comp. also the following lines from *Sir Degrevant* (Halliwell, *The Thornton Romances*, p. 178):

"He was ffayre mane and ffree,
And gretlech yaff hym to gle,
To harp and to sautré,
And geterne fful gay;

Well to play in a rote,
Of lewtyng, well y wote,
And syngyng many suet not,
He bare the pryes aey."

From the *Pilgrymage* I may be allowed to quote the following passages:

Youthe answers to the pilgrim, 1179:

"I wyl be ffethryd, & ga ffle,
And among, go sportë me;
Pleye at the cloos, among, I shal,
And somwhyle Rennyn at the bal
Wyth a Staff mad lyk an hook;
And I wyl han a kampyng crook;
Ffor I desyre, in my depos,
ffor to han noon other croos.
And among, I wyl nat spare
To hunte ffor hert, ffor buk & hare;
Somtyme ffysshe & cachchë fowlys,
And somtyme pleyen at the bowlys;
Among, shetyn at bessellys,

And affter pleyn at the merellys,
Now at the dees, in my yong age,
Bothe at hassard & passage;
Now at the ches, now at the tablys,
Rede no storyes but on ffablys,
On thyng that ys nat worth a lek;
Pleye at the keylës & the quek;
Somwhyle my wyttys I applye
To herë song & menstralcye,
And pleye on dyuers Instrumentys:
And the ffyn of myn entent ys
To folwe the best off my coráge,
And to spendë my yonge age
In merthe only, & in soláce,
ffolwe my lustys in ech pláce."

The damysele says, 11604 ff.:

"Gladly ffolkys I conveye,
Swych as louë paramours,
To ward the voode, to gadre fflours,
Soote rosys & vyalettys,
Ther-off to make hem chapelettys
And other fflourys to her plesaunce
And in thys weye I teche hem daunce;
And also, ffor ther lady sake,
Endyte lettrys, & songys make
Vp-on the gladë somerys dayes,
Balladys, Roundelays, vyrelayes.

I teche hem ek, (lyk ther ententys,)
To pleye on sondry Instrumentys,
On harpe, lut, & on gyterne,
And to revelle at tavérne,
Wyth al merthe & mellodye,
On rebube and on symphonye;
To spendë al the day in ffablys,
Pley at the ches, pley at the tablys,
At treygobet & tregetrye,
In karyyng & in Iogolory:
And to al swych maner play,
Thys the verray ryhtë way."

The fox flatters the raven, 14263 ff.:

"ffor trewly, as I kan dyscerne,
Ther ys harpë nor gyterne,
Symphonyë nouther crowde,
Whan ye lyst to syngë lowde,

Ys to me so gracyous,
So swete nor melodius
As ys your song with notys clere."

Pride observes in her speech, 14301 ff.

"Thys belwes ek (yt ys no drede)   Thys ffoutys ek, w*ith* sotyl musys,
Causeth (who-so taketh hede)   And thys shallys loudë crye."
Bombardys and cornemusys,

l. 2408. Comp. what Lydgate says on the invention of the game in the *Troy-Book* II, 11 F ii f. :

"of the chesse the playe moste gloryous
Which is so sotyll and so meruaylous
That it were harde the mater to discryue
For though a man studyed all his lyue
He shall ay fynde dyverse fantasyes
Of wardes makynge and newe Jupartyes
There is there in so great a dyuersyte
And it was firste founde in this cyte
Durynge the sege lyke as sayth Guydo
But Jacobus de vitriaco
Is contrarye of oppynyon
For lyke as he maketh mencion
And affermeth fully in his aduyse
How Philometer a philosopher wyse
Unto a kynge to stynte his crueltee
Fonde firste this play and made it in Caldee."

In Caxton's *Game and Playe of the Chesse* (ed. William E. A. Axon) we read p. 11 : "Thys playe fonde a phylosopher of Thoryent whiche was named in Caldee Exerses or in greke philometor."

Comp. farther, *Roman de la Rose*, l. 6975–6982 :

"Athalus,
Qui des echez controva l'us,
Quant il traitoit d'arismétique ;
Et verras en Policratique
Qu'il s'enflechi de la matire
Et des nombres devoit escripre
Où ce biau geu jolis trova,
Que par demonstrance prova."

See also the note of Marteau (II, p. 417), from which I may be allowed to quote the following interesting remarks : ". . . d'autres attribuent cette invention à Palamède, pendant le siége de Troie. On en fait aussi honneur à un certain Diomède, qui vivoit du temps d'Alexandre. Frère Jean de Vignay, dans son *Traité de la moralité de l'échiquier*, dit que le jeu des échecs fut inventé par un roi de Babylone, et que depuis, ce jeu fut porté en Grèce, ainsi que Diomède le Grec en fait foi dans ses livres anciens. Jérôme Vida, dans son poème sur les échecs, a feint que l'Océan, qui avoit joué de tout temps sous l'onde avec les Nymphes marines, apprit ce jeu aux Dieux célestes qui assistèrent aux noces de la Terre, et que dans la suite Jupiter ayant débauché Scacchide, nymphe d'Italie, il lui enseigna ce jeu pour prix des faveurs qu'elle lui avoit accordées ; et qu' enfin cette fille, qui lui donna son nom, l'apprit aux hommes. Sarrazin, dans sa curieuse dissertation sur ce jeu, croit que les Indiens l'apprirent aux Persans, ceux-ci aux Mahométans, et que ce fut par le moyen de ces derniers que ce jeu passa en Europe."

2459 ff. *Phoebus and Daphne*] The story is found in Ovid, *Met.* I, 452 ff. and Hyg. *Fab.* 203. Comp. Chaucer's *Troilus* III, 726–28 ; *Knightes Tale* 1204–6 ; *Conf. Am.* I, 336 ; *T. of Gl.* 112–16 ; see Schick's note.

2459–60. marginal note. Comp. *Virg. Eclog.* x, 69 : " Omnia vincit amor."

2460. *attamen*] O.E. *atemian* = subdue. A totally different word is *attamen*, from O.Fr. *atamer* = pierce, try, begin. We find it in Chaucer, *Nonne Preestes Tale*, Prol. 52 : "And right anon his tale he has attamed"; also in Lydgate, *F. of Pr.* I, 14 F. i: "Hercules .. high emprises proudly dyd attame"; 1, 15 F. iv *b* : "thus in her writing to hym she dyd attame." Hoccleve, *R. of Pr.* 2795 :

"Hem deyneth naght an accioun attame
At comun lawë.

2508. *Love and Deduit duelle y-fere*] Why and in how far Amours and Delectacion must go together is pointed out in *É. A.* fol. 29 *a* and *b*.

2535 f. Comp. *Pilgr.* 11758 :

"And lynë ryht vn-to the gaate
The weye I held."

In l. 11751, I think, we have also to read *lyne ryght :*

" by the samë gatë go
Wher as she stodë, lynë ryght."

Troy-Book I, 6 D iii *b* :

"And lyne ryght a-gayne the wromes hede
They holde it."

2558–2592. The pleasures in the garden of Deduit are described in a similar way in *De Vénus*, st. 221 ff. Comp. especially st. 242.

2568–92. The allusion to the portraits on the wall is Lydgate's work. The original reads—(Fol. 11 *b*) :

" Plus ne ten diray mais tu verras   Et com y vit Ioyeusement.
Bien que cest quant tu y venras   Et Il ne veult viure aultrement
En ce delittable vergiez   Briefment Il na cure de vie
Se seult esbattre *et* herbergier Ou Il ait orgueil ne enuie
Amours plus voulentierz quailleurs Ne nulle angoisseuse tristresse
Car ce li samble li meilleurs   Il ne veult que droite leesse
De tous les lieux ou Il sembat   Et Ieux et Ioye et amour toute."
Pour ce quadiez on si esbat

2636. further, O.E. fyrðrian, fyrðran = help, assist, promote, advance, is used frequently in Lydgate. Comp. *Pilgr.* 8122 : " yt sholde hem furthre neueradel."

9869 f. :   "Wych to me was no forthryng,
            But perturbaunce."

20913 f. :   "helpe hym that he myghtë spede,
            To ferthre hym in hys gret nede."

F. of Pr. I, 8 C iv *b*. :

"J bring a great witness,
My feathers head, and his deadly visage
Ayeinst nature to forthern your vyage."

And, a little later, "forthering .. of your ryght." Also in Chaucer and his followers the word is frequent. Comp. *Romaunt* 3504, *Parl. of Foul.* 384, *Troilus* I, 1707, *Legend*, Prol. A 484, 1477, 1618 ; Gower, *Conf. Am.* III, p. 185, 7 ; p. 188, 13.

2766. *tapite*] The word is not frequent. Comp. Fab. *Duor. Mercat.* 194 : "Her ioiful somer is tapited al in greene." *Book of the Duch.* 258 ff. :   "and al his halles
            I wol do peynte with pure golde,
            And tapite hem ful many folde
            Of oo sute."

Of more frequent occurrence is the subst. *tapit*. Comp. *F. of Pr.* I, 1 A iv *b*. : "For god and kind with freshnes of colours—and with their tapites, & motles of gladnes—had mad þe place aboundant in swetenes."
  2788 ff. marginal note. The reference to Pliny proves correct. See *Nat. Hist.* xii, 17-19. From Pliny we learn also why Diana is placed under an ebony tree. Comp. *Nat. Hist.* xvi, 214, where we read that the statue of the goddess at Ephesus was made of ebony. There is no mention of the Queen of Saba presenting King Solomon with the gift of ebony. In I. *Reg.* x. 11 ff. only "ligna thyina" occurs. Perhaps *Ezech.* xxvii. 15 suggested the comment which the annotator gave: "Filii Dedan . . dentens eburneos et ebeninos commutaverunt in pretio tuo." Dedan (Dadan) and Saba are frequently spoken of together. Comp. Wetzer and Welte, *Kirchenlexikon*.
  3081. For similar expressions see *Pilgr.* 9573: "as blynd as ys a ston"; 9834, "blynd as a ston."

9697 f.:	"Seyng cler he shold ha noon, Na mor than hath the coldë ston."
13902 f.:	"ffor they be dowmb in their spekyng, As an ymage wrouht off Tre or stoñ."
20921:	"as dowmb as stok or ston."
20927:	"ffor he ys ded, as ston or tre."
T. of Gl. 689:	"dovmb stil as eni stone" (comp. Schick's note).
1184:	"dovmb as eny stoñ."

Hoccleve, too, has such phrases: *Reg. of Princ.* 1496, ".dombe as ston."

1804:	"Myn hert is also deed as is a stoon."

3186. *to stonde in grace*] Comp. l. 1367. Also in other works of Lydgate. *F. of Pr.* I, 8 C v *b*:
  "Which was his wife *and* stode wel in his grace."

I, 15 F iv:	"He was enamered with the semelines and desyrous therof to stonde in grace."
	"no woma*n* so fresh ne faire of face that able were to stonden in his grace."

Chaucer uses the expression in *Prologue* 88, where we read of the squyer that he had borne him wel "in hope to stonden in his lady grace."
  Troilus ii, 714: "Now were I wys, me hate to purchace, With-outen nede, ther I may stonde in grace."

III, 472:	"So wel his werk and wordes he bisette, That he so ful stood in his lady grace."

See further iv, 10; iv, 1393 and Legend 1014.
In Hoccleve, *R. of Pr.* 1833 we read:
  "If þat þou stonde in his benevolence."
  3217. One of the stock phrases of Chaucerian literature. I confine myself to giving some instances which I have collected from Gower's *Conf. Am.* See I, p. 234:
  "Who so therof be lefe or loth With Deianire forth he goth;"

II, p. 24:	"for no thing that slouthe voucheth I may foryete her lefe ne loth."
p. 27:	"were hem leef or were hem lothe To ship he goth."

p. 65 :   " be him leef or loth
                    To Troie with hem foth he goth."
p. 153 :   " be hem lef or be hem loth
                    They suffre."
Comp. also II, p. 384, 5 ; III, p. 50, 25, and p. 180, 9.

3255. *davnce on) hir ryng*'] follow her desire or instigation. A similar expression is " to go on somebody's dance," comp. *Pilgr.* 17882 :
      " with this hand, I can adaunce
      Alle thys trwauntys everychon
      Wych that on my dauncë gon."

3259 ff. *Europa*] Ovid, to whom Lydgate refers, tells the story, *Met.* ii, 836 ff. It is repeatedly touched upon in Lydgate's writings ; see Schick's note on ll. 117–20 of the *T. of Gl.* Comp. also Chaucer, *Legend,* Prologue 113 ; *Troilus,* iii, 722 f. The author of the *É. A.* touches once more upon the story on fol. 42. With the first marginal note may be compared Isidor, *Etym.* xiv, 4, 1 :
      "Europa Agenoris regis Libyae filia fuit quam Jovis ab Africa raptam Cretam advexit."

3261–4. *Danae*] Lydgate's original, later on, gives a detailed account of the story. See *É. A.* fol. 42 b. The classical sources are Ovid, *Met.* iv, 608 ff. ; Hyg., *Fab.* 63 ; Hor., *Carm.* iii, 16, 1 ff.; Apollod., *Biblioth.* ii, 4.

3363–69. The sweetness of false delight ending in bitterness is a favourite theme of Lydgate and contemporaneous writers. Comp. the similar passage later on, 4015–4061, especially 4038–40. See further *Romaunt* 3229 f. and 3279–86 ; Hoccleve, *R. of Pr.* 721, 1299. In this connection might be mentioned those expressions which speak of " suger hiding galle, poysoun and tresoun," or of "gladnes medled with greuaunce." See *Troy-Book,* Prologue A ii *b*:
      " With sugred wordes vnder hony soote
      His galle is hyd lowe by the roote."

I, 5 C iii *b* : [Fortune] " can vndre sugre shrowde hir poyson."
Pilgr. 14286 ff :   " the blast of fflaterye
                    The wych, with hys sugryd galle,
                    Euery vertu doth appalle."
14704 f. : " In tast lyk sugre ; but the galle—Ys hyd " (viz. flattery). *Chorle and Bird,* Halliwell, p. 186 :
      " sugre strowed that hydethe fals poyson."
Secrees 677 : "Ther sugre is soote ther galle doth no good " (viz. of flatterers).
880 :   " Wheer double menyng hath ony existence
            Ther growith ffrawde And covert fals poysoun
            And sugryd galle honyed with Collusyoun."

889 : "[flatterers] Be outward sugryd And galle in existence."
F. of P. I, 7 C i *b* : " All worldly gladnes is medled with greuaunce "; " His littel sugre tempred with much gall " ; I, 8 C ii : " All worldly blisse is meint with bitternesse " ; C iii *b* : " Thus aye is sorowe medled with gladness." I, 10 D vi *b* :
      " Though þe roses at midsomer be ful sote
      yet vnderneth is hid a full sharpe spine ;
      some fresh floures haue a full bitter rote
      and lothsom gal can suger eke vndermine."

I, 12 E iii : " ay her (viz. Fortune) gladnes is meint with some enuy."

I, 13 E v b : " though a tale haue a fayre visage,
It may include ful great decepcion,
Hid vnder suger, gall and fell poyson."
Gower, *Conf. Am.* iii, p. 281 :
" all such such time of love is lore,
And lich unto the bitter swete,
For though it thenke a man first swete,
He shall well felen ate laste,
That it is soure and may nought laste,
For as a morsel envenimed,
So hath such love his lust mistimed."

3370. Comp. the description of Chymere in Isidor, *Etym.* xi, 3, 36 : " Fingunt et Chimaeram triformem bestiam : ore leonem, postremis partibus draconem, media capream." Another description of the fabulous beast is found in *F. of Pr.* I, 1 A vi b :
" the beast monstrous and sauage,
which called is the chymere of licye :
specially when he is in his rage,
which monstre had to his auantage. [!]
head of a Lyon as bokes determine
wombe of a Gote and tayle serpentine."

As to the quotation of the marginal note see *Epistola Valerii ad Rufinum* (Hieronymi operum Mantissa, ed. Vallarsi, xi, col. 240 ff.), cap. 2 : " Chimaeram nescis esse miser quod petis : vel scire devoves, quod triforme monstrum illud insignis venustetur facie leonis, olentis maculetur ventre capri, anguis insidietur cauda virulentae." How well this letter was known by Chaucer is pointed out by Koeppel in *Anglia* XIII, p. 181 ff.

3378. *Rammys*h *taraged as a goot*] Comp. Isidor, *Etym.* xii, 1 14 : " Hircus, lascivum animal, et petulcum, et fervens semper ad coitum, cuius oculi ob libidinem in transversum aspiciunt, unde et nomen traxit. Nam hirqui sunt oculorum anguli secundum Suetonium. cuius natura adeo calidissima est, ut adamantem lapidem, quem nec ignis, nec ferri domare valet materia, solus hujus cruor dissolvat." Comp. note on l. 6842.

3387 f. *Venus is seyde of venym*] Comp. 4581 : "Venus ys sayde of venquysshing." See further *Pilgr.* 8150 : " Venus ys sayd off venerye"; Fulg. *Mythol.* ii, 4 : "Venerem dici voluere, aut secundum Epicureos bonam rem, aut secundum Stoicos vanam rem."

3396 ff. *The tavern of Venus*] It is the same fiction that we have in the beginning of our poem with regard to Fortune. I refer once more to *Secrees* 249, where we hear of "the licour of Cytheroes tonne." Comp. note on l. 47 ff.

3398. *ypocras*] O.Fr. ipocras : a kind of cordial, once a favourite beverage. For its preparation see Halliwell, *Minor Poems* 216 : " of win and spices is maad good ipocras." The drink is also mentioned *Pilgr.* 12830, *Troy-Book*, ii, 58. In *Chaucer* the word occurs, *Phisic. Tale* 306. *Pyment* is wine with a mixture of spice or honey. Comp. Gower, *Conf. Am.* iii, p. 8 : "never pinent ne vernage—Was half so swete "; Chaucer, *Mill. Tale* 192.

l. 3414. *triacle*] O.F. *triacle :* a mediaeval compound of various ingredients formerly believed to be capable of curing or preventing the effects of poison. With regard to the history of the word see Morley, *Lib. of Engl. Lit.* p. 21. Its original meaning is preserved in the following instances : *Pilgr.* 7719, " No tryacle may the venym saue " (viz. of " A Tongë venymous ") ; and again 15337 f. :

"I tourne ek by collusïoun
Tryacle to venym *and* poysoun."

Æsop, iv, 148 :

"Ageyne verray poyson ordeyned is triacle."

Roman de la Rose, 13048 ff. :

"Car il ne resuscitera,
Se déables n'i font miracles,
Ou par venins ou par triacles."

Frequently the word adopts a more general meaning. See *Assembly of Gods*, x, 12 :

"To rowne *with* a pylow me semyd best tryacle." (Comp. Triggs's note.)

Pilgr. 67f.: "A-geyne whas strokë, helpeth no medycyne,
Salue, tryacle, but grace only dyvyne."

Fab. *Duor. Mercat.* 446 :

"His freend to hym abrochyd hath the tonne
Of freendly triacle."

How the plage was sesyed in rome, st. 6, 1 (Add. MS. 29729):

"Not golde potable nor pured quintessense
not Rewe barbaryn nor Alpharike Triacle
surmownte the power of myghty pestilence."

Ordenaunce of *a presesyon*, st. 14, 5 (Add. MS. 29729):
"goostly tryacle and owr lyves boote—
ageynst the sorowes of worldely pestelence."

See also Chaucer B. 479 and C. 314. In *Piers Plowman* 11, 146, Love is called "a triacle of heven." *De Triacle et de Venin* is the title of an interesting poem in A. Jubinal, *Nouveau Recueil de Contes, Dits, Fabliaux*, I, p. 360 ff.

3416. See also l. 3454–58. Comp. *Pilgr.* 8158 ff. :

"in thys bataylle
Ther geyneth power noon, nor myht,
Nor other rescus but the fflyht,
ffor flyht ys only best diffence ;
And ffor to makë résistance
A-geyn hyr dredful mortal werre,
The ffyht *with* hyre ys best a-ferre."

And again 8175–8193. In *Romaunt*, 4777–81, we read :

"But if thou wolt wel Love eschewe,
For to escape out of his mewe,
And make al hool thy sorwe to slake,
No bettir counsel mayst thou take,
Than thinke to fleen."

Note on l. 3489 may also be consulted.

3418–20. Comp. *Romaunt* 3229 f. :

"Hir aqueyntaunce is perilous,
First softe, and aftir[ward] noyous."

3421–31. The transformation is told in Ovid, *Metam.* xiv, 154 ff. Comp. Hyg., *Fab.* 125, 156, 199. The drink of Circe is again mentioned in l. 4093–4101. Allusions to this antique sorceress are numerous in Chaucer, Gower, and other works of Lydgate.

3489–94. Comp. *Romaunt* 4677–79, where Raisoun says of the God of Love :

"For if thou knewe him, out of doubt,
 Lightly thou shulde escapen out
 Of the prisoun that marreth thee."

3502–5. Comp. *Romaunt* 4643 ff. :
"Thou felle in mischeef thilke day,
 Whan thou didest, the sothe to say,
 Obeysaunce and eek homage."

3521 ff. There are two other accounts of Jason's story in Lydgate's works: *Troy-Book* i, 5–7, and *F. of Pr.* i, 8. Comp. Schick's note on l. 62 of the *T. of Gl.* The verses of the *Troy-Book* often remind us of our poem. Comp., for instance, the following lines :

(A. v): "And who that wolde to encrease his glorie
 This Ram of golde wynne by the victorie,
 First he muste of verry force and myght
 Vnto oultrance with this bullys fyght
 And them venguysche alderfirste of all
 And make them humble as any oxe in stall
 And to the yok and do them ere the londe."

In the *R. de la R.* the story is told l. 9843 ff. and 13827–13860. Comp. also Chaucer, *Legend* 1580 ff. and Gower, *Conf. Am.* ii, 236 ff. In the *É. A.* fol. 39, the story is referred to once more.

3525. Comp. *F. of Pr.* I, 8 C ii : "Out of Colchos when they ·gan remewe." *Troy-Book*, II, 11 F i : "by perce whan he went."

3528. Comp. *F. of Pr.* I, 8 C ii : "The ram which bare þe fleese of gold."

3595. The French text is here much shorter and simpler. It reads (Fol. 15 a) :
"Car cil qui sont layens happe
 Il sont assez mieulx attrappe
 Que nest en enfer tantalus
 Cest la maison de dedalus
 Qui si soubtilment fu tissue
 Que nulz ne puet trouuer lissue."

The house of Dedalus is mentioned once more in the French original; see l. 77 of Körting's text. Chaucer, too, has allusions to this miraculous house: *Legend* 2012 ff. ; *Boetius* III, pr. 12, 165 ; and *Hous of Fame* 1320 ff. :
"An hous, that *domus Dedali*,
 That *Laborintus* cleped is,
 Nas maad so wonderliche, y-wis,
 Ne half so queynteliche y-wrought."

Comp. also Skeat's note on this passage and Schick's note on l. 84 of the *T. of Gl.* I think the *R. de la R.*, which frequently touches upon the story of Jason, must again be held responsible for such allusions. Of course many classical authors also tell the story. Comp. Virgil v, 588 ; Ovid, *Met.* viii, 158 ; Deodor. I, 61. 97 ; iv, 77. I am unable to explain what *clowthy* means. Are we, perhaps, to read *clew-thyng* or simply *clew* ? Comp. *F. of Pr.* i, 8 C iv *b* :
"who that entred his retourne was in vein,
 Without a clewe for to resort ageyn ; "

Chaucer, *Legend* 2140 f :
"His wepen, his clew, his thing that I have said,
 Was by the gayler in the hous y-laid . . . ; "

in l. 2016 we hear of "a clewe of twynne"; in Gower, *Conf. Am.* ii, p. 306, Adriagne gives Theseus "a clue of threde."

3620 ff., marginal note. The quotation is from *Etym.* xi, 3, 30 f.

3668. Comp. *F. of Pr.* I, 9 D iv *b*: "was neuer man that stode in worse plite." Chaucer, *Troilus* ii, 711 f.:

"Paraunter he mighte have me in dispyt,
Thurgh which I mighte stonde in worse plyt."

Phrases like "to stonde, spiourne, be enhanced in a plyt" are used very frequently in Hoccleve; see *Reg. of Pr.* 63, 1221, 1362, 1468, 1733, 3587.

3685 ff. The marginal note refers to *Ezech.* viii. 14: "Mulieres sedebant plangentes Adonidem."

3685. *Adonydes*] As far as I know this rather unusual form occurs only here. In *F. of Pr.* I, 15 F v, we find *Adones*, rhyming with *pereles*. The usual form is *Adoun*, comp. *T. of Gl.* 64; *F. of Pr.* F v; *Black Knight*, 386; Chaucer, *Knightes Tale* 1366; *Troilus* iii, 721 (Adoon). See Schick's note on l. 64–66 of the *T. of Gl.* The story found its way directly from the *R. de la R.*, where it is told in the same detailed manner as in our poem, in l. 16347 ff.; comp. also 10895–897. Ovid tells the story in *Met.* x, 503 ff.

3727. This line seems to have been almost a standing formula. See Chaucer, *Parlement of Foules* 195: "The dredful roo, the buk, the hert and hinde." Gower, *Conf. Am.* ii, p. 45:

"She sigh the bestes in her kinde,
The buck, the doo, the hert, the hinde."

p. 68: "With hert and hinde, buk and doo"; "As buk and doo and hert and hinde." Comp. also the following lines from Lydgate's *Pilgr.* 8098 ff.:

"Huntyng for hert outher for ynde,
Chasyng for Rayndeer or for Roo,
Huntyng for buk outher for do?"

3751–3802. The story of Venus and Mars ensnared by Vulcan is a favourite theme of mediaeval authors. We find it in the *R. de la R.* 14445–786, also in Gower's *Conf. Am.* ii, p. 148 ff. Chaucer based his *Compleynt of Mars* upon it. Comp. also *Knightes Tale* 1525 ff.; *Troilus* iii, 22 724 f. For other allusions to Mars and Venus in Lydgate's writings, see Schick's note on l. 126–28 of the *T. of Gl.*

With l. 3791 f. is to be compared Chaucer, *Hous of Fame* i, 138 f.: "Vulcano,—That in his face was ful broun." Gower, *Conf. Am.* ii, p. 149:

"his figure,
Both of visage and of stature,
Is lothly and malgracious."

These traits are in accordance with the portrait of Vulcan given by the mythographers; see Albr. l. c. V: "Vulcano deo ignis, rustico turpissimo, in conjugium erat consignata." I may here refer to the "locus classicus" of the story of Venus and Mars: Homer, *Odyssey* viii, 266–366.

3755. There is no doubt that our author refers to the bed in the *Roman de la Charette* which is pierced by a lance. Comp. *Hist. Litt.* xv, p. 257.

3773. *compass* = contrivance, plotting. Comp. Chaucer, *Hous of Fame* 461 f.:

"How, maugre Juno, Eneas,
For al hir sleighte and hir compas,
Acheved al his aventure."

Gower, *Conf. Am.* i, p. 238, "his sligh compas." In Chaucer as well as in Gower we also find the form *compasment.* See *Legend* 1416; *Conf. Am.* i, p. 237, 19. In the *Temple of Glas* 871 we have the verbal noun *compassing* with the same meaning. The verb *compassen* occurs several times in Chaucer and Gower. See *Romaunt* 194, *Legend* 1414 and 1543; *Conf. Am.* i, p. 240, 14, and 263, 23; iii, p. 161, 4, etc. I find it also in other works of Lydgate. See *F. of Pr.* 1, 8 C iii. :

"This Medea voyde of shame and drede,
Compassed hath of wilfull false hatrede,
that Theseus the sonne of king Egee,
with newe poyson shal deuoured be."

C iv : "by full false treason—she compassed the destruccion"; I, 10 D vi : "This he compassed full falsly of malice"; I, 11 E i [Tyestes] :

"compassed a mene
By sleighty wyles that wer incomparable
To corrupt my wiues chastitie."

3798. *tachchis* = manners, qualities; the word has the same meaning in Chaucer, *Hous of Fame* 1777 f. :

"Ye masty swyn, ye ydel wrecches,
Ful of roten slowe tecches."

Also in *Romaunt* 6517 :

"riche men han more tecches
Of sinne, than han pore wrecches."

Hoccleve, *Reg. of Pr.* 3364: "wykked teichës and vices eschue." The word usually means *defect,* Fr. tache, see Körting 8004. Instances are numerous. See l. 6183 of our poem; *F. of Pr.* 1, 13 E v : "weomen .. haue no tatche of mutabilitie"; Chaucer, *Against Women Unconstant* 18 : "That tache may no wight fro your herte arace." *Troilus* iii, 934 f. :

"wrecches wol not lere
For verray slouthe or othere wilful tecches."

3802. *wilde fire*] Here the expression does not mean a disease, erysipelas, although it is frequently found in the execrations of that time. Comp. Chaucer, *Reves Tale* 252 : "A wilde fyr up-on thair bodyes falle." *Marchantes Tale* 1008 :

"A wilde fyr and corrupt pestilence
So falle up-on your bodies yet to-night."

In our passage *wilde fire* means a fire not easily put out. Comp. *Wife of Bath's Prol.* 373 : "Thou lyknest it (viz. woman's love) also to wilde fyr." *Troy-Book* I, 2 A v :

"Out of whose mouthe leuen and wylde fyre
Lyke a flawme euer blased out."

Gower, *Conf. Am.* ii, p. 200 :

"A wilde fire into the depe
They caste among the timber werke."

The French for l. 3802 reads: "Elle vouldroit quil fust ore ars."

3803–96. The French has only 40 ll. The idea of placing the fatal well into the garden of Deduit originates from the *R. de la R.* which relates the history of the unfortunate lover in l. 1487 ff. Lorris's source was Ovid, *Metam.* iii, 407 ff. Our poem touches once more upon the story from l. 4258–63.

3812. *tarage*] Old French *terrage, tarrage, tarage.* Comp. Furnivall's note on l. 9462 of the *Pilgr.* The word does not occur in Chaucer, but there are some more instances in Lydgate's writings. See l. 3931 and 3943 of this poem. Comp. further *Secrees* 1886: "[Watrys] Which tarage haue of foreyn dyvers sondys," and 2001: "Of tarrage and stok good and holsom wyne."

Pilgr. 9457 f.: "the ffrut ....
         Bereth the tarage off the tre."
9462:   "The bud hath tarage off the roote."

Chorle and Bird (Halliwell, p. 180): "holsom fressh tarage" (viz. of wine); and further (p. 192):
         "frute and trees and folke of every degre
         Fro whens they come they take a tarage."

Tretis of the kynges coronacion st. 2, 4 (Add. MS. 29729):
         "arthoure was knyghtly and charles of gret prise
         And of all these thy grene tender age
         ..... shalle take a tarage."

Troy-Book, Prol. A i b:
         "The rootis vertue thus can the sent renewe
         In euery parte the tarage is the same."

F. of Pr. I, 13 E v.:
         " of the stocke the fruite hath hys tariage (!),
         pilgrimes may go ful ferre in their passage
         But I dare say, how farre that euer they go
         there bideth some tarrage of y^t they cam fro."

E V b.: "tonges that haue a tarage of treason." In his glossarial index Steele interprets the word by *flavour;* this sense would be perfectly suitable in some cases; in other instances, however, the meaning is more general, and means perhaps *kind* or *quality.*

ll. 3897 ff. The whole chapter numbers only 58 ll. in the French, just half the number employed by Lydgate. The story of Pyramus is only briefly treated (Fol. 16):

         "Ainsy se la lettre ne ment
         Se mua anchiiennement
         Par maniere assez merueilleuse
         Un mourier par la mort piteuse
         De P*y*ramus et de tisbe
         Qu*a*nt Ilz furent si destourbe
         Pour la grant paour du lyon
         Quil en prirent occasion
         Deulx occire a leurs proprez mains."

For the primary source comp. Ovid, *Metam.* iv, 55 ff. How much this classical tale was in favour with Middle English poets is shown by Schick's list in his note on l. 80 f. of the *T. of Gl.* To the instances given by Schick might be added *Amor vincit omnia*, st. 3 f. (Add. MS. 29729).

3941. *lake*] The word occurs in Chaucer, *Sir Thopas* 147:
         "He dide next his whyte lere
         Of cloth of lake fyn and clere
         A breech and eek a sherte."

It means a kind of white linen cloth. *Laken* is not only a common Dutch word (comp. Skeat, *Student's Chaucer*), but also a Low-German expression for *blanket.*

3955 ff. Comp. Ovid, *Metam.* iv, 125 f.:
         "Arborei fetus aspergine caedis in atram
         Vertuntur faciem."

The changing colour of the fruit I think gave rise to this fable. See Plinius, *Nat. Hist.* xv, 97 : "Moris sucus in carne vinosus, trini colores, candidus primo, mox rubens, maturis niger."

3995. algate] O.E. algeats = altogether. Here the meaning is *under all circumstances, at any rate.* Comp. *Pilgr.* 2178 :

"Thus sholde every shepperde do,
Resoun algatë techeth so."

Troy-Book I, 6 D ii b :

"And if sole that thou wylt algate
Thy purpose holde."

F. of Pr. I, 23 G v b : "we algate shall dye." In Chaucer the word occurs, also in the extended form *algates*, often enough; we find it also in Gower's *Conf. Am.* iii, p. 55, 23 ; p. 16, 22, and p. 355, 14 ; in Hoccleve's *Reg. of P.* it is very frequent, comp. l. 1248 (algatës), 1828, 1986, 2055, 2240, 2943, 2991 (al-gatis), 3495, 3667, 3961 (algatës) 4659 (algatës), 4827.

4001–14. Comp. Plinius, *Nat. Hist.* xvi, 51 : "Hanc Sextius smilacem a Graecis vocari dicit : et esse in Arcadia tam praesentis veneni, ut qui obdormiant sub ea cibumve capiant, moriantur." Comp. also what Pliny later on (64) tells of the ash-tree (fraxinus) : "tantaque est vis, ut ne matutinas quidem, occidentisve umbras, cum sunt longissimae, serpens arboris eius attingat, adeo ipsam procul fugiat." In a similar way the Physiologi fabulize about the tree Peridexion.

4022–32. *a serpent daring under flours*] One of Lydgate's favourite figures of speech. Comp. *Pilgr.* 15158 ff. :

"ffor I resemble the serpent,
Wych, vnder herbys fressh *and* soote,
Ys wont to daren by the roote."

Troy-Book I, 5 C iii :

"vnder floures depeynt of stabylnesse
the serpent dareth of newfangelnesse."

F. of Pr. I, 19 G iii :

"She [viz. Dalilah] like a serpent daring vnder floures,
or lyke a worme that wroteth in a tree,
Or like an adder of manyfolde couloures,
right freshe appering and faire vpon to see
For shrowded was her mutabilitee
with lowlihede," etc.

I think we must make the *R. de la R.* responsible for the frequency of this figure. Comp. l. 17270–17300. The lines of Virgil referred to in this passage read :

"Qui legitis flores et humi nascentia fraga
Frigidus, o pueri, fugite hinc, latet anguis in herba." (Egl. iii, 92 f.)

Comp. Marteau's note 15 in vol. iv.

4112. *Empedokles*] philosopher, poet and physician, born after 500 B.C. at Agrigentum in Sicily, died about sixty years old. Comp. Horat. *Ep.* I, 12, 20 ; Cicero, *De Orat.* I, 50 ; for further references see Überweg-Heinze, *Geschichte der Philosophie des Altertums*, 8 Aufl. 1894. The story about Ætna is rejected as fictitious by Strabo. As to the story itself see the account in Lemprière, *Class. Dict.* p. 324. The *R. de la R.* refers to this story in l. 17739 ff.

4113 f. The original reads : "Qui trop mellancolieux fu." "Fols et melancolieux," a frequent expression in O.F. poetry.

4116. The French reads:
(fol. 16):
"Car le feu dont Venus esprent
Est plus ardant qui garde y prent
Et plus nuist anchois con lestaigne
Que li feux dethna la montaigne."

4127–4226. In the original, this chapter contains only 41 lines. The 20 lines referring to the story of Icarus and Phaethon are expanded into 66 lines. As to the story of Icarus see *Met.* viii, 183 ff.; Hygin, *Fab.* 40; *R. de la R.* 5468 ff. Comp. also *Hous of Fame* 920 ff. Phaethon's story is told in Ovid, *Met.* ii, 47 ff. Comp. also *Hous of Fame* 941 ff.; *Troilus* v, 663–65.

4178. *fethres white and donne*] Comp. *Pilgr.* 3830: "the skyës dyrke & donne"; *T. of Gl.* 30: "skyes donne"; see Schick's note; *Balade gyuen vnto þe king henry* (Add. MS. 29729, fol. 145 b), st. 2, 4; "skyes donne."

4191. *a-vale*, O.Fr. avaler = to come down, fall. Comp. *Pilgr.* 14245: "Thys wynd kan maken hem avale;" 20783 "avale a-doun."

4194. *A mene ys good in alle thing*] A favourite theme with M.E. writers—*mene, mesure* is the same notion which in M.H.G. poets figures as *mâze*. Comp. Wilmanns, *Leben und Dichten Walthers von der Vogelweide*, p. 238 f. and iii, 493. Comp. *F. of Pr.* I, 9 C iii b:
"who climeth highest, his fal is fardest down
a mene estate is best, who could it knowe,
twene high presumig & bowig down to low."

Countenance de table (Add. MS. 5467 Fol. 68):
"Be meke in mesure not hasty bot tretable
Ouermoche is not worth in nothing."

In Chaucer's *Book of the Duchesse* 881 f. the lover, praising his lady, tells us:
"In alle thinges more mesure
Had never, I trowe, creature."

Hoccleve, *R. of Pr.* 1335:
"Mesure is good; let hir þe gye and lede,
Be war of outrage";

in l. 2420 f. the poet says of a king:
"If he his tongë with mesures reyne
Gouernë, than his honur it conserueth."

Male Reglê 356: "let the mene thee souffyse."

4265 f. Comp. *Troy-Book*, II, 11 F i:
"suche as coude with countenaunce glade
Make an Image that wyll neuer fade
To countrefete in metall tree or stoon
The sotyll werke of pygmaleon."

4265–4280. Ovid, to whom Lydgate (but not the French poet) refers, tells the story of Pygmalion, *Met.* x, 243 ff. Again the simplicity of the French text contrasts with the prolixity of Lydgate's version in a striking manner;
(fol. 16 b): "Et pymalions ensement
Y ayme vne ymaige dyuoire
Quil meismez cest chose voire
Auoit fait a ses proprez mains
Et laoure et sert soirs et mains
Et a soy meismez estriue
Comme se ce fust chose viue."

Comp. with these last two lines ll. 4279-80 of our poem:
"Which made hym selfe [for] to stryve,
Lyche as hyt had[de] ben) alyve."
Pygmalion plays an important part in the *R. de la R.* l. 21593-21877.
See Marteau's note 75. In Lydgate's original we hear again of Pygmalion
later on, see *É. A.* fol. 37. Comp. also Chaucer, *Phis. Tale* 13:
"lo I, Nature,
Thus kan I forme and peynte a creature,
whan that me list; who can me countrefete?
Pigmalion noght, though he ay forge or bete,
Or grave, or peynte."
4227-4344. Comp. with these 118 lines the corresponding 58 lines
in the French text. ll. 4242-51 read in the French simply:
"Car Il se fait
Bon chastiier par aultrui fait."
4284. Pasiphae, like Medea and Mirra, is referred to in *De Planctu
Naturae*, l. c. p. 450: "Pasiphae etiam hyperbolicae Veneris furiis agitata,
sub facie bovis sophistice cum bruto bestiales nuptias celebrans, paralo-
gismo sibi turpiori concludens, stupendo bovis conclusit sophismate."
The story is told in Ovid, *Ars. Am.* i, 295 ff.; it is referred to in Chaucer,
Wife of Bath's Prol. 733-36.
4287. The story of Mirra is narrated in *Met.* x, 298; Hyg., *Fab.* 58,
275; Boccaccio, *De Cas. Vir.* and Lydgate's *F. of Pr.* (i, 15). See again,
De Planctu Naturae, l. c.: "Mirrha etiam cupidinis aculeis stimulata in
patris dulcore, a filiae amore degenerans, cum patre matris exemplavit
officium."
4300. There is no reference to Phaedra in the *R. de la R.*, nor in Alanus
ab Insulis. But the classical sources of her story are very numerous.
Comp. Hyg., *Fab.* 47, 243; Virg., *Æn.* vi, 445; Ovid, *Her.* 4, 74;
Ars. Am. i, 511 ff. The story has found a pathetic treatment in the
Hippolyt of Euripides and Seneca, it is contained in Boccaccio's *De Cas.
Vir.* and Lydgate's *F. of Pr.* (i, 12). Phaedra, sister of Ariadne, is also
mentioned in Chaucer, *Hous of Fame* 419, and in *Legend* 1970 ff.
4302. For the classical sources for the story of Tereus, see Hyg., *Fab.*
45; Ovid, *Met.* vi, 424 f.; Virg. *G.* 4, 15. 511. In a later part of the
French original the story is told at great length. See fol. 37 b and 38
of the Dresden MS. See also Chaucer's *Legend of Philomela* in the
Legend of Good Women 2228 ff. and *Troilus* ii, 64-70; Lydgate's *T. of
Gl.* 97-99 (see Schick's note), and, last not least, the detailed account in
Gower's *Conf. Am.* ii, 313 ff.
4307 ff. The French original only devotes three lines to this story.
Comp. Ovid, *Met.* viii, 6 ff.; *Trist.* ii, 393; Hyg., *Fab.* 198; Boccaccio's
Tragedies and Lydgate's *F. of Pr.* i, 8. Comp. Chaucer, *Legend* 1907 ff.,
Parl. of Foul. 292, and Skeat's notes.
4329 ff. I refer back to the note on l. 3521 ff. Comp. also Alanus ab
Insulis, *De Planctu Naturae* l. c. p. 450: "Medea vero proprio filio
novercata, ut inglorium Veneris opus quaereret, gloriosum Veneris de-
struxit opusculum."
4333. The story of Phillis is told in Ovid, *Her.* 2; see also *Ars. Am.*
ii, 353. f.; *Trist.* ii, 437; Hyginus, too, has a short account; *Fab.* 59 and
243. Comp. Schick's note on l. 86-90 of the *T. of Gl.* Schick's references
prove how very popular the story was in the Middle Ages.
4336 ff. Dido, too, is a figure often quoted in mediaeval authors.
Comp. the instances which Schick gives in his note on l. 55-61 of the

T. of Gl. The reference to Virgil is only in Lydgate's version. The author of the French original found the story in the *R. de la R.*

4337. *hest* with the meaning of *promise* is not very frequent, although not uncommon in M.E. Comp. Chaucer, *Troilus* v, 355 : "she nil hir hestes breken for no wight"; *Frankeleyns Tale* 336: "holdeth your heste."

Holy Rood 74 : "That thai had bene cumen right
To the land of heste."

In Hoccleve's *Reg. of Pr. hestes* occurs four times : 1593, 3694, 4821, 4968, but always with the significatiom of *laws, orders*.

4497. *nat a myte*] mite, O.Fr. mite = a small coin, is frequently used to signify something very small or unimportant. Comp. Hein, *Über die bildliche Verneinung in der mittelenglischen Poesie* (*Anglia* xv, p. 134): "Keine münze wird in der mittelenglischen poesie haüfiger im bildlichen Sinne gebraucht als mite. Dieses wort kehrt überhaupt zur wiedergabe des an wert geringsten bei den me. Lichtern im vergleich zu allen andern bildern am häufigsten wieder."

4583. *roune*] to speake lowe, to whisper. Comp. *Troy-Book* 953 : "Some rownynge and some spake a-brode"; *F. of Pr.* I, 19 G ii *b* : "with hys (viz. Samson's) wife they (viz. Philistes) priuely gan rowne"; Chaucer, *Squiers Tale* 208 : "Another rowned to his felawe lowe." Gower, *Conf. Am.* ii, p. 307 :

"Theseus in a prive sted
Hath with this maiden spoke and rouned."

Hoccleve, *Male Regle* 172 : "rownyngly. I spak no thyng on highte." *R. of Pr.* 1271 :

"seint Ambrose, astonëd sore of this
Anon right rowned to his compaignye."

The verb is used transitively in Chaucer, *Hous of Fame* 2043 ff. :

"every wight . .
Rouned ech in otheres ere
A newe tyding prevely."

4678 ff. *The noble sentence of Caton*) is taken from Dist. iv, 28 :

"Parce laudato : nam quem tu saepe probaris,
Una dies, qualis fuerit, ostendet amicus."

Comp. Schick's note on l. 295 of the *T. of Gl.*

4715–26. The statement that Lycaon

"slough and mordred with his honde
Hys gestys soothly euerychon)"

is an addition of Lydgate's. According to Ovid, *Met.* i, 196 Lycaon was changed into a wolf, because he had tried to murder Jupiter himself, who was his guest. Comp. also Hyg., *Fab.* 176 ff. Gower tells the story of Lycaon in *Conf. Am.* iii, p. 204 f. Comp. also *F. of Pr.* I, 14 F i *b* f.

4927 ff. The quotation of the marginal note is taken from Ovid, *Ars. Am.* iii, 61 ff. :

"Dum licet, et veros etiamnum degitis annos,
Ludite : eunt anni more fluentis aquae ;
Nec quae praeteriit, iterum revocabitur unda,
Nec quae praeteriit, hora redire potest."

5120 ff. *Regia solis erat*] Thus begins the beautiful description in Ovid, *Metam.* ii, 1 ff.

5379–81. Passages in which the blindness of Cupid is mentioned are very frequent. Comp. *Pilgr.* 8135 f. : "Cupide—The blyndë lord"; *F. of Pr.* I, 14 T iii *b* : "blynd Cupide"; I, 23 G vi : "Poetes sayen

he is to blind to ben a Judge"; and again, "He is depaynt like a blynd archere." Chaucer, *Legend* 169-70:
"And al be that men seyn that blind is he,—
Al-gate me thoughte he mighte wel y-see."
Hous of Fame 136-37: "Cupide—Hir (viz. Venus) blinde sone"; *Romaunt* 3703: "The God of love, blinde as stoon"; Gower, *Conf. Am.* i, p. 43: "love is blinde and may nought se;" further, p. 328: Cupide
"which loves cause hast for to guide,
I wot now wel that ye be blinde;"
iii, p. 16: "The boteler (viz. of the two tons of Jupiter), which bereth the key,—Is blinde"; iii, p. 351: "the blinde god Cupide;" p. 369: "This blinde god."

5411-5514. The model of our poet's description is the *R. de la R.* But the two different bows and sets of arrows are by no means the invention of Lorris. We find them already in the works of his predecessors. Comp. for instance *De Venus la Deesse d'Amor*, st. 247-250:
"Icele cambre estoit la ou li deu d'amors
Auoit tos ses repairs, ses delis, ses retors.
Iluec uei deus koeures qui pendoient a flors,
Qui bien estoient paint des roses et de flors.
Et ens en l'un des koeures qui pendoit plus aual
Auoit saietes, li fer sont de metal,
Et li alquant de plonc: qui en ert naures par mal,
N'amera mais en cest siecle mortal.
A l'autre koeure qui pendoit par engin
Auoit saietes, li fer erent d'or fin;
Qui en ert naures al soir et al matin,
Ce fait amors torner a sa [maniere] enclin.
Li dex d'amor, quant se uait deporter,
De ces saietes fait auoec lui mener,
Contre ses dars ne se puet nus tenser,
L'un fait hair et l'autre fait amer."
Comp. *The Court of Love* 1315 f.:
"The Golden Love, and Leden Love thai hight:
The ton was sad, the toder glad and light."

Spencer also speaks of Cupid's "bow and shafts of gold and lead" (*Colin Clout* l. 807).

For other allusions to Cupid's different species of arrows see Schick's note on l. 112-16 of the *T. of Gl.*

In the story of Daphne told by Gower, Cupid casts a dart of gold through the heart of Phoebus, whilst he wounds Daphne with a dart of lead. See *Conf. Am.* i, p. 336, and again iii, p. 351 and 352.

5691-5696. The prolixity of this passage is obvious. Comp. what is said in Gower's *Conf. Am.* ii, p. 124-25 relative to the epitaph of Iphis:
"And for men shall the sothe wite
They have her epitaphe write
As thing, which shulde abide stable,
The lettres graven in a table
Of marbre were and saiden this:" etc.

6048 ff. *adamant*] The reference in the marginal note is to Aristoteles, ΠΕΡΙ ΟΥΡΑΝΟΥ ii, 2. This stone is also mentioned in some of the physiologi. See the lists in M. F. Mann, *Der Bestiaire Divin*, p. 31 ff. Lauchert's remarks about the origin of the chapter *De Magnete* (*Geschichte des Physiologus*, p. 32) are at least inaccurate. The mediaeval books on natural history, too, know the attractive power of the magnet. Comp. Isidor, *Etymol.* xvi, 4. 1 ; Vincentius Bellovacensis, *Speculum Naturale* viii, 19 f.; Brunetto Latini, *Livres dou Trésor* (ed. Chabaille), p. xi, where the editor gives an interesting account on the occurrence of this stone in Early French literature. It forms, of course, a component part of the different lapidaries. Comp. Marbod § xix ; first French Version, 19 (Pannier, *Lapidaires Français*, p. 50) ; *Lapid. of Modena* 21 (Pannier, p. 101); *Lapid. of Berne* 21 (Pannier, p. 130); *Lapid. of Cambridge* 18 (Pannier, p. 160).

l. 6079 ff. *awmber*] The yellowish translucent fossil resin found chiefly along the southern shores of the Baltic. Its electric properties were even known to the Ancients. Electric, called from the Greek name ἤλεκτρον. The gift of attraction perhaps was the reason that a piece of amber was used as an amulet to attract lovers. Comp. Isidor, *Etymol.* xvi, 8. 7 : " Ex ea fiunt decoris gratia agrestium feminarum monilia, vocari autem a quibusdam *harpaga*, eo quod attritu digitorum, accepta caloris anima, folia, paleasque, et vestium fimbrias rapiat, sicut magnes ferrum." Cp. further Isidor xvi, 8. 6 and 24. 1 ; xvii, 7. 31 ; *Spec. Nat.* viii, 103 f. Solinus cap. xx, 8, etc.

6123 can only mean : which, with regard to their figures, exhibit a great variation. The French reads: " Moult de merueilleuses figures."

6158. *Emeraudys grene*] smaragdi. Comp. Isidor, *Etymol.* xvi, 7. 1 ; *Spec. Nat.* viii, 99 ff.; Pannier, l. c. p. 41, 86, 118, 150, 244, and 262. The emerald was chosen on account of its wholesome effect upon the eyes.

6169 ff. See also ll. 6800–14 and 6873–6899 of our poem. Comp. *F. of Pr.* I, 8, C v. :

"Innocentes can not deme amys,
Namely of wiues that ben found true
Clerkes may write, but doutles thus it is,
of their nature they loue no thinges newe,
Stedfast of hert, they chaunge not their hew."

And again C v b. :

"sely women kepe thier (!) stedfastnesse,
aye vndefouled saue sumtime of their kind,
They muste puruay whan men be found vnkind."

The fickleness of the female sex is often touched upon in Middle-English and Old French poetry. Comp. *Troy-Book* i, 1845–1904 and iii, 4276–4342 ; *R. de la R.* 18820–36, 16996–17020, 10307–10330. *La Contenance des Fames* in A. Jubinal, *Nouveau Recueil de Contes* ii, p. 170 ff. The irony of Lydgate reminds me of two *other* poems in Jubinal's collection, *De la Femme et de la Pye*, l. c. ii, p. 326, and *Des Femmes*, l. c. II, p. 330. Comp. also *Li Epystles des Femes* and *L'Evangile as Fames* in Jubinal, *Jongleurs et Trouvères*, p. 21 ff. and 26 ff.

6195 ff. Literally Chaucer's favourite line. See *Knightes Tale* 903 : "For pitee renneth sone in gentil herte." Compare further *The Tale of the Man of Lawe* 562, *The Marchantes Tale* 742, *The Squieres Tale* 470, *Legend* 503. See Skeat's note on this line in his *Oxford Chaucer.*

The more general idea that *pite* and *gentilesse* are companions is also often expressed in mediaeval allegorical love-poetry. Comp. *De Venus la Deesse d'Amor* st. 183 :

"En cent mil cuers gentis n' i a un seul felon,
Humilite, gentillece, pitie sont compaignon."

Chaucer, *Legend* 1078 ff. (Dido and Aeneas) :

"Anoon her herte hath pitee of his wo,
And, with that pitee, love com in also ;

And thus, for pitee and for gentilesse,
Refresshed moste he been of his distresse."

Troilus III, 402 f. may also be compared.

6217 ff. On the fading away of youth and beauty there is a similar passage in *F. of Pr.* I, 1 A vi.

6262 ff. Comp. *F. of Pr.* 1, 13 E v:

"their husbondes in causes smal or grete
Whatsoeuer they say, they cannot counterplete.
Blessed be God þe hath them made so meke,
So humble and fearefull of their condicions
For though men would causes *and* matter seke
Ayeins their pacience to fynd occasions,
They have refused al contradiccions,
And them submitted throw their gòuernaunce
Onely to mekenes and womanly suffraunce
I speake of al, I speake not of one,
that been professed vnto lowlines,
thei mai haue mouthes, but langage haue thei none
al true husbondes can beare herof witnes,
for wedded men, I dare right well expresse,
That haue assayed and had experience,
Best can record of witly pacience.
For as it longeth to men to be sturdy,
And sumwhat froward as of their nature,
right so can weomen suffer patiently,
And all wronges humbly endure,
Men should attempt no maner creature,
And namely wemen their mekenes for to preue
which may wel suffer while no man doe them greue."

See what ll. 6791–6800 relate about meekness. With this passage may be compared *R. de la R.* 9495–9500.

6268. Comp. *F. of Pr.* I, 13 E IV.:

"thei mai haue mouthes, but langage haue thei none
al true husbondes can beare herof witnes."

I, 23 G v: "A mouth he hath, but wordes hath he none." Comp. also Schick's note on l. 823 ff. of the *T. of Gl.*

6276. The reference to the *philisophre* proves correct. Comp. Aristotle, ΠΡΟΒΛΗΜΑΤΑ, B. 3.

6300–14. Comp. *F. of Pr.* I, 19, G ii *b*.; further the last entry in the Add. MS. 29729, warning the false pity of ever-weeping women (vol. i, p. xxviii). The *R. de la R.*, too, points out how easily women are moved to tears.

6310. Comp. *Troilus* IV, 150 f.:

"the teres from hir eyen two
Doun fille, as shour in Aperill, ful swythe."

6342. How well women are able to keep within the bounds of propriety is also told in the *R. de la R.* 9697 ff., and 9740 ff.

6350. Comp. *F. of Pr.* I, 1 A vii: "false lust doth your bridell lede"; I, 3 B iii *b*: "Pride of Nembroth did the bridell lede"; I, 7 C i:

"fortune dyd his bridle lede
To great richesse."

I, 8 C iv: "feined fa[l]senes doth the brydle lede"; I, 20 G iv *b*: "doubleness dyd their brydle lede." Comp. also Schick's notes on l. 878

and 1197 of the *T. of Gl.* Similar phrases are used by Hoccleve, see *R. of Pr.* 365 f. and 2871 f.

6361–6374. Comp. *F. of Pr.* I, 19 G ii *b*:

"But weomen haue this condicion,
of secret thinges whan they haue knowleging
They holne inward their hertes ay freting
Other they must dye or discure,
So bretle of custome is their nature ....
Such double trust is in their weping
to kepe their tonges women cannat spare,
Such weping wiues euil mot them fare
and husbandes I pray god yeue them sorow,
That to them tel their counsail eue or morowe."

l. 6387–88. Cp. *Pilgr.* 14311 f.: "They blowe many a blast in veyn, They seuere the chaff fer fro the greyn." *Ryght as a rammes horne*, 7, 6 (Add. MS. 29729): "we dyde the cokkel from the puryd corne." *Pilgr. Perf.* (W. de W.) 134 *b*: "As the flayle tryeth þe corne from the chaffe."
Similar expressions might be collected from contemporaneous writers. Comp. Chaucer's *Leg.* Prologue A, 529): "Let be the chaf, and wryt wel of the corn." Gower, *Conf. Am.* I, p. 32: "The chaf is take for the corne"; p. 231: "bringe chaffe and take corn"; ii, p. 59: "To winne chaffe and lese whete."

6389 ff. *Serpent*] The notice that the serpent stops up its ears is found in the Bible, *Ps.* lviii, 5. Lauchert (p. 21, note 1) believes that this very passage has given rise to our story, which is found in Greek MSS., good Latin ones, and mediaeval versions of the *Physiologus*. Comp. Isidor's *Etym.* xii, 4. 12 (aspis); Brunetto Latini i, 5. 139; and *Spec. Nat.* xx, 20 f. See also Gower, *Conf. Am.* i, p. 57, etc. An allusion to our story is made in *Old English Homilies* (ed. Morris) ii, p. 49. For allusions in German and Italian literature see Lauchert, p. 173 ff., 190 and 198.

I think that the writer of the marginal note had in mind the passage from Isidor above referred to: "fertur autem aspis, cum coeperit pati incantatorem, qui eam quibusdam carminibus propriis evocat, ut eam de caverna educat, illa cum exire noluerit, unam aurem ad terram premit, alteram cauda obturat et operit."

6402–15. Comp. *F. of Pr.* 1. 13 E v:

"Fayth and flattery they been so contrary,
they may together hold no soiour,
Nor simples which that cannot vary,
May neuer accord with a baratour.
Neither innocence with a losengour.
Neither chastitie cannot herself apply,
Her to confourme unto no ribaudye."

Further *R. de la R.* 10289–302:

"Car il n'est fame, tant soit bonne,
Vielle ou jone, mondaine ou nonne,
Ne si religieuse dame,
Tant soit chaste de cors et d'ame,
Se l'en va sa biauté loant,
Qui ne se délite en oant :
Combien qu'el soit lede clamée,
Jurt qu'ele est plus bele que fée,
Et le face séurement,
Qu'el l'en croira legierement ;

    Car chascune cuide de soi
    Que tant ait biauté, bien le soi,
    Que bien est digne destre amée,
    Combien que soit lede provée."

6438 ff: *Panther*] Comp. the researches of Lauchert, p. 19. To the best of my knowledge, the animal forms a component part of each of the western physiologi. It is also contained in the fragment of the O.E. physiologus. Isidor (xii, 2. 8) does not mention the sweet breath of the animal, but the accounts of Brunetto Latini (i, 5. 196) and of Vincentius Bellovacensis (xix, 99 f.) have all the traits of Lydgate's representation.

With regard to the statement that women have as many virtues as there are spots on the panther compare the German poet Hugo of Langenstein, who uses the same simile with relation to Christ (*Martina* 96, 111, etc.). Allusions to the sweet breath of the animal are very numerous; the sanative power of this breath is likewise often mentioned, see Lauchert, p. 175 ff., 183, 185, 187–90, 193, 199, 200, 201. In the Prov. physiologus the effect of the breath is said to be deadly.

6448–92. Comp. what is told in the *R. de la R.* (8597 ff., 14180 ff., 15031 ff.) about the greediness of women.

6523 ff., marginal note. *In arduis nidificat*] Comp. Job xxxix, 27: "in arduis ponet nidum suum."

6528 ff. *Eagle*] Originally the physiologi know nothing about the eagle's sharp eyes and the experiment of testing the young birds' strength of sight, but in the Old French bestiaries and in the physiologus of the Waldenses these traits are contained. Isidor (xii, 7. 2), Brunetto Latini (i, 5. 147) and Vinc. Bellov. (xvi, 35) also relate the story of the old eagle testing his young. For literary allusions comp. Lauchert, p. 171 ff., 183, 191, 196 ff., 199.

6546–49. Comp. Hoccleve, *R. of Pr.* 3579 ff.:

    "but ve*r*ray god & man
    Conseyued was thoruȝ þe humilite
    Whiche he be-heeld in þat blyssed woman."

Gower, *Conf. Am.* 1, 152:

    " That other point I understood,
    Which most is worth and most is good
    And casteth lest a man to kepe,
    My lorde, if ye woll take kepe,
    I say it is humilite,
    Through whiche the high Trinite
    As for deserte of pure love
    Unto Marie from above
    Of that he knewe her humble entente
    Hir owne sone adown he sente
    Above all other, and her he chese
    For that vertu, which bodeth pees."

And further, ii, p. 186:

    " For by that cause the godhede
    Assembled was to the manhede
    In the virgine, where he nome
    Our fleshe and verray man become."

These passages are to be traced back to St. Bernard's saying: " Beata Maria, ex virginitate placuit Deo, sed ex humilitate co*n*cepit deum." Comp. p. 129 of Furnivall's edition of the *R. of Pr.* I refer also to the allusion to the mother of Christ in *Le Dit des Femmes*. See Jubinal, *Nouveau Recueil*, ii, p. 334.

6554–86. How modest and simple and innocent women are is pointed out at great length in *F. of Pr.* 1, 20 G iii *b* f. I may be allowed to quote the following stanzas:

> "Of one deuise they holde them not apaide
> they must ech day haue a straunge wede,
> If any be better then other araied
> of frowarde grutching they fele their heart blede
> For euery eche thinketh verely indede,
> a morowe pryeng in a myrour bright,
> For to be fairest in her owne sight.
> They can their iyen and their lokes dresse
> To drawe folkes by sleightes to their eure,
> And somwhile by their frowardnesse,
> And feyned dau*n*ger they can of men recure
> What euer they lyst, such is their auenture,
> Agein whose sleightes force nor prudence,
> May not auaile to make resistence.
> With co*n*streint weping and forged flatterie
> subtill spech farcid with plesaunce,
> And many false dissymuled maladye,
> Though in their herts they fele no greuau*n*ce
> And with their couert sobre daliau*n*ce,
> Though underneth the double serpe*n*t dare,
> Ful many a man they haue brought in their snare.
> O swetnesse full of mortalitie,
> serpentine with a pleasaunt visage,
> unstable ioye ful of aduersitie,
> O most chaungeable of heart and of corage
> In thy desiers hauing this auauntage,
> what euer thou list to daunt and oppresse,
> Such is thy fraunchise Bochas bereth witnesse."

The *Troy-Book* dwells upon the envy and vanity of women in book i, l. 2672–2699. Comp. also *R. de la R.* 8793 ff., 8849 ff., 13871 ff.; further Lydgate's ballad, *Ryght as rammes horne*.

Women's art of dissimulation is pointed out in another passage of the *Troy-Book*. Comp. i, 2072–96.

6565 f. ˙At that time women used to wear horns at their ears, and to these horns they fastened their veils. Against this foolish fashion inveighs a *Ballad on the forked head-dresses of ladies* (Halliwell, *M. P.*, p. 46). In France, too, this fashion reigned more than two centuries. Comp. *Hist. Litt. de la France*, xxiii, p. 248. In French literature we find a *Dit des Cornetes* (Jubinal, *Jongleurs et Trouvères*, p. 87); see also *La Contenance des Fames* (Jubinal, *Nouveau Recueil*, II, p. 176). Jean de Meung alludes several times to this folly in fashion; see *R. de la R.* 13895 ff.:

> "Sus ses oreilles port tex cornes,
> Que cers, ne bués, ne unicornes,
> S'ils se devoient effronter,
> Ne puist ses cornes sormonter."

In a note on this passage Marteau refers to the miniatures of that time. Another allusion from Meung's *Testament* is also quoted in *Hist. Litt.* xlii, p. 248. Comp. E. Gattinger, *Die Lyrik Lydgates*, p. 58 f., and my remarks in *É. A.* p. 250.

6584–86. A counterpart to these lines is found in Chaucer, *Tale of the Man of Lawe* 174 f.:
"Housbondes been alle gode, and han ben yore,
That knowen wyves, I dar say yow no more."

6604. *Ruby*] Red sapphire. Comp. note on l. 6685.

6640–42. *pose*, O.E. gepŏs; comp. Sweet, *A.S. Dictionary*. Bosworth-Toller gives *gepôs*; this, however, is certainly wrong as is evident from the form *wiþ gepôsu*. The word is comparatively rare, and it occurs, as far as I can see, only twice in Chaucer, in both cases rhyming with *nose*. *Reves Tale* 231 f.:
"He yexeth, and he speketh thurgh the nose
As he were on the quakke, or on the pose."
Manciple's Prologue, 61 f.:
"he speketh in his nose,
And fneseth faste, and eek he hath the pose."

6623–56. With regard to the delegation of Genius, the priest of Dame Nature, comp. Alanus, *De Planctu Naturae*, l. c. 479 B f.; *R. de la R.* 20029 ff.; Gower, *Conf. Am.* i, 48 ff. The rather witty turn which the narrative of Alanus assumes in our poem is not original, it was suggested by the *R. de la R.*

6635. To curse "with bell and book," or, "with bell, book, and candle," a phrase popularly used in connection with a mode of solemn excommunication formerly practised in the Roman Catholic Church. After the formula had been read and the book closed, the assistants cast the lighted candles they held in their hands to the ground so as to extinguish them, and the bells were rung together without order (*Cent. Dict.*). Comp. *Cursor Mundi*, 25038:
"Pilate betokenis feinde of helle,
Cursed he is wiþ boke and belle."
Chron. Gr. Friars 27: "Sir Edmonde de la Poole was pronuncyd a cursed opynly with boke, belle, and candell."

6685. *Saphirs oriental*] The sapphire found in the Orient is of the best quality. See *Etym.* xvi, 9. 2: "Saphirus caerulea est cum purpura, habens pulveres aureos sparsos, apud Medos optimus." *Spec. Nat.* viii, 93: "Hic lapis hominem reddit castum, & firmat in bonis animum .. Sed oportet vt ille, qui portat summo studio castitatem seruet. Orientales Saphiri sunt optimi." In Pannier's edition the stone is treated on p. 39, 84, 115, 149, 247, and 266. Comp. also Marbod, § 5. See also the notes of Skeat, *Piers Plowman*, b. 2, 14, and Bertha M. Skeat, *The Lamentatyon of Mary Magdaleyna*, p. 11.

6691–95. *Vnycourne*] It is not apparent from Lydgate's text, why the "beste Surquedous" is used as a symbol of *verecundia* = shame, sense of shame; neither is the statement of the marginal note that this animal lives in the wildest thickets a natural *tertium comparationis*. The physiologi and other mediaeval books on natural history relate how the unicorn in the presence of a virgin loses its ferocity, and thus may be easily captured. Comp. Isidor xii, 2. 13; *Livres dou Trésor* I, 5. 201 (comp. the note of Chabaille, p. xii f.); *Spec. Nat.* xix, 104. If *verecundia* is taken in the sense of *reverence, veneration*, this story sufficiently accounts for the unicorn being chosen here as a symbol. There is no instance in the love-poetry where the unicorn is referred to in the same sense as in our poem. But the story of the physiologi has frequently given rise to a simile. Comp. Lauchert, p. 186 f., 190, 193, 199, 200, etc.

6696. Our alteration is proved correct by the French text which reads: "LI senestre portoit lymaige—Dun lieure fuitiz et sauluaige."

6719. Comp. Isidor, *Etym.* xvi, 7. 9; *Spec. Nat.* viii, 106. The question why the maiden's two Rooks bearing a mermaid and a lark in their shields were made of topas is sufficiently answered by the following passages from Vinc.: "Topazion enim trogoditarum lingua significationem habet quaerendi ... in aspectum suum singulariter prouocans aspicientes."

6738. *Calaundre*] The description of the calandra forms a component part of almost all the physiologi of Europe. The mediaeval books on natural history contain also the fable about this miraculous bird. Comp. *Speculum Naturale* xvi, 44; Brunetto Latini i, 5. 156; Bartholomaeus de Glanvilla, *De Propr. Rerum* xii, 22. In the common editions of Isidor the bird is not mentioned, but in Cod. Tolet. xii, vii a description of it is added. As to the accounts given by ancient natural philosophers, see Lauchert, p. 7. In mediaeval literature there are frequent allusions to this bird. Comp. Lauchert, p. 169 and 198 ff. For further instances see *Archiv Oesterr. Geschichtsquellen* ii, p. 581; note on Chapter xxvi of the *Physiologus of Crisostomus*; *The Wars of Alexander* (ed. Skeat), l. 5603.

6775–6821. According to Lydgate the dove is meant
"to expresse
The loulyhede and the meknesse
That women) han) of her nature."
Therefore he qualifies the bird as "humble and meke," comp. l. 5368, where Cupido is called "Symple and as dovwe meke." In the marginal note *fraunchise* is the quality signified by the dove; but the word is undoubtedly to be taken here in a wider sense: it might be translated by *innocence*, *harmlessness*; otherwise there would be no sense in the clause "quia felle caret et nullum ledit," which, by the by, is quite in accordance with the writers on natural history in the Middle Ages. Comp. Isidor xii, 7. 61; Brunetto Latini i, 5. 157; *Specul. Vincentii* xvi, 53: "Columba felle caret: rostro non laedit."

6778–6784. *Eliotropia*] Comp. Isidor, *Etym.* xvi, 7. 12: "Magorum impudentiae manifestissimum in hoc quoque exemplum est, quod admista herba Heliotropio quibusdam additis precationibus, gerentem conspici negent." *Spec. Nat.* viii, 67: "hic lapis gestantem in longa vitae tempora producit, sanguinem stringit, venena fugat, & contra dolos tutum facit." Marbod. § xxix: "Nec falli poterit lapidem qui gesserit istum.—Tot bona divino data sunt huic munere gemmae,—Cui tamen amplior hic esse potentia fertur—Nam si jungatur ejusdem nominis herba,—Carmine legitimo, verbo sacrata potenti,— Subtrahit humanis oculis quemcunque gerentem." *Lapidarium omni voluptate refertum* etc. (Wien), D, iii *b*: "Dicitur autem reddere hominem bone fame: & large uite: & *contra* fluxum sanguinis & uenena ualere. Dicitur autem *quod* unctus herba sui nominis: fallit uisum ita ut hominem prohibeat uideri. Inuenitur autem pluries *in* ethiopia: cipro & india." Consult Pannier, p. 55, 137, 167, and 235.

6790. *Pelican*] How the story of the pelican killing and reanimating its young probably originated is pointed out by Lauchert, p. 8 ff. There are only a few physiologi which do not contain it. Comp. the lists drawn up by Mann, p. 31, etc. Of mediaeval encyclopædias which contain this story, I adduce Isidor xii, 7. 26; Brunetto Latini, i, 5. 168; *Specul. Naturale* xvi, 127. In our poem the killing of the young birds is not mentioned; we only hear that the pelican is ready to sacrifice its heart's blood. Allusions to this readiness of self-sacrifice are numerous in the different branches of literature, see Lauchert, p. 169 ff, 183, 190, 201 ff., 204 f. In the marginal note to our text we read that the pelican "ex indignatione" kills its young in order to reanimate them: this is the original form of the story. With regard to allusions, see Lauchert, p. 170, 190, 202, 204 ff.

6828 ff. *Alcest*] The story is told in Hyg., *Fab.* 50 and 51; comp. also Apollod. *Biblioth.* i, 9. 15. For the mention of Alcestis, and poetical treatment of her story, I refer to Schick's note on l. 70–74 of the *T. of Gl.* I only adduce the instances I collected from Lydgate's writings, *T. of Gl.* 70 ff.:

" And aldernext was þe fressh[e] quene,
I mene Alceste, the noble trw[e] wyfe,
And for Admete hou sho lost-hir life
And for hir trouth, if I shal not lie,
Hou she was turnyd to a dai[e]sie."

Secrees, ll. 1305 and 6 :

" Whan the Crowne of Alceste whyte and Red
Aurora passyd ful fresshly doth Appere."

There is also to be mentioned a ballad of the Add. MS. 29729, fol. 157 *a* (comp. Halliwell, *Minor Poems*, p. 161), and the report in *F. of Pr.* 37 *b*.

6842 and 6892 f. Like the magnet, this stone is contained in the physiologi, but its peculiarity of yielding only to goats' blood is not always mentioned. With regard to the oldest accounts, see Lauchert, p. 28. Of mediaeval physiographers compare Isidor xvi, 13. 2 ; *Speculum Naturale*, viii, 39. The lapidaries, of course, deal also with the adamant, see Marbod § 1; earliest French version of his treatise, 1 (Pannier, p. 36) ; *Lapidary of Bern*, 1 (Pannier p. 109) ; *Lapidary of Cambridge*, 1 (Pannier, p. 145). How often the hardness of the adamant is referred to, is visible from Lauchert's list (p. 179, 204, and 206), which might easily be enlarged. Comp. for instance, l. 4385–86 of the *Romaunt*.

6847–50. The albeston, too, is a symbol of indelible and quenchless love. See Isidor, *Etym.* xvi, 4. 4 : "*Asbestos* Arcadiae lapis, ferrei coloris, ab igne nomen sortitus, eo quod accensus semel nunquam extinguitur . . . . . . in templo quodam fuisse Veneris fanum (dicunt) ibique candelabrum, et in eo lucernam sub dio sic ardentem, ut eam nulla tempestas, nullus imber extingueret." Comp. the instances adduced in *New Engl. Dict.*

6849. *Dyuers* has here the meaning of *extraordinary, renowned*. See also l. 5338 and 5574. Comp. O.F. *divers* = singulier. The French reads here :

" une pierre moult Renommee
Qui estoit abeston nommee."

6853. *turtle*] Comp. Lauchert, p. 26, etc. In the physiologi, the crow was originally the symbol of matrimonial faith ; it is not until the time of the late Greek versions that this bird is replaced by the turtle-dove. As classical allusions to this bird, Lauchert adduces Aristoteles H. A. ix, 7 and Aelian iii, 44. Isidor does not relate the story, but Brunetto Latini (i, 5. 172) and Vincentius Bellovacensis (xvi, 143) have it. In Early English literature the turtle is frequently referred to as an example, either of faith in general, or of widow's faith. Comp. *Homiliae catholicae* (ed. Thorpe), i, p. 142: "Þa turtlan getacniað clænnysse : hi sind swa geworhte, gif hira oðer oðerne forlyst, þonne ne secð seo cucu næfre hire oðerne gemacan"; *Old English Homilies* (ed. Morris), ii, p. 49 ; see also l. 355 of Chaucer's *Parlement of Foules*: "The wedded turtel, with hir herte trewe"; *Milleres Tale* 520 : " Lyk a turtle trewe is my moornynge." *Marchantes Tale* 833. Shakespeare refers to the turtle as an emblem of chaste and faithful love in the following passages : *Winter's Tale*, v, 3. 132–35, and iv, 4. 154 f.; *Love's Labour's Lost*, iv, 3. 211 ; *Merry Wives*, ii, 1. 82 f., and iii. 3. 44; *Troilus*, iii. 2. 184 f. Comp. further *The Phoenix and the Turtle*.

Comp. with the line quoted from *Parl. of Foul*. the reading of Alanus ab Insulis, *De Planctu Nat.* (Migne 210, 436 c): "turtur suo viduata consorte, amorum epilogare dedignans, bigamiae refutabat solatia." For allusions in German literature comp. Lauchert, p. 154.

6890–6930. Comp. *R. de la R.* 16027 ff. See also note on l. 6169 ff. With the lines 6906–12 may be compared what is said in the *Troy-Book*, I, 6 D i b:

"Alas that she was so debonayre
For to truste vpon his curtesye,
Or to quyte hir of hir genterye,
So hastely to rewe vpon his smerte!
That thei wyll gladly of routhe and pyte,
Whan that a man is in aduersyte,
Saue his lyfe rather than he shulde deye."

6931 ff., marginal note. The quotation is taken from Ovid's *Remedia Amoris* 139 f:

"Otia si tollas, periere Cupidinis arcus,
Contemptaeque iacent et sine luce faces."

6969 ff., marginal note. With the quotation from Ovid may be compared *Remedia Amoris* 691 f.:

"Artibus innumeris mens oppugnatur amantum,
Ut lapis aequoreis undique pulsus aquis."

6975. *Tiger*] Comp. Lauchert, p. 40. Only in Armenian physiologi is the story of the tigress handed down. Lauchert is inclined to believe that it is derived from Pliny's account of the manner in which the cubs of the tiger are taken away (viii, 18. 66). None of the Latin MSS. hitherto known contains the story of the use of mirrors, but we find it in Old French and Provençal physiologi; there is moreover a *Physiologus of the Waldenses* in which it is given. In the *Hexaëmeron* of Ambrosius and in the *Spec. Nat.* (xi, 112) the hunter throws a "sphaeram de vitro" in the way of the animal. See Lauchert, p. 40 and 142; further, Chabaille, *Livres dou Trésor*, p. xii, note 3. Brunetto Latini, too, knows the story, see i, 5. 199. In Isidor it is wanting. The French original of Lydgate, which here, as in all other cases, simply gives the name of the symbol, later on, in a detailed account, enlarges upon the story of the mirrors, see *É. A.*, fol. 26 b. Comp. with this passage the following lines which Lauchert quotes from a poem of the Sicilian Inghlifredi, *Poeti del primo secolo*, i, p. 136:

"Sono amato da lei senza inganno:
A ciò mio mente mira,
Si mi solleva d'ira,
Come la tigra lo speglio sguardando."

Sometimes the story of the mirror is transferred to other animals, see Lauchert, p. 188.